Hope and the Purple Onion

Jaque Banas Shank

Hope and the Purple Onion

LBO Publishing
PO Box 872
Joshua Tree, California 92252

www.JaqueBanasShank.com

ISBN 978-0-9826089-7-5

Table of Contents

A Note from Susan Mucklow

In 1980, Jaque Banas Shank unveiled the ache in my Christian walk. She introduced me to the concept of journalizing God's word as a means of eliminating the ache of a seemingly silent God, and life changed.

I am thankful to have been her friend and to have worked with her for nearly forty years. Through these years of collaboration, I had the joy of investing my heart into the fabric and foundation of Visionwriters International. Jaque and I labored to work out the details of its structure, and to refine a strategy that could be duplicated to help others to hear God's voice consistently.

Jaque and I operated in tandem. She was the visionary and dynamic public speaker. Jaque had written short study guides to include the practice of daily dialogue with God, but she considered herself a speaker and a teacher, rather than a writer, and often wondered why God asked her to write. However, her obedience proved God's wisdom. As the message evolved, the manuals also needed to evolve. A fan of teamwork, as Jaque began the task of revising each manual, she utilized my gifts to hone content and bring continuity.

Our writing partnership continued while bringing the manuals into their current form, but when Jaque was called home, I felt tentative to make the changes that would clarify or bring congruity to her teaching without noting my additions as separate quotes. Previously, my insertions or clarifications were woven together cohesively with hers. I have continued in that vein now, as long as Jaque's point could remain intact. However, if more explanation has been added, my input is inserted as a quote.

In her final months, Jaque asked me to finish what we had started by bringing continuity to her remaining manuals and other writings. I miss her final seal of approval, but she used to say, "If you want to know what I meant, go ask Susan. She articulates the heart of my message better than anyone." I do not make that claim, but she trusted my ability to convey her heart to others, and that is humbling.

I write this for the sake of those who do not know me or understand how the process occurred in the past. If I can mitigate misunderstanding, it is my heart to do so. Please receive my efforts in Christ...

May the God of your hope so fill you with all joy and peace in believing - through the experience of your faith - that by the power of the Holy Spirit you may abound and be overflowing (bubbling over) with hope.

ROMANS 15:13 (AMPC)

INTRODUCTION

Years ago the Lord whispered the word *journalize* in my heart. As I looked up the word in a dictionary, I understood He wanted me to put His words in writing. Through this practice, I came to understand that growth is a process. As I sought to maintain a daily surrender, I kept this understanding in the foreground. I exercised grace throughout the discipline of making journalizing a regular point of contact, a place where I began to dive deeper into the wells of His presence.

Journalizing gained potency when I realized His Spirit was asking me to write the vision of Christ as He lives through me. The exercise became a tool to make the Father's thoughts real to me. Christ lives in every born again believer by His Spirit. When I understood His kingdom was in me, I began to experience the atmosphere of righteousness, peace, and joy in the Holy Spirit.

In order to live a full life I had to begin from a correct frame of reference. In Christ, I found that correctness. Being born from above is a prerequisite for hearing the voice of God. For this reason, journalizing, as I ascribe, is used correctly only in the hands of those who are born from above and who revere God's word as the final authority.

Through His word, and by His Spirit, He reveals the heart of prayer to those who let Him reveal Himself as He chooses. Who is God? How will He direct us toward faith-filled prayer? How does He lead and guide us into all truth? What is the true nature of the Vine in which we abide and how does *that* influence the way we pray? The answers to these questions change everything. The Lord reveals Himself through His word, His Spirit, and in times of prayer. You and I cannot know any more about God than He chooses to reveal. He is *that* big; we are *that* small. It is my hope that this study will broaden our view of God so that He might broaden our view of His intention for prayer.

Journalizing is written prayer. To write the vision of who God is will mean taking a journey into the loving heart of God. The Lord uses this writing tool as a means to speak to us and to bring us to understanding. He reveals His consistency through this method of communication. Our reactions to His Lordship (and life in general) are filled with a wide range of fears, absurdities, and emotional outbursts. His presence will stabilize our emotions. Even on our most painful and agonizing days, we learn to trust Him as we discover that He does not pull away from our neediness. At its core, journalizing is meant to lead us to the will of God so that we can do the will of God. It is a map guiding us to maturity.

After new birth, surrender to God through written dialogue with God is a potent next step. Journalizing God's word in His presence ensures a progressive maturation of the soul that causes a baby Christian to realize who he is in Christ. I believe this ripening must begin through an intensely *personal* relationship with God where the question "Who am I?" gets a final answer. In my generation, this ripening has been largely neglected in the body of Christ, so this study and the submission it prescribes, if done in earnest, will enlarge the soul to experience union with God. This union will bring the experience of peace and confident trust forever, which is the actual effect of righteousness (see Isaiah 32:17).

Until we actually realize that we are the pulsating body of Christ on earth, walking, talking and thinking like Christ, we will not fully understand our responsibility as Christians. Thus, God's purpose is to bring man's soul into a conscious understanding of who he is and *why* he is here. Prayer becomes a great clarifier of the vision. To receive an answer to prayer is really the same thing as enjoying your position in Christ. Understanding prayer becomes a baseline for *possessing* that which we are promised in covenant with God.

We are made to live and dwell in relationship with God. Prayer, in its many forms, is the avenue by which we enjoy relationship with Him in our everyday lives. Receiving answers is about hearing God.

The only way to know God is to come into His presence so that a *personal* relationship might be developed. We cannot relate to God vicariously through other people. God does not relate to us through a leader, minister, priest, spouse, friend, or mentor. As babes, we are fed and cared for by others, but as we mature, our relationship with God becomes direct. A good mentor will teach us, from an early age, how to come into the Lord's presence so that the Lord can reveal Himself, even unto babes.

As we seek to make all that is in our heart and mind present to God, to bring ourselves into conversation with God, to be and to project the vision as the Son of God puts it into our soul, then we begin to know God and to be free. I believe this is the most important message for Christians anywhere at anytime.

Personal soul management is an ongoing process where we begin to experience Spirit-led changes. We live from a faith that knows it is His life working out His will *to do* in us. Those who will begin this study from such a standard of faith will of necessity take God seriously and surrender to the invitation to write down His instructions with a ready heart to obey them, not in our own strength, but by receiving His strength to do so. This is what walking the talk looks like, for faith is full of spontaneous works born from a genuine, personal, and intimate relationship with God, and not from the letter of the law. Obedience to the law is false obedience, not born from the love of God. Anything not born of love will not reap God's rewards.

Hearing the voice of God is the heritage of every disciple of Christ. I believe this study is a deep desire in the heart of God. I pray you are blessed in doing it, and that you become transformed by the reality of the Gospel through the complete renewal of your mind.

Living Loved,

Jaque Banas Shank

HOPE IS FOR CHRIST

But give reverent honor in your hearts to the Anointed One and treat him as the holy Master of your lives. And if anyone asks about the hope living within you, always be ready to explain your faith with gentleness and respect.

1 PETER 3:15 (TPT)

Herman, the Purple Onion

There once was a purple onion named Herman; I gave him a name so that I could tell the tale of his plight. I purchased Herman from the grocery store because I've always liked purple onions. The reason this particular onion inherited a name is because I never actually got to *taste* this onion. You see, when I brought him home I put him in my vegetable basket with the other vegetables. I didn't notice him again until he was the last veggie in the basket; he was hollow inside and as light as a feather. Herman was dead; he was alive when I got him, but now he was a goner. I imagined Herman once had a personality. I imagined that, before I brought him home, Herman had anticipated his life and all that he had been created for. He probably imagined himself decorating a fine salad, accompanying a bell pepper on a sizzling plate of fajitas, or perhaps adding the perfect finale to a cheeseburger.

I imagined that after weeks of sitting in the basket, with no attention from me, he said to himself, "I wish I had stayed in the grocery store with my brothers. At least I would have a chance of being purchased by someone who had a plan for my life. But here I sit, alone in a basket, lost and forgotten. I'd rather be chopped up and fed to the animals than to die never having fulfilled my purpose at all!"

I buried Herman in the trash that day, but I knew he was an object lesson from God. The Lord said, "Every created thing needs to live with purpose and with the hope of fulfilling its calling." Suddenly, I could relate to Herman; I realized I was also created for a specific purpose and at that time I did not know what it was. Because of Herman, I had a newfound desire to connect with my purpose. Strange, but true, Herman is the reason this study manual exists. On that fateful day, I discovered a hope that I'm going to relate to you so, "lettuce" proceed!

Habit of Permanent Expectancy

This book approaches the subject of hope. I have always loved the acrostic for hope - the *Habit Of Permanent Expectancy.* Hope creates a habit - something we repeat until it becomes a part of our disposition. After awhile, we can call it our pattern. Hope creates positive habits for us so that the 'good thing' becomes mechanical - something we can do unconsciously. Hope underlies all spontaneous movement and delight; hope is the basis of true passion and with hope, the hope of Christ Himself, we have a future to look forward to.

Where do hope-filled habits come from? Hopeful habits come from permanent expectancy. We all crave permanence. We crave a stable, continuous, constant, everlasting, and abiding life of peace. We all crave positive expectancy. We want to anticipate the prospect and likelihood that good is on the horizon.

Throughout this study, I will use pregnancy as an analogy for hope. When a woman is pregnant, she is *expecting*. There is a positive anticipation (hope) that at the end of her term, a newborn baby will arrive. As believers, we are developing the habit of permanent *pregnancy*. In the physical, that is not appealing, but spiritually speaking, to be continually pregnant with the love and vision of God is thrilling. When we deliver one desire, we expect another. We are always pregnant with His agenda, and His purpose in and through us.

Even when a situation looks dismal, hope will teach us to expect God to show up on the scene. It will become our habit to do so. To live in God, with a high anticipation of His being, from moment to moment, brings greater joy than any other endeavor.

Hope is based on the fact that God is immutable, unchangeable, permanent, and always the same. He had a specific design and purpose for each of us before the beginning of time or the foundation of the earth. He knows us perfectly, and always had you and me in mind.

My little children, for whom I am again suffering birth pangs until Christ is completely and permanently formed (molded) within you...

GALATIANS 4:19 (AMPC)

God's plan for all of us is for Christ to be fully formed in us. Christ is the Seed that grows in us, as us, through the nurturing of our relationship with Him. Christ is our Hope, and hope is for Christ in us. If we get ahold of this, our study on the subject of hope will not be complicated, and life will get easier. We complicate life by seeking meaning apart from the formation of Christ in us. *God's* hope is always for the simplicity of Christ in us.

This is not another book to read; it's a tool to help develop a habit of repetition for nurturing our relationship with Christ. Our goal is to develop a pattern of hearing His voice and conforming to His image. This study manual is a tool to help develop a habit that uncovers real hope, the hope that God put inside us, the hope that cannot fail or disappoint us because it is built on better promises.

It is important that we come to understand the purpose of our unique existence. God has a specific plan for each and every one of us, and whenever we find it, and walk it out by faith, we become the most satisfied people on earth. This is our birthright. As we continue on this journey, we can expect to see *hope* that leads to the ecstasy of our souls.

Hope and Choices

Life is a series of choices that we all *hope* to define correctly for ourselves. We can choose to love God or to scrutinize Him. We can choose to discover our hope or go on living in despair. Our choices determine our disposition. We can choose to open our hearts and learn to trust God in all things, or to keep walking in cloudy doubt.

Hope is the opposite of suspicion because it has no doubt regarding the goodness of God. It's also the opposite of passivity because hope enflames passion.

When we choose to believe God, we are choosing to know the reason for the hope that lies within us. If hope is a gift within us, then faith and its corresponding action are also gifts.

Hope causes us to make the most of time; it also helps us see there is hope for our brothers and sisters. To hope is to see others as they 'can be' and to do what we can to help them be all they can be. Hope helps us understand that we are not what we feel, we are what we *choose*, for if we choose what we feel we will often choose doubt, but if we choose to live by truth, we choose life!

Free choice is another word for what the Bible calls faith.

NORMAN GRUBB

God's Hope vs. Man's Hope

Blessed be the God and Father of our Lord Jesus Christ! According to his great mercy, he has caused us to be born again to a living hope through the resurrection of Jesus Christ from the dead.

1 PETER 1:3 (ESV)

Hope, apart from God, is no hope at all. We are meant to hope with God's hope. Man's hope always falls short because it is nothing more than wishful thinking. The hope of man is not based on certainty. God's hope is Christ, the living hope of the Gospel.

In the infant stage of growing up in Christ, we can have a problem with hope. In spiritual infancy, we are like children in need of a parent. Infants need more care than toddlers, and toddlers need more care than adolescents, etc. If we have children of our own, we know that the habit of taking care of the baby is necessary. We love our child, and as an infant, he or she requires more of our time, energy, and life. We look for patterns that we can create to take the best care of the baby.

Likewise, as spiritual infants, we create a habit to take care of our newly created selves in Christ. We look for new habits to help us learn to listen for and to hear His voice. We embrace the habit of journalizing because we want to be closely knit to Christ in us. The time it takes can be overwhelming; but as Christ in us, as us, grows, then we see a scripture like Galatians 2:20 and we come alive.

> *I have been crucified with Christ [that is, in Him I have shared His crucifixion]; it is no longer I who live, but Christ lives in me. The life I now live in the body I live by faith [by adhering to, relying on, and completely trusting] in the Son of God, who loved me and gave Himself up for me.*
>
> GALATIANS 2:20 (AMP)

It takes a spiritual insight to read a verse and have it come alive. To understand that it is no longer us who lives, but rather Christ, is a revelation. Life takes on new meaning as we live with a determination to see ourselves decrease so that His life can increase in us.

> *Even when we were dead (slain) by [our own] shortcomings and trespasses, He made us alive together in fellowship and in union with Christ; [He gave us the very life of Christ Himself, the same new life with which He quickened Him, for] it is by grace (His favor and mercy which you did not deserve) that you are saved (delivered from judgment and made partakers of Christ's salvation).*
>
> EPHESIANS 2:5 (AMPC)

God did not give us a life like Christ's, He gave us the very life of Christ Himself. We do not have to wonder, "Gosh, what would Jesus do?" Instead, we can draw from His very life in us, work out our own salvation, and listen to His voice day by day. We do not need to live *like* Christ. We simply need to see the life He is unfolding in us, as us. It is much better to have His life, than a life like His. As we grow spiritually, we begin to realize that He has no problem being Himself.

Problems occur when we think we need to mimic Him, or do something to please Him. There are ideas, opinions, thoughts, and religious attitudes to let go of before this new life can spring up and work for us. What is our part? Do we need discipline to make our life better or to become more like Jesus? Do we need a little more knowledge, another book, or another hour of prayer? Can we earn a life like Jesus? Our work is to let go of those false ideas. Our work is to let go, and let *Him* flow.

Hope...For the Future?

Most people associate hope with goals and plans for the future. We would love to know the future or try to control future events with goals, strategies, and fortitude. Yet, this is not living by faith. When we decide to live by faith, we agree to walk in the dark. We live by the unknown ways of the Spirit instead of living by what we think we know. We think we need to know our future. We want to make the right choices for our future. We plead with God to help us make right choices, but we can trust Him with the unknown because, what we *do* know is that He is trustworthy.

Hope is about making a choice. We are inundated with choices every day. However, there is a supreme choice. It is not a choice of career, spouse, vacation, style, spending, saving, or relationship. Let us shelve all that and understand that hope is for Christ to increase in us. If we will begin right there, everything else that needs to be known will be known when it needs to be known. We hope in God; we do not hope in the uncertainty of riches, armies, strength, health, beauty, or intelligence.

> *As for the rich in this present world, instruct them not to be conceited and arrogant, nor to set their hope on the uncertainty of riches, but on God, who richly and ceaselessly provides us with everything for our enjoyment. Instruct them to do good, to be rich in good works, to be generous, willing to share [with others]. In this way storing up for themselves the enduring riches of a good foundation for the future, so that they may take hold of that which is truly life.*
>
> 1 TIMOTHY 6:17-19 (AMP)

We set our hope on God, who ceaselessly provides us with everything for our enjoyment. By knowing Him, we know the reason for the hope that lies within us. We hope to see the life of Christ manifesting in us because to see Him is to see the new creation. What is the new creation? The new creation is Christ, the first born from among the dead, giving Himself to each of us by being born again in us, as us. How do we stir up this hope? We fan the flame by looking to Jesus, the author and finisher of our faith.

This study is intended to help us give focused attention to the hope of the Gospel, which is Jesus Christ. Over the years, I asked God to teach me about hope. I just wanted better time management and goal setting, or a greater sense of purpose and clear direction. Eventually, He was able to show me that He is the source of wisdom behind everything else I sought. To seek Him was the straight line I was looking for.

We want to be a better discerner, and a better chooser. However, every choice we need to make (past, present, and future) is found in Him, right here and now. We would rather God improve our choosing because we want to be seen as wise. We also like to feel like we are in control. We like to believe that what we *do* defines our choice. We fail to see in these moments that right *choosing* comes from right *being*, not from right *doing*. Christ is our hope of choosing right. We have no greater assurance than the assurance of knowing that Christ is our right *being*. Knowing Him becomes our greatest discipline.

We want the choices we make to be the best. We want our roadmap to be clear, direct, and to lead to the perfect destination. We want every goal to hit the bull's-eye with no more hits and misses. We want to choose correctly, permanently. These are true desires.

We can tie these desires to the idea that Christ is our only hope of consistently making right choices. Hope is for actualizing Christ in us. Every decision we make (which house to buy, car to drive, clothes to wear, career to pursue, etc.) is elementary when we are assured that we have chosen from Christ within. In choosing from Christ, the choice no longer matters. What we choose is no longer what counts - Who we are choosing from, does!

We make a big deal out of the choices we make. If we have made good choices, we feel proud of ourselves. If we have made bad choices, we have excuses and people to blame. We make a big deal out of the endless list of possible choices and their potential consequences. We think this way because we are choosing from ourselves, not Christ. We may ask for God's help in choosing, and get upset when it does not work out, but what the Lord really wants us to see is that choosing is not about one way being the right or wrong way - it is about choosing from Christ.

We often choose based on the fear of man. We choose based on what our spouse, parent, friend, pastor or spiritual advisor will think. As soon as we bring the fear of being misunderstood into the equation, we are not choosing from Christ and we will likely regret the choice. It is not good enough to want to be understood for the choices we make - making higher choices is about living with the assurance and confidence that comes from knowing that we chose from His life in us.

To grow into confident choices, we need to give focused attention to Christ, growing up in us, as us. The new creation in us cannot remain in the shell, or as a seed. We must nurture it, fertilize the soil, speak words, water it, shed tears and laughter, apply faith and hope, and give it all the time it needs to grow up in us.

Thanks, Herman

Herman was a fine onion. What is amazing is how God can use everything for His glory. To walk into a kitchen, find a dead onion in a little veggie coffin, and have the presence of God fill the room, is incredible. When I first wrote this study, I thought people were going to laugh at me. Who writes a book based on a purple onion? Nonetheless, God breathed His inspiration through a dead onion. In the end, Herman did not die with his purpose unfulfilled. He was not part of a salad or a sandwich, but he fulfilled an even higher purpose. Herman was not the first bit of penicillin that I have made. A lot of produce has grown mold under my care. However, God chose Herman to teach and inspire hope in me. This little onion became more famous in death than in life; he died, and God used his death to inspire hope in others.

Herman's purpose was to inspire a new study, but I chose to write or not to write. If I had not chosen to write, my encounter that morning would be long forgotten. God animated an onion, gave it a name, filled in a back-story, and said, "Now go…write down all the words I will teach you about hope."

I chose to incubate the story. Like a woman, pregnant with child, Herman's lesson was kept in a nice, dark, and meditative place so it could grow. I sat at the Lord's feet, and listened as He stirred my thoughts of Herman. As it incubated, I saw that a purple onion had been chosen by God to give pleasure, and I did not take pleasure in it while it was alive. In the end, redemption prevailed; but between Herman's death and the newness of life that he inspired, there was much to learn.

We have a choice everyday; we will incubate hope and let Christ increase in us, or not. There is so much more to see. We want to become someone new; we want to become Christ in us. We do not want to have new things as much as we want to become someone new. We want to enjoy our real life and our true nature. We want to know Him, as He is in us. The more we see Him, the more we will be like Him. So, again, we will use journalizing as a tool to open our hearts, teach us to pray, and to fill us with hope.

Over the years, I have used these studies in various group settings. People would come discouraged because they had not applied themselves as diligently as they had hoped. I would say to them what the Lord always said to me, "Do one thing right, just one thing - show up! If you did not journalize, or answer your heart work, then just *show up* for class. That is the one 'right thing' that you can do this week. Then, let tomorrow morning start a new week filled with *hope* for a better endeavor."

Throughout this study, we do our best to apply ourselves. We show up, reach for the goal, but trust Him when our inconsistencies surface. We do not intentionally choose hopelessness. God is not asking us to be anything but available. We are not adequate; if we are trying to be adequate then we need pride knocked off our shoulder. Nobody is adequate; God is looking for availability.

Persistence in Faith

> *And will not [our just] God defend and protect and avenge His elect (His chosen ones), who cry to Him day and night? Will He defer them and delay help on their behalf? I tell you, He will defend and protect and avenge them speedily. However, when the Son of Man comes, will He find [persistence in] faith on the earth?*
>
> LUKE 18:7,8 (AMPC)

The story of the widow and the unjust judge is a lesson in persistence and faith. Will the Lord find us persistent in His faith when He appears? Are we showing up, ready and available? The encouragement is always to 'just show up.' Even if we sit to do a journal and nothing seems to be there, we can go ahead and write something in faith. Prime the pump, just show up. Maybe all we write is, "I love you and care about you." That is okay; it is not our job to manufacture a profound word. If we supply a little water to prime the pump, He will give us back a well. It may not be today, but today's persistence is noticed. We show up, and let God do what He wants to do.

Journalizing the Word of God

Journalizing is conversing with God in writing. In so doing, we give Him the full attention He deserves. God speaks and we listen - we speak and God listens - on paper. Journalizing encourages us in our faith by asking us to believe that God wants to involve Himself with us and it provides a means for us to stay in the process until we bear more fruit. Over time, the Lord proves that we are not alone, for He is not silent. Our ears are trained to hear Him and He trains our hearts to obey.

To journalize is to write down the words and insights we hear God speaking as the eyes of our hearts are opened by His presence. Journalizing is done by faith - as though Christ is speaking directly to us and is interpreting the truth of His word openly into our lives. Jesus sent the helpmeet, the Holy Spirit, to teach us God's will. By repeatedly listening to and obeying Him we come to know the truth, for it is the truth we *know* that sets us free. What we hear with our ears we forget; what we see with our eyes we remember; what we take the time to attentively write, we understand; and when, with understanding, we obey what we see from our hearts, our lives are forever transformed.

Bearing Fruit

> *I will give you the treasures of darkness and hidden riches of secret places that you may know that it is I, the Lord, the God of Israel, Who calls you by your name.*
>
> ISAIAH 45:3 (AMPC)

> *He made darkness His secret place; His canopy around Him was dark waters and thick clouds of the skies.*
>
> PSALM 18:11 (NKJV)

After writing studies that included the practice of journalizing, I saw a need for a structure to help turn good intentions into reality. I founded a ministry called Visionwriters International in answer to this need. Four basics that I exercised in my personal life were woven into the structure that God impressed upon me. My goal was to help people connect with God in a way that brings lasting change, so discipline, accountability, relationship, and community became footings to help develop the how-to that supports the want-to. People intend to love God but often lack follow-through. I founded Visionwriters International to help facilitate good intentions.

Lack of follow-through makes us an easy target for condemnation. As we practice discipline, accountability, relationship, and community, God pulls us through the condemnation to the higher call of conviction, which leads to our personal best. As we commit to working out our salvation with the Lord, we gain confidence in our own hearts that we *really are* new creations in Christ. We learn to open ourselves to God's love and forgiveness and walk in the newness of life.

Discipline

A majority of Christians state their ache in much the same way: "I'm not bearing fruit," or, "I'm not seeing radical transformation in my life." We want to be someone new; we want our new life in Christ to affect every other relationship we have in a positive way.

Asking questions, getting answers, gaining understanding, and acting on truth is the basis for every cycle of growth. To seek God first is our first right choice, and making this choice each day is the key to growth, but consistently choosing to seek Him requires discipline. We all desire consistency, but our busy lifestyles swallow such desires and complicate what we want most. Still, it is our responsibility to return and seek God; no one else can do this for us.

Discipline affects the way we do things, which also affects the way we feel about ourselves. Although our goals are within reach, failure to attain those goals robs us of self-respect. Why do we fail to act compatibly with our goals? Are we really that undisciplined? I believe lack of vision is the problem. "Where there is no vision [no redemptive revelation of God], the people perish" (Proverbs 29:18a AMPC). Vision imparts passion and passion becomes discipline, because people always end up doing what they love. The primary use of discipline is for seeking the vision of Christ-in-us. Discipline happens in cycles; first, we surrender, as best we can, to the pursuit of Christ in our journals. Then, as we recognize Him by the writing of His hand upon us, our passion for Him grows, and as our passion grows, our discipline grows, as does our desire to obey Him.

As we receive the vision of His life in us, He affirms and loves us in writing - yet He also disciplines us, as would any loving Father. Through being disciplined, we learn to exercise discipline. We find we are able to pledge ourselves to the choices He asks us to make. We can use marriage as an effective metaphor to illustrate this. If married, we wed our spouse "for better or worse, for richer or poorer, until death do us part." We take responsibility for this commitment even in times of conflict. We face our shortcomings and are loyal to the marriage, no matter what. Over the course of time, our marriage prospers because commitment works, regardless of our shifting feelings. In a like manner, passionate faith helps us stay committed to our godly choices regardless of fluctuating feelings. Likewise, our relationship with Him keeps us stable in the things to which He commits us.

Holding fast to our passion for Christ, we understand that although we chose Him once for all, we still need to choose Him every day. As a continual connection by intimate conversation makes a good marriage, a strong relationship with God depends on a continual connection of hearts. Stabilizing our choice for Christ is like planting a seed in the ground and then nurturing that seed until the fruit of Christ increases and the lie-weeds of the old self diminish. Continually feeding the vision of Christ in us feeds our passion, and thus our discipline.

A double-minded man, as described in James, is simply a man who refuses to make that deliberate choice every day. If he will not stay focused on the vision of Christ, how can he expect to receive anything from the Lord? Discipline is the road to maturity. By it, we practice patience and the principle of little by little, every day. By discipline, we enjoy the journey, instead of being consumed with the destination. God's reality becomes undeniable to us. The discipline of abiding in the Vine inflames our passion to a continual readiness for the next right choice.

> *Obey me and live! Guard my words as your most precious possession. Write them down, and also keep them deep within your heart.*
>
> PROVERBS 7:2-3 (TLB)

> *Do not merely desire peaceful relations with God, with your fellowmen, and with yourself, but pursue, go after them!*
>
> 1 PETER 3:11B (AMPC)

Accountability

Accountability is a crucial ingredient of growth; it sometimes involves conflict, and is always a two-way street. In fellowship with other believers, we are held accountable by one another, and hold one another in accountability. Because of accountability, we can give a reason for the hope that lies within us. We are accountable for writing the vision of Christ in us and for sharing Christ with others. If people see Christ in us, it is because He is the One building His character in us.

Accountability means we are responsible. We are willing to be interconnected as one body. Our personal growth affects others and so does our unfruitfulness. We are accountable to one another to work out our own salvation and to face God with difficult questions. We are committed to the sometimes-painful process of hearing the truth spoken to us in love, and to speaking in the same fashion to others. The fear that we are not changing is dissolved when we connect with people willing to be held accountable.

In pursuing our relationship with Christ, we are never alone. The body of Christ is a network that reinforces our desire to know Him. We guard one another in prayer, loving support, and Christian accountability. Christians are never truly isolated, nor do we feel the need to pretend to be more than we are. Accountability reinforces the foundation for growth and develops a valuable support system.

During this study, we are accountable to God to meet with Him in our daily journal. We give heartfelt response to our Heart-work and join with others in our study group with happy participation. We press toward the mark, understanding that we are not condemned for our shortcomings but encouraged with more grace. As we gather with others, the hope is that we always give answers priority over problems. We are humble enough to confess our weaknesses, yet Christian enough to profess Christ as our strength.

We trust the desire to become someone new, knowing it means we will walk away from old patterns. In the spirit of accountability, we sometimes need to challenge one another in ways that may feel uncomfortable. Nevertheless, Christ's love for all of us is irresistible; it wins our hearts completely so that we thrive in the atmosphere of accountability. We actually find it amazing that we may have once thought we could grow and mature without it.

> *Now we exhort you, brethren, warn those who are unruly, comfort the fainthearted, uphold the weak, be patient with all. See that no one renders evil for evil to anyone, but always pursue what is good both for yourselves and for all. Rejoice always, pray without ceasing, in everything give thanks; rejoice for this is the will of God in Christ Jesus for you.*
>
> 1 THESSALONIANS 5:14-18 (NKJV)

> *[Oh, I know, I have been rash to talk out plainly this way to God!] I will [in my thinking] stand upon my post of observation, and station myself on the tower or fortress, and will watch to see what He will say within me, and what answer I will make [as His mouthpiece] to the perplexities of my complaint against Him. And the Lord answered me, and said, "Write the vision, and engrave it so plainly upon tablets that every one who passes may be able to read [it easily and quickly] as he hastens by. For the vision is yet for an appointed time, and it hastens to the end [fulfillment]; it will not deceive or disappoint. Though it tarry, wait [earnestly] for it; because it will surely come, it will not be behindhand on its appointed day."*
>
> HABAKKUK 2:1-3 (AMPC)

Relationship

Christ died to give us an unimaginable covenant relationship with God. We have what the whole world wants - the ability to become who God made us to be. Everyone wants to be someone new; the fear of 'not changing' is universal. We all want to be known, loved, and accepted for who we are, and yet we all know we can be more. In the long and short of it, we want connection, we want relationship, and we want covenant.

Covenant is God putting us in a place of honor, granting us the right to a relationship of the most intimate nature with Him. Covenant gives us exclusivity with God, a personal relationship with ourselves and others, and a place of shelter from a worldly system that has no room for Him. As we grow in this covenant relationship, we begin to understand what it means to give ourselves to one another.

The quality of our relationships with other people reveals the state of our relationship with the Lord. In other words, our relationship with God is never better than our relationship with the most significant persons in our lives. It's a hard saying, but working out our relationship with those closest to us is the working out of our salvation with God. If what we say we have with God is not changing our relationships with others for the better, then our connection with God is not working as it is designed to work. Remember, we cannot be healed in denial; we can only be healed in those things we admit. If we are hurting, we have most likely fallen asleep in the ache of our unbelief and need to take an honest look at ourselves. We need to repent our way back to God.

> *"But this is the covenant that I will make with the house of Israel after those days, says the Lord: I will put My law in their minds, and write it on their hearts; and I will be their God, and they shall be My people. No more shall every man teach his neighbor, and every man his brother, saying, 'Know the Lord', for they all shall know Me, from the least of them to the greatest of them, says the Lord. For I will forgive their iniquity, and their sin I will remember no more."*
>
> JEREMIAH 31:33-34 (NKJV)

Community

Community develops as we exercise discipline, accountability and relationship. My hope is that you will use this study manual with a committed study group, and that you find the ease to be yourself, receive correction, offer truth, and praise God for His presence in each member of His body. In community, we are certainly not trying to fix each other but are rather providing a safe atmosphere so others can heal and convert themselves. Community is a place where we come to receive and give support. In true community, the fear of man flies out the door because we will not pretend with one another. In other words, community is the place we practice being most like ourselves. A healthy community includes the clashing and chaos necessary for growth without the splits that happen in less secure groups.

Community becomes a gathering of mature and loyal people who seek first to understand, then to be understood. Here, relationship comes before issues, and people are more important than opinions.

We can do more in community than we could do alone. Christ's fullness is in our unity; together we can change the world. "They will know we are Christians by our love," the song goes. His fruit is maturing and His character in us will draw all sorts of people to Christ.

In the final analysis, discipline, accountability, relationship, and community weave together to become a safety net. Discipline is built on the structure of vision and passion. It provides the tracks we need to give our train a destination and a sense of clear direction about where we are headed. Nevertheless, if we fall off the track because our vision of Christ is too vague, accountability is the net that catches us before we plunge over the cliff. Accountability works because we keep showing up, *no matter what*. We understand that no matter what happens, we need each other, and we need to be held accountable. Because God loves us, He gives us one another so that we will have this safeguard. However, even if people fail to hold us accountable, the relationship based on Christ Himself will place our value before our issues and love us back home. In real relationship, those who are most mature will act from their Christ-selves and love God's prodigal sons and daughters home. The last layer of the safety net is community. If we do not quickly return after the first three nets fail to catch us, the prayers of a loving community will enlarge the ache of our unbelief until it testifies against us, and we are no longer willing to live on pig slop.

> *My son, never forget the things I've taught you. If you want a long and satisfying life, closely follow my instructions. Never tire of loyalty and kindness. Hold these virtues tightly. Write them deep within your heart. If you want favor with both God and man, and a reputation for good judgment and common sense, then trust the Lord completely; don't ever trust yourself. In everything you do, put God first, and he will direct you and crown your efforts with success. Don't be conceited, sure of your own wisdom. Instead, trust and reverence the Lord, and turn your back on evil; when you do that, then you will be given renewed health and vitality. Honor the Lord by giving him the first part of all your income, and he will fill your barns with wheat and barley and overflow your wine vats with the finest wines. Young man, do not resent it when God chastens and corrects you, for his punishment is proof of his love. Just as a father punishes a son he delights in to make him better, so the Lord corrects you. The man who knows right from wrong and has good judgment and common sense is happier than the man who is immensely rich! For such wisdom is far more valuable than precious jewels. Nothing else compares with it. Wisdom gives: a long, good life, riches, honor, pleasure, peace. Wisdom is a tree of life to those who eat her fruit; happy is the man who keeps on eating it.*
>
> PROVERBS 3:1-18 (TLB)

Righteousness, Peace, and Joy

> *For the kingdom of God is not meat and drink; but righteousness, and peace, and joy in the Holy Ghost.*
>
> ROMANS 14:17 (KJV)

If God rewards those who diligently seek Him, what is His reward? His kingdom; it consists of righteousness, peace, and joy. These three elements are the crux of all we hope for - the essence of all we long to be and do. In the end, righteousness, peace, and joy correspond in sequence to God, others, and ourselves.

Righteousness

Righteousness is when, by our first faith in Christ's sacrifice, we are suddenly found to be right with God. It is a gift so completely given that upon our discovery of it, we begin to hunger for God like never before. Righteousness is our stable connection to God. Because of righteousness, we have confidence to hear, trust, and obey His will. When we are righteous in God's sight, we boldly live our lives by faith. We have an unusual confidence in the future, for righteousness is our eternal security. Because of righteousness, we no longer have to live second-guessing ourselves; we have discernment to choose what needs to be chosen and to let go of everything and anything that needs to be let go. Righteousness is at the heart of our identity, and the reason that our hearts can no longer condemn us. To believe in Christ and yet not comprehend His reward of righteousness is like not ordering or writing checks after a rich benefactor has placed a billion dollars in our checking account. Pursue righteousness - crave the gift - hunger for the understanding of it, for this reward is great and we cannot afford to neglect it. It is the core of all our longing and the foundation of God's delight in us.

Peace

When we are right with God, everything becomes right with ourselves. Peace is finding answers inside us and recognizing His answers as they come through others. We believe God is here in our circumstances, and we trust Him in our hearts. The fear of man is the number one enemy of our peace, proving we do not grasp our righteousness with God. Our fear of other people speaks louder than words because we will risk displeasing God for the sake of pleasing them. We forfeit our peace when we compromise ourselves and our beliefs just to supposedly be 'right' in someone else's eyes. When we grasp righteousness we will have peace, for we will finally accept ourselves in Christ. Self-acceptance is always the crux of our peace, and righteousness with Christ is the crux of our self-acceptance. To keep receiving God's reward we will stay on a steady diet of truth and love, for this is what it takes to free us from the fear of man so that we can have peace.

Joy

Joy is the manifestation of righteousness and peace. We experience joy when we act confidently as our true selves and are then completely free to accept others. Joy is experienced in the atmosphere of acceptance - the safest atmosphere in which to grow. Joy is not dependent on circumstance. Neither persecution, trial, nor tribulation can suppress joy, for it is God's divine happiness, eternal in nature. Joy is at the heart of extravagant giving; joy is the natural spring from which God's goodness flows. Simply put, joy delights in God. It equates to trust, for joy has found that final resting place in God. Joy underlies the fact that God exists to give Himself away. When joy is pure, we also exist to give ourselves away, for our joy cannot be contained within ourselves. Joy is contagious; it is God's strength spreading His kingdom around the globe. "Thy kingdom come, Thy will be done on earth as it is in heaven." This is why we are on the earth, for in righteousness, peace and joy the children of God will usher in God's kingdom.

> *Seek (aim at and strive after) first of all His kingdom, and His righteousness [His way of doing and being right], then all these things taken together will be given you besides.*
>
> MATTHEW 6:33 (AMPC)

> *Not every one who says to Me, Lord, Lord, will enter the kingdom of heaven, but he who does the will of My Father Who is in heaven.*
>
> MATTHEW 7:21 (AMPC)

When discipline becomes delight, it is easy to flow into accountability, relationship and community with God and with others. Please enjoy discipline, accountability, relationship, and true community with a committed group of classmates. Discover the light of Christ in you and in one another.

THE HOPE OF THE GOSPEL

'For I know the plans that I have for you,' declares the Lord, 'plans for welfare and not for calamity to give you a future and a hope.'

JEREMIAH 29:11 (NASB)

LESSON 1, DAY 1 - *Better Promises*

☐ DAY 1 - READING ASSIGNMENT

God knows how He planned that Christ, slain before the foundation of the world, should become the Hope of the world. In looking at hope, we behold desire. Christ Himself becomes our desire as we behold Him.

With hope, we learn that the thing we are hoping for is the thing that we desire, but true hope, just like Christ as the Hope of the Gospel, is not based on wishful thinking. Hope commonly used means, "I hope I will get it, but the probability is slight." In the Hope of the Gospel, God has put Christ in the middle of our heart, and He becomes hope that is based on better promises; it is based on the certainty and absolute infallibility of God, His atttributes, and His Word.

Hope always brings joy; hope is dramatically different than wishful thinking. Hope holds the promise that *possessing* the good thing that is desired is not only possible, but also probable. Wishful thinking is accompanied by pain, anxiety, and disappointment because it holds no such promise. Hope is confidence in a future event; its well-founded expectation of good sets it apart from wishful thinking. We have good reason to expect this *good* that is hoped for in Christ. Hope is sound desire, and faith is the greater passion for that desire.

Throughout this lesson, we will revisit hope's acrostic (habit of permanent expectancy), the awareness that the journey *is* the destination, and the analogy of a chicken with an egg and/or pregnancy. Discovering our hopes and learning how to incubate hope are important counterparts.

Jaque's Journal

Jaque, I am your hope and expectation, I am your goal. With your attention focused on Me, strength is renewed, energy is increased, and you have power to do what you cannot do. I am your hope to be who you were always created to be, but could never manage to become on your own.

The journey is the destination, Jaque. Learn to focus your attention on Me and not on a desired outcome. My destination for you is always the moment you are in. The end result that you want is not what I want for you. My end result is the journey itself; how you take this journey through life is My good goal for you. Are you living with the Habit Of Permanent Expectancy? Are you creating habits that allow the practice of My presence to be both conscious and unconscious?

Jaque, a habit is important because, once something is a habit, it would be difficult for you NOT to do it. Hope, positive expectation grounded in Christ, is a firm habit. You are alive, which means you expect something from moment to moment. There is no shortage of new desires. With the Habit Of Permanent Expectacy comes the promise of good outcomes. The habit is the end result. The good outcome is not reserved for a future date; the good outcome is the joy, peace, patience, and confident assurance that you experience along the way. Practice this mindset with Me, for the means to all your ends, is the end. The way you get there, Jaque, sets the quality of your life.

From the 'hoping way of life' in you, I will cause My hopes and desires for Christ in His Jaque form to be made known to you along with all the particulars. Your patterns will be new, according to the Christ way. Your history will be transformed - all you have done or will do, and all that has ever been done to you, will go back only as far as Calvary.

This is the way of eagles who lift their wings and mount up to the sun. This is the way of Jaque, who lifts her wings and mounts up close to God because you are living the life of, and from, someone entirely new.

Lord, I love the 'hoping way of life' in me. You are the strength of my wings, Lord, and they are stretched out to You. My only ambition is to mount up close to You.

The means to the end is the end. The *way* we get to a result is the result that matters. *How* we perceive each new moment determines the quality of our life. It is not *what* we are living; it is *how* we are living it. Are we living our life in joy or struggle? The point the Lord is making is that *how* and *why* is more important than *what.*

Potential From On High

But ye shall receive power, after that the Holy Ghost is come upon you...

ACTS 1:8 (KJV)

In Luke 24:49, Jesus told His disciples to wait for what the Father promised - the Holy Spirit - because the Spirit is our power from on high. Other translations say that the Holy Spirit will clothe us with power from on high. It gives a new meaning to the phrase 'power suit'!

Hope holds potential. When scripture tells us we will receive power from on high, the word for power is 'dunamis' in the Greek. *Dunamis* is a word that means latent power, or the *potential* for power, such as dynamite. If we carry a stick of dynamite in our pocket, it has the potential for power, but if we never strike a match and ignite its fuse, it still has the potential of power, but it lacks the actual force or energy of its intended power. A stick of dynamite has powerful potential, but it is benign until it encounters the fire that will cause it to explode.

Hope gets its potential from Christ. Every true desire of a new creation is conceived in Christ. Hope, like a chicken sitting on her eggs, keeps desire safe and alive until faith can ignite its latent power.

The Miracle of Conception

Every desire that we have is like an egg, full of latent potential. A woman may have hundreds of eggs during ovulation, yet the chance of getting pregnant in a given cycle is surprisingly low. In the window for conception, there are all sorts of hurdles that egg and sperm must overcome. When conception does occur, it is a miracle of individuality and latent potential.

Likewise, there are hurdles and obstacles that thwart our desires. This is why God gives us so many desires and why it is understood that each one is only filled with *latent* power or potential. Each desire is like and an egg, looking to be fertilized, hoping for conception. Hope is the only reason we ever pursue a desire. Every little hopeful 'egg of desire' is full of Christ - it is full of unique possibility. If a desire is conceived, it will take on its distinctive form in our lives according to the specific detail and delight that is within that one egg (desire).

There are an unlimited number of ways that Christ could be Himself in us. We have different desires, unique gifts, and distinctive personalities. Our desires are equally unique. If we think about all the ways He could potentially express Himself through us, we would pursue as many desires as we could. He is waiting for hope to turn into a request for Him to fertilize each new desire. If the possibilities are limitless, then we need to reach for the stars. Thinking our desires are unimportant, we limit the expression of His uniqueness in us. To live with high hopes of how He could express Himself through us, brings greater joy than any endeavor and brings hope to the world around us.

☐ DAY 1 - REFLECTION

Define HOPE:

____

____

____

____

Define PASSION:

____

____

____

____

☐ DAY 1 - JOURNALIZING ASSIGNMENT

Now may our Lord Jesus Christ Himself and God our Father, Who loved us and gave us everlasting consolation and encouragement and well-founded hope through [His] grace (unmerited favor), comfort and encourage your hearts and strengthen them [make them steadfast and keep them unswerving] in every good work and word.

2 THESSALONIANS 2:16,17 (AMPC)

Study Suggestions

- Use a Bible translation that is accurate and easy to understand. A few good options are The King James Version Easy Read (also known as The Sword Bible) The New American Standard Bible, and The Amplified Bible. The Message Bible, The Passion Translation, and The Mirror Bible are enjoyable to read but note that they are paraphrased versions rather than direct translations.
- Read the verses around the assigned scripture to stay in context.
- Use a commentary to help you understand the Scripture in light of the historical setting, context, and the original language in which it was written.
- It would be highly beneficial for you to follow a plan to read the whole Bible each year.
- When defining a word, make use of a dictionary, concordance, thesaurus, and other reference materials of your choosing.
- When answering daily Reflections you may prefer more space than the few lines that are provided. Feel free to use a separate notebook or to use margin space to expound your answers.

Instructions for Journalizing

- ❖ We start by coming to our journals in faith knowing that God is, and that He rewards those who diligently seek Him.

And without faith it is impossible to please him. For whoever would draw near to God must believe that he exists and that he rewards those who seek him.

HEBREWS 11:6 (RSV)

- ❖ We believe that the word is alive and active and that Jesus is the word, so we come to the journal expecting Him to show us how the Scriptures apply to our daily lives and situations.

In the beginning was the Word, and the Word was with God, and the Word was God...and the Word became flesh and dwelt among us, full of grace and truth.

JOHN 1:1, 14 (RSV)

For the word of God is living and active, sharper than any two-edged sword, piercing to the division of soul and spirit, of joints and marrow, and discerning the thoughts and intentions of the heart.

HEBREWS 4:12 (RSV)

- ❖ Trusting that the Bible is our authority, we read our assigned verse(s) with a reflective heart. Reading the verse then reading it again as if we have never read it before, we sit quietly and ponder, asking the Holy Spirit to speak into our hearts. We listen with the intent to obey.

All scripture is inspired by God and profitable for teaching, for reproof, for correction, and for training in righteousness, that the man of God may be complete, equipped for every good work.

2 TIMOTHY 3:16-17 (RSV)

- ❖ We know that God has given the Holy Spirit to guide us, so we ask Him for understanding and discernment.

But the Counselor, the Holy Spirit, whom the Father will send in my name, he will teach you all things, and bring to your remembrance all that I have said to you.

JOHN 14:26 (RSV)

- ❖ Because we believe that God calls us by name, we begin a journal by writing our name. If journalizing is new to you, practice by paraphrasing the verses. Write as if God is speaking the verse directly to you. Look for the way the scripture applies to your life and write down what you believe He is saying in your heart. Let Him speak to you about everything that concerns you; then let Him speak to you about how everything concerns HIM. Let the writing flow; allow the Holy Spirit to expand the meaning of Scripture and apply it directly to your life.

To him the gatekeeper opens; the sheep hear his voice, and he calls his own sheep by name and leads them out.

JOHN 10:3 (RSV)

❖ For more help see the Appendix on Journalizing and Other Helps on page 265.

Lesson 1, Day 2 - *Hope Broods*

☐ Day 2 - Reading Assignment

Desires are like eggs which start small, like an embryo. We barely believe they are from God, yet they remain. Even when we try to suppress them, they resurface. Eventually, we realize that our true desires *are* from God and that they need to be taken care of.

Imagine a hen sitting on her eggs to warm, nurture, and faithfully protect them until the season comes for them to hatch. A faithful hen will not leave her eggs unattended, for she knows, if she does, a poacher might steal them and eat them. A hen named "Hope" will sit and warm those eggs, brooding over them until they get mature enough to hatch.

Hens lay eggs. Less commonly known, hens lay eggs with or without a rooster. Fertilized eggs require the mating of the hen and rooster. If the hen has mated and she lays an egg, then that egg is fertilized. If the hen has not mated and she lays an egg, then that egg is unfertilized. Only a fertilized egg will produce a chick!

We want our desires to be fertilized, and that requires Christ. Desires are fertilized as we meditate on (become intimate or *mate* with) the personal words, visions, and hopes that He sparks in our heart.

Jaque's Journal

Jaque, you had no hope, no promise. In the world without God, you who were once so far away, were brought near through the blood of Christ. You were far from your potential, far from a heart of true desire, but now, in Christ, you have an anchor that holds you steadfast in your hopes.

As you journalize the scripture, Jaque, you write Christ into your life. You pen what promises you can receive for today. The Spirit takes the scriptures, and gives them back to you in ink form. I am the hope in this writing, I am the journal of your heart, here I am, Jaque, in ink form, ink that is penned into spiritual thought and etched on the fiber of your soul.

To write a vision of hope is to hold fast and cherish that hope for as long as it takes to fertilize. Journalizing is a potent way to cherish Christ. It is the way of a disciple who waits to see what Christ will say within them, and who then captures the words in writing for meditation at a later time.

When you capture My words, Jaque, you create the Habit Of Permanent Expectancy, you incubate desires in a dark place, as in a womb. Like a hen on her eggs, you brood over My words and the desires they ignite. Nobody else can see it yet, this embryo of desire that impregnates you. It is ours; an expression of Christ in you, your hope of glory.

Nobody else can see it, Jaque, but you are incubating eggs when you meditate on My word in your journals. You will experience joy each time a new desire is born. Joy will come gently, and blow its breath upon your soul.

You will see and receive vision through the joy that hope provides. With vision, comes great joy. It comes as a free gift, one that you did not earn. Joy comes and lands softly, like a butterfly on your shoulder. When My Spirit lands, you just 'see and know'...effortlessly.

Christ is your mystery, Jaque, hidden deep in your heart; and until Christ is received in each recess of your heart, the mystery is yet to be known within that particular recess. Little by little, I am received by you; little by little, I take over the hidden recesses of your being.

Father, all I want to do is submit my thoughts and feelings to the glory of this mystery. I want to live as though 'You and I' is all there is...

The All in All

We will talk a lot about hope and desire, but first we must see that everything begins and ends in Christ.

> Christ is the All in all. If a true desire is sparked, it is by Christ. If it is conceived, it is by Christ. If an embryo is formed, it is by Christ. If we give birth to a purposeful goal, it is by Christ. All of our hope begins and ends in Christ. When we are impressed to pray, He is the impetus. If we see more clearly today than yesterday, He is the vision. We can trace all goodness, all inspiration, and all divine influence to His touch and to the nod of His head in our direction. He moves in us, and our response is a nuance of His grace.
>
> SUSAN MUCKLOW

If we have hope, it is because of Christ. Wishful thinking, however, is pure fantasy and we can have that all by ourselves. Fantasy causes a lot of pain. To comfort ourselves with vain imaginations that hold no promise alienates us from reality. With idealism and perfectionism at its core, fantasy will destroy all hope for real relationships. Christ does not offer fantasy; He offers Himself - the foundation of hope. As the All in all, Christ is the hen who sits on the egg, and He is the chick inside the egg. He is pregnant with vision in us, *as* us.

Jaque's Journal

> *Jaque, I have plans for your yesterdays, todays, and tomorrows.*
>
> Lord, how do you have plans for my yesterdays? How do You transform yesterday? Isn't it too late to plan for a day that has passed? Isn't hope for the future? How can I have hope for yesterday? I can look back at the past and say, "Oh Lord, I see how You spared me from even greater sorrow," but that doesn't *change* the past.

Jaque, Christ is your hope for yesterday, as well as tomorrow. He is the same yesterday, today, and tomorrow. Your hope of realizing My glory in the past is Christ in you today. Christ transforms how you interpret the past, and He causes you to recognize My use of all things for good. What do I purpose from the compost heap of your past? It may seem like manure to you, but manure is good for flowers. Jaque, does a flower grow in the center of your heart?

Yes, Lord, an everlasting flower of joy. Sometimes you send rain as water, but mostly you shine and let it grow up out of the compost pile of yesteryears. I see it Lord; yesterday is not a mistake or a sad story. Today I see how good it was, and is, for me. Because of yesterday and because I love You, I will endeavor to see all things according to Your purpose. I have a beautiful flower growing in my soul, it is an eternal and everlasting joy. It is a sweet fragrance to me everyday. Thank you for such an exquisite flower; this flower would not be in my soul if yesterday didn't look like manure.

Yes, Jaque, it is time to start seeing the greater view of what I do with all that has happened to you. I am the All in all. The past is not what it seemed to be. To see My purpose is to see with a new set of eyes. Hope is your hat, Jaque, your helmet, your thinking cap, and your covering. This is good because it protects you from hopeless thinking. Your hope is unwavering in Christ, He has carried you over the threshold to faith where your confidence for eternal security is strong and cannot be broken. Such hope causes you to speak boldly and fearlessly to the world around you. Christ is My mystery, and it takes faith to understand this mystery in you. You do not 'understand' in order to believe, you must first 'believe' in order to understand. To believe is to act on something in obedience to faith.

How you interpret yesterday has everything to do with your world-view and how you see the future. Jaque, people see the future in the context of yesterday; they interpret everything according to history - according to how they interpret the past. If you want hope for the future, you have to start interpreting the past differently. The past has a new interpretation in Christ. Don't think that your interpretation of the past is the right interpretation, for I have a different interpretation. In My interpretation, Christ is the All in all...

The significance of our past is in knowing that God uses everything for good. It does not matter what happened, or how badly people treated us. God brings flowers out of dung - blossoms of peace, joy, hope, love, and every wonderful thing that God wants us to inherit.

☐ Day 2 - Reflection

What is the importance of brooding over God's word and the intimate words He speaks in our journals?

____

____

____

____

☐ Day 2 - Journalizing Assignment

For whatever was written in earlier times was written for our instruction, so that through endurance and the encouragement of the Scriptures we might have hope and overflow with confidence in His promises.

Romans 15:4 (AMP)

Your future is bright and filled with a living hope that will never fade away. As you listen to me, my beloved child, you will grow in wisdom and your heart will be drawn into understanding, which will empower you to make right decisions.

Proverbs 23:18,19 (TPT)

Lesson 1, Day 3 - *Hope Takes Patience*

☐ Day 3 - Reading Assignment

When we think of hope, we can think of a mother. A mother waits out her term of pregnancy, and approximately nine months later, a little homo sapiens is born. If that momma were an elephant, she would have to wait almost two years for her little one to arrive. Apparently, elephants are more patient than human beings. Even more patient is Christ, who waits as long as necessary for us to reach maturity!

A mother hen is a good analogy if we want to picture how to care for our 'hope eggs' - even Jesus compared Himself to a mother hen once (Luke 13:34). When it comes to brooding over our hopes, we exercise patience, like a mother. A pregnant woman does not go to the delivery room until it is time. She does not say, "Oh, I went to the doctor this morning and he told me I am pregnant. So, I am going to go to the hospital this afternoon to deliver my baby." There is the understanding that the baby has to grow and develop within the safety of the mother's womb for about nine months. She does not doubt the doctor or the presence of the baby just because she has to wait for the baby to arrive. She knows the baby will come when it is time.

> *Do not, therefore, fling away your [fearless] confidence, for it has a glorious and great reward. For you have need of patient endurance [to bear up under difficult circumstances without compromising], so that when you have carried out the will of God, you may receive and enjoy to the full what is promised.*
>
> Hebrews 10:35,36 (AMP)

Carrying to term, then delivering hope is like pregnancy. We cannnot fling away our confidence that the baby will arrive. We need patient endurance. We may bear up under difficult circumstances, but when we have carried out the will (and hope) of God we will enjoy the fruit of what was promised. God's hopes in us are His will for us.

Whether a baby in a mother's womb, or hope in the womb of our heart, it takes time to grow. When we understand the formation process, we can enjoy nine months of pregnancy - or however long it takes our 'hope baby' to grow. Like a woman with child, we use our time wisely by doing things in expectation of what is coming. We get the nursery ready - paint walls, decorate, buy a crib, rocking chair, diapers, clothes, blankets, and the perfect teddy bear. A baby is coming; we want to be ready for the new arrival.

Why do we have a problem with patience? Our problem with patience, in part, is that we live in a world of instant mashed potatoes and chicken-in-a-minute. The Kingdom of God is not 'instant' in nature. Good things take time. Hope takes time because God works through *our* thoughts, desires, and requests. He works through our unique design and what fits with our purpose and joy. He knows what He put in us, and He knows what was corrupted; therefore, He knows what needs to be put on or taken off.

As we know ourselves in Christ, we start to choose different eggs (different desires, hopes, plans and actions). It is important for us to understand that *we* get to choose what we will hope for. He gives us the glorious opportunity to participate with Him in the development of our true expression in Christ. What we choose is filled with latent potential.

What is the 'hope egg' that we want to choose, or give expression to? Why did I choose to write about hope? I could have chosen from several hundred thousand subjects - but I chose an egg called Hope. *This* time, it was hope; another time it could be joy. However, this I know, whatever I choose, I will have to sit on it, incubate the egg, the word, or the subject, for a long time. When I got 'pregnant' with the word 'hope', I did not understand what the word meant. I knew I needed it, but I had to sit and incubate the word before I ever comprehended its meaning. I had to prepare my mind for the action He might require. I set my hope on the grace that I would receive as the revelation came. As I did, the word grew into an entire study.

> *Therefore, preparing your minds for action, and being sober-minded, set your hope fully on the grace that will be brought to you at the revelation of Jesus Christ.*
>
> 1 PETER 1:13 (ESV)

> Here's the progression: As Jaque incubated the word 'hope,' her understanding increased. A single word (hope) was fertilized and became an egg (a desire to write a study manual). The egg was filled with latent potential. As long as it was *just an idea,* the potential was present, but dormant. It had the *potential* to be a study manaul but first the 'baby' had to form (be outlined), and be born (written). As this egg grew in Jaque, it was not visible to her or others; but when it was born, we could all see the baby that had been growing. Once it was born, it was no longer latent; it reached its potential when it was no longer a figment of her imagination and it became a tangible study manual.
>
> Now, the baby (the study manual) has a new potential all its own. It has the *potential* to cause continued spiritual growth in Jaque *and* in others. The Lord used a word to create a study that could facilitate a life of learning. The word was weighty in Jaque because she *believed* in the vital importance of learning to incubate true desires in Christ.
>
> SUSAN MUCKLOW

We Do Not Play Church

A word like hope will lead to other words like faith and love, or joy. However, it all begins with hope; hope is the seed. We start with one true desire - the desire for Christ. Christ is our very first hope, our first *genuine* desire. Our desire is to know Him, not to play church. We do not want to pretend to have it together at church, but fall apart when we are at home. God intends to be a living reality in our life at all times.

Does a church building make God real? Is He more real *outside* of a church building? God *is* Reality; He becomes a reality in some churchgoers and in some non-churchgoers. Whether we attend church or gather in small groups, let us choose not to play church with God. Instead, let us make *knowing Him* our determined purpose.

But whatever former things I had that might have been gains to me, I have come to consider as [one combined] loss for Christ's sake. Yes, furthermore, I count everything as loss compared to the possession of the priceless privilege (the overwhelming preciousness, the surpassing worth, and supreme advantage) of knowing Christ Jesus my Lord and of progressively becoming more deeply and intimately acquainted with Him [of perceiving and recognizing and understanding Him more fully and clearly]. For His sake I have lost everything and consider it all to be mere rubbish (refuse, dregs), in order that I may win (gain) Christ (the Anointed One), and that I may [actually] be found and known as in Him, not having any [self-achieved] righteousness that can be called my own, based on my obedience to the Law's demands (ritualistic uprightness and supposed right standing with God thus acquired), but possessing that [genuine righteousness] which comes through faith in Christ (the Anointed One), the [truly] right standing with God, which comes from God by [saving] faith. [For my determined purpose is] that I may know Him [that I may progressively become more deeply and intimately acquainted with Him, perceiving and recognizing and understanding the wonders of His Person more strongly and more clearly], and that I may in that same way come to know the power outflowing from His resurrection [which it exerts over believers], and that I may so share His sufferings as to be continually transformed [in spirit into His likeness even] to His death, [in the hope] that if possible I may attain to the [spiritual and moral] resurrection [that lifts me] out from among the dead [even while in the body].

PHILIPPIANS 3:7-11 (AMPC)

☐ DAY 3 - REFLECTION

Name one of your desires, how it will become a fertilized egg, what you can do to prepare for its manifestation, and what it might look like when it finally hatches.

____

____

____

____

☐ DAY 3 - JOURNALIZING ASSIGNMENT

Let us not become weary in doing good, for at the proper time we will reap a harvest if we do not give up.

GALATIANS 6:9 (NIV)

But if we hope for what we do not yet have, we wait for it patiently.

ROMANS 8:25 (NIV)

LESSON 1, DAY 4 - *God Uses it All*

☐ DAY 4 - READING ASSIGNMENT

God will use everything *from* our past to create hope *for* our past, present, and future. As an example, I had a lot of discouragement from my past relationship with conventional church modalities. I always felt dissatisfied and often contended with the thought that I was a rebel in His church. Eventually, I realized the Lord *meant* for me to feel dissatisfaction, for He used it to build structure into study manuals that could support His presence as our only Source of satisfaction. I would not have found His path if it were not for that nagging sense of lack and dissatisfaction. He intended it as a call on my life from the very beginning and it took every ounce of frustration, emptiness, and ache to get me to the point of seeking His answers. The ache was always for more of Him. The inclusion of daily journalizing into study manuals, and even the approach I took in my home fellowship group, became solutions to a personal problem that God intended me to solve.

My search was for Him; I came to His word to behold Him, and I continued in His word to behold Him. Now I stay, in part, because of you. I am becoming a "self for others." My heart is for His people. I have a deep and passionate love that I cannot begin to comprehend. I cry deeply with His love for the Church. That which was infuriating me and left me feeling dissatisfied, is now the very thing that my heart yearns for. I want the Church to press into the Kingdom so badly that it has become part of my life's story. I would not have picked me for this job, but God used my frustration to forge a desire in me to be part of the solution. God knows what He is doing - I trust Him and we keep going!

Sit On It

If God is real, then let us *hope* to see Him and to be His yielded vessel. When I chose to incubate the word 'hope,' it was because of an innate *hope* that He put in me; I *knew* there was something for me to do with that word. It required more than just wishfully thinking that a revelation would fall out of the sky. The old saying "sit on it" was what I heard in my heart. It was like the Lord said, "Sit on it, Jaque! Go incubate this thing - get quiet, shut the doors. Tell everybody, 'No I cannot see you right now, I am incubating a 'word baby' and in order for it to grow in me, my understanding must grow. I am in desperate need of *hope*, so for a season, I need more time to sit, listen, study and learn, so that I can see what the Lord will say within me…about hope!'"

This is how a new desire takes shape. We give it our focus and it becomes our passion; it becomes the very reason we get out of bed in the morning. We awaken with a readiness to get to a quiet place where we can hear what else He will say about the new hope that we have been brooding over together. Whatever hopeful words we need, our passion has grown and we find we *must* have God in His real manifested form as it pertains to this, His latest desire in us. We are not interested in playing church - we want something much bigger than that - we want the Kingdom of God to be revealed in us, and we *have* to have it.

Compared to everything else we can look at in life, nothing comes close to the realness of God. Everything that *is* real comes out of the Kingdom. The passion to go after all the latent potential that is within each desire comes out of the Kingdom. The potential is waiting for someone to expect it, to draw it out and into the tangible realm. Christ is the mother heart of God in each of us. As we learn to expect Him, He supplies all the hope-filled expectation that is needed to give birth to His vision in us.

Jaque's Journal

> *Jaque, Christ is the golden goose who continuously lays golden eggs of hope. He brings definition to your desires when He calls a desire by its real name. Once you understand which desires are real to you, it is as if an egg has been laid. The egg has hope, but you still cannot see what is in the egg. You are hopeful even though it is invisible; it is very real to you, though unseen. Hope will nurture the invisible reality until faith manifests the chick in the egg. Every egg of desire is an embryo of Christ. So every*

hatchling is an uncovering, a revealing of Christ Himself in another form. Everything you give birth to is another revelation of Christ in you, as you.

The Lord is speaking the language of unity. He is asking us to see Him in all things. Is someone hoping for a child, a new career, to run a marathon, or to learn to play the piano? The manifestation of every hope we have is an embryo of Christ; an *expression* of Christ is in each of our desires. Everything we hope for is a revealing of Christ in another form, and every time we see Him, we have more hope.

Jaque's Journal

Jaque, hope enables you to enter into My presence, it reaches into the invisible region of heaven where the Father lives in you. Father's oath, Father's promise, is the anchor. It is what hope is based on. The promise of God is the anchor of hope, it settles into the soul and it cannot be aborted or broken. Hope is the reason you reached, Jaque. It gave you the unction to hold fast, and to desire holiness and rightness for your life. You can never stop hoping, even if you tried. I have given you this anchor; just to know that 'I Am' anchors you. To explore Me, sets the anchor even deeper. The more you hope in Christ, the more Christ is seen and recognized as your only hope of glory, and the simpler your life gets. The more you hope for Christ, the less you want material goods. You want less of fame and recognition, and more of Him. You want less complications, and more ease; you want less busyness, and more solitude or contemplation. As your hope in Christ grows, you want less form and structure and more freedom and spontaneity. You hope for less of what you used to hope for as you desire more of the inner life of heaven. The goal is for Christ to increase and for you to decrease.

Passion causes hope to get hotter as it (hope) waits for, and broods on, Christ. We are waiting for the manifestation of our hope, for a revealing of Christ in another form, and as we hover over our hope, it becomes the earnest feeling of our mind. In other words, the mind is renewed. We sit on our hope-filled desire through meditation and study and His presence makes incubating an egg an easy task. We stay pregnant and go full term; we never abort our hope.

The seed of Christ is still growing in each of us. Our reverence for His word should always be increasing. As He speaks His word to us, it leads, and we follow. His Word, spoken clearly and personally in our hearts, increases love's vision - Christ.

☐ Day 4 - Reflection

How do new desires take shape?

____

____

____

____

☐ Day 4 - Journalizing Assignment

No matter what, I will continue to hope and passionately cling to Christ, so that he will be openly revealed through me before everyone's eyes. So I will not be ashamed! In my life or in my death, Christ will be magnified in me. My true life is the Anointed One, and dying means gaining more of him.

PHILIPPIANS 1:20,21 (TPT)

Hope deferred makes the heart sick, but desire fulfilled is a tree of life.

PROVERBS 13:12 (NASB)

This hope [this confident assurance] we have as an anchor of the soul [it cannot slip and it cannot break down under whatever pressure bears upon it] - a safe and steadfast hope that enters within the veil [of the heavenly temple, that most Holy Place in which the very presence of God dwells], where Jesus has entered [in advance] as a forerunner for us, having become a High Priest forever according to the order of Melchizedek.

HEBREWS 6:19,20 (AMP)

LESSON 1, DAY 5 - *Faith, Hope, and Love*

☐ DAY 5 - READING ASSIGNMENT

We give thanks to God always for all of you, making mention of you in our prayers; constantly bearing in mind your work of faith and labor of love and steadfastness of hope in our Lord Jesus Christ in the presence of our God and Father, knowing, brethren beloved by God, His choice of you; for our gospel did not come to you in word only, but also in power and in the Holy Spirit and with full conviction.

1 THESSALONIANS 1:2-5 (NASB)

An act of faith, a labor of love, and a steadfast hope in Christ, work together. Faith pleases God because it demonstrates our assurance that God will do what He has promised. Love inspires hope, hope ignites faith, and faith involves heaven in the process. Hope, etched on our heart, directs all our efforts in faith and in love. Hope inspires, faith moves, and love unites. Sharing our hopes with one another is a life-affirming exchange of faith, hope, and love.

SUSAN MUCKLOW

Faith (as passion) causes hope to get hotter. Hope without faith is still just wishful thinking. We cannot separate hope from faith and love. Faith is the *substance* of things hoped for...faith is the tangible egg that hope sits on. When faith is full, it is hot enough to produce further results. Faith gets the heat from hope to produce results, for faith without heat is dead. Faith without hope is only a hen with an *empty* egg. It is not fertile, there is no chick in the egg, until hope and faith work together in love. Love is the foundation that hope and faith sit on.

Faith and hope work together by love. What mother hen (hope) would tend eggs if not for love? So love activates hope which spreads to faith, and the result is the *manifestation* of that which we hope for. Faith, hope, and love remain…the greatest of these is love. God so loved us that He gave us His Son, the very *Hope of the Gospel*. Christ is the mother hen of our faith eggs! He is also the chick in the egg! He is the All in all.

Faith, hope, and love work together; we don't see separation, for they never work independently. To separate one from the other would be to lose the essence of each. Their power is in their unity. They are attributes of God and none can be separated from the other. They are a part of the whole nature of God, the God who never differs from Himself nor is any shadow of turning found in Him. They are a part of Him *all* the time.

Jaque's Journal

Father, I know I have not yet captured all there is for me, but one thing I know, the past does not equal the future in You, so I won't fret over the past. By-gones are by-gones. I let go, not recalling the mistakes of the past, to press on to the future, to all that lies ahead in Christ. My supreme goal is to win the heavenly prize, to know those desires that You've placed in me and to incubate them, to brood over them until they turn into the burning passions that get the job done. You love me Lord; I am full of faith and hope. My job is nothing short of expressing Christ to the world in His Jaque form. Christ is calling me upward to these things.

Jaque, to do this is to attain what is true. Seek the excellence of Christ through a powerful testimony. Know that excellence is the power (passion) to live from My Spirit, not relying on the law or the performance of the flesh, but fully trusting your passion in Me to carry you to the end goal. Faith is passion, and hope anticipates what it will, by passion, acquire.

Love for others produces passion, for love is the most passionate force on earth. Passion (faith) works by love even as love is expressed through passion (faith).

Our highest calling is to stay pregnant with godly hope by abiding in His presence. Our goals in Christ must continually inspire us, therefore we continue to journalize His words to us. The constant sense of His goodness will keep our hope anchored to Him. We live in changing times, but that can be said in any decade. How do we navigate a changing culture that presents so many challenges? Our most vital need is to make a permanent habit of expecting God. We expect God to show up and to be God in the midst of every future unknown. Furthermore, we rest in the knowledge that He is good. If God is not good, then there is no rest at all. Apart from the knowledge of His goodness there is only the fear of torment.

Jaque's Journal

Jaque, all expectation, all true hope, is predicated upon My goodness - the foundational groundwork of all anticipation. I am good, and I do not force My attention upon you. It is easy for Me to have you in My thoughts at all times, but if you would know Me then you need to direct your focus towards goodness. Your attitude determines how you experience My reception of you. If you expect goodness, you will soon see that I am not slow to give it. But if you expect harshness, you will deem Me cold and aloof. Your heart determines how you know Me. To the humble heart, I am good. In My goodness, I show that to live well and be happy means hoping in Me and expecting Me in all goodness and favor. It means carrying an uplifting attitude toward Me. My word shows how good I am, even though your attitude can either reject or receive it. You choose how to know Me, Jaque. The choice is yours to make. This is My gift to you - 'choice' - the rudder of your ship. Where will your soul sail today? On seas of goodness, or seas of tumult? Let goodness open your horizon so your hopes are full of the light of My goodness. Then nothing but "goodness" will be your experience - no matter what the circumstance. In light of My goodness, all your desires offer hope and a future.

Father, I wholly devote my heart and mind to you. Thank you for choosing me to know goodness and to be utterly delighted by it. I expect you to present Yourself as awesomely good.

Journalizing His word elevates our view of God. He will unveil His goodness through a simple practice that helps us maintain our focus on His goodness even in the midst of personal trial, cultural corruption, or societal deviance. His life in us is the very hope we need to hope with. He is the one constant and only permanence; our hope is in Him.

He anchors our hope so that our words and actions begin to align. If our hope is in God, then we will not be plagued by futility. If our hope is in God, we will experience the assurance that what we are hoping for will come to pass. We experience this confidence because our hope is anchored in the integrity of His word, His promise, and His reality.

☐ DAY 5 - REFLECTION

How does an understanding of the goodness of God affect our hope?

Consider it All Joy, Abundant Life, Eternal Hope & expectant faith & passion

☐ DAY 5 - JOURNALIZING ASSIGNMENT

I find more joy in following what you tell me to do than in chasing after all the wealth of the world. I set my heart on your precepts and pay close attention to all your ways.

PSALMS 119:14,15 (TPT)

My soul has been cast far away from peace; I have forgotten happiness. So I say, "My strength has perished and so has my hope and expectation from the Lord." Remember [O Lord] my affliction and my wandering, the wormwood and the gall (bitterness). My soul continually remembers them and is bowed down within me. But this I call to mind, therefore I have hope. It is because of the Lord's lovingkindnesses that we are not consumed,

> *because His [tender] compassions never fail. They are new every morning; great and beyond measure is Your faithfulness. "The Lord is my portion and my inheritance," says my soul; "Therefore I have hope in Him and wait expectantly for Him." The Lord is good to those who wait [confidently] for Him, to those who seek Him [on the authority of God's word]. It is good that one waits quietly for the salvation of the Lord. It is good for a man that he should bear the yoke [of godly discipline] in his youth. Let him sit alone [in hope] and keep quiet, because God has laid it on him [for his benefit].*
>
> LAMENTATIONS 3:17-28 (AMP)

LESSON 1, DAY 6 - *A Measure of Faith*

☐ DAY 6 - READING ASSIGNMENT

The Holy Spirit will always 'connect the dots' of God's Word and interpret its meaning in our heart. We understand according to our current level of faith and, by understanding, we acquire more faith. That is a good goal, for with increased faith we can advance God's Kingdom and diminish Satan's effect on earth.

What exactly is faith? We are in a world where bad things happen to everyone, even those with full faith, but still, what is faith? Faith is beyond what our natural mind has to say in defense of it. Faith is the substance of things hoped for. Faith is substantiated or made manifest when all our hope is in God. Although every believer has a measure of faith, faith grows on the food that feeds it - the Word of God. It does not grow by praying for more faith. So how much food does faith require on a daily basis? Practically speaking, a seed of faith, like a baby, needs to be fed and exercised if it is to grow. It is not enough to say, "I have faith," because we all have faith. The real question is what is happening with the measure of faith that we have been given. A great gift was imparted; what are we doing with it?

> *So then faith cometh by hearing, and hearing by the word of God.*
>
> ROMANS 10:17 (KJV)

> *For through the grace given to me I say to everyone among you not to think more highly of himself than he ought to think; but to think so as to have sound judgment, as God has allotted to each a measure of faith. For just as we have many members in one body and all the members do not have the same function, so we, who are many, are one body in Christ, and individually members one of another. Since we have gifts that differ according to the grace given to us, each of us is to exercise them accordingly: if prophecy, according to the proportion of his faith; if service, in his serving; or he who teaches, in his teaching; or he who exhorts, in his exhortation; he who gives, with liberality; he who leads, with diligence; he who shows mercy, with cheerfulness.*
>
> ROMANS 12:3-8 (NASB)

> Romans 12 shows us that God has given each of us the grace and the faith to exercise or operate in our own unique gifting. In a word, we have been given the grace and faith to be *ourselves*. When Paul's audience was thinking of themselves "more highly than they ought," Paul's response to their pride was to clarify that not only are *spiritual gifts* a work of God's grace, but so is the *faith* that is necessary to exercise those gifts. He eliminated human boasting from the equation. In essence, faith is evidenced when we do what we were gifted to do. The gifts differ according to the grace given to each of us, and so we exercise the gifts according to the portion of faith that was given to accompany the gift.
>
> SUSAN MUCKLOW

I believe love is the reason for this gift of faith. Love is the vision and mystery of Christ in us, *as* us (Colossians 1:27). According to the Word of God, love is the only thing that never fails (1 Corinthians 13:8).

The word of God is the understanding, maintenance and preservation of our very selves. It is the preservation of all our hopes and desires. The Word of God is Christ living in us, as us. His word feeds our faith and faith pleases God (Hebrews 11:6). Reading scripture, devotion, giving to the poor, acts of kindness or extreme sacrifice, means nothing if not done by faith. All that matters is faith, expressing itself through love.

> *If I speak in the tongues of men or of angels, but do not have love, I am only a resounding gong or a clanging cymbal. If I have the gift of prophecy and can fathom all mysteries and all knowledge, and if I have a faith that can move mountains, but do not have love, I am nothing. If I give all I possess to the poor and give over my body to hardship that I may boast, but do not have love, I gain nothing. Love is patient, love is kind. It does not envy, it does not boast, it is not proud. It does not dishonor others, it is not self-seeking, it is not easily angered, it keeps no record of wrongs. Love does not delight in evil but rejoices with the truth. It always protects, always trusts, always hopes, always perseveres. Love never fails.*
>
> 1 CORINTHIANS 13:1-8 (NIV)

For in Christ Jesus neither circumcision nor uncircumcision has any value. The only thing that counts is faith expressing itself through love.

GALATIANS 5:6 (NIV)

Because God is love, He sent His Word to heal and deliver us (Psalm 107:20). He sent His word to give us a safe place to dwell, to lift our thoughts, heighten our expectations, impact us with hope, and to substantiate (give substance to) the Kingdom of God within us.

Remember that God works *through* mankind. He doesn't work alone, He works through our thoughts, our desires, our requests. If our vague prayers were answered, our faith would never grow because we wouldn't know it was *His* answer. He delights in making it very clear that He *is* God, and that He hears *specific* requests and sends *specific* answers. In this way it is apparent that God is rewarding and fulfilling the desires of our unique and individual hearts.

Hope is the evidence of God. God *is*, so hope broods on Him. We, by hope, anticipate God's goodness, therefore we are *moved* to action! Hope is the expectation that *always* gets what it anticipates. Faith is the substance of things we are hoping for, the evidence of our expectation! Our highest purpose and desire on earth is to express Christ to the world through the form He takes in us. He is the final Hope of the Gospel.

We begin a study in hope by placing our hope in Christ. If our hopes are in Him, we remain in the safety of His counsel, for were it otherwise, it would be easy to misplace our hopes and put them in other people, places and things. But we want to learn right from the start how to possess our desire *in Him*. He is the ultimate hope; He is the All in all. We begin, not by separating the things we hope for *from* Christ, but by putting them right in the middle of Him. *He* is the sum of all that we desire, all we will ever want.

Being human, we easily think in separate terms. We have Christ, then we have our desires, and then we have our things. But in Spirit and in Truth, He is the *sum total* of all our desires. He is the Way, the Truth, and the Life.

The hope with which we hope is always and forever Christ in us. We cannot love until His love is shed abroad in our hearts, so we cannot hope with frail human hope - we hope with God's hope just as we love with God's love. Our certain hope is none other than the hope *of* God Himself dwelling within us. This is what is meant by Christ *is* our hope.

☐ Day 6 - Reflection

Write down your understanding of Galatians 5:6 (the only thing that counts is faith expressing itself through love).

____

____

____

____

☐ Day 6 - Journalizing Assignment

For God alone my soul waits in silence and quietly submits to Him, for my hope is from Him. He only is my rock and my salvation; my fortress and my defense, I will not be shaken or discouraged.

Psalm 62:5,6 (AMP)

May the God of hope fill you with all joy and peace in believing [through the experience of your faith] that by the power of the Holy Spirit you will abound in hope and overflow with confidence in His promises.

Romans 15:13 (AMP)

LESSON 1, DAY 7 - *Want Them More*

☐ DAY 7 - READING ASSIGNMENT

If there are true desires that have not manifested, we have to *want* them more. There are many areas of our life where it seems we have failed. However, we have not failed until we fall down and *refuse* to get back up. Falling down is not failure, as long as we get up and learn from our falling and rising. If something diverts our attention, and we fail to nurture our egg, then we need to *want* it more than we want the distraction. If the egg is important, we will come back to it. We may fall, but we get back up on our nest and continue warming our hope.

Honestly, some desires 'come and go' because they are not that important to us yet. This is part of the process of growing up and learning to discern values and desires. They may even be true desires…just not for now; perhaps later we will be ready for them. Later we may be able to pick them up and to carry them to term.

Sometimes we may find that our own desires are not clear to us. Not to worry, for the Lord is faithful. He will filter, sift, and sort until we are able to see what we do and do not desire. When hopes are tied to the kingdom of heaven within us, then heaven will define our every desire.

Jaque's Journal

Jaque, the Spirit causes you to know, and you do know, when you listen. This knowing is what you must live by - it is the knowing of faith. The problem is not that you do not know your true desires, hopes, and dreams; it is that you have not quieted your inner state enough to listen and hear. Wake up now and listen! You believe I am here, so listen!

Jaque, listen for My knowing voice in you. Take the pause between stimulus and response so you can hear what I say. Give Me time. Slow down all of your actions and in the stillness you will realize that you have the mind of Christ.

Let this be your treasure! More than anything else that you want in this world, you want to hear Me. So, listen.

I will speak, and in your heart you will begin to see My hope and vision; your eyes will be sound and full of hope. You will have delight in My plans for you, and obedience will be sweet. With Me at the helm of your hope, you'll never lack for new ventures. I'll tell you all that you need to hope for - and what I don't speak about, you don't need to worry about. There are hopes that are not for you, and plenty of hopes that I will give to others.

Lord, Father, Christ, and Spirit! All I have ever wanted in the whole world is to hear You. The sound of Your voice makes me know that I am safe.

Hope is a journey. Whether we are talking about hopes in need of nurturing, hopes that are for a later time, or hopes in need of refinement and personalization, we keep in mind that the journey *is* the destination. We focus our attention on Him, not on a desired outcome. His destination for us is the present moment. The results that we often want are not what He wants for us. His desired result is the exercise of joy in the journey; *how* we take this journey through life is His goal for us. Are we living with the habit of permanent expectancy? Are we creating a habit to practice His presence daily? Remember, a habit is important because, once something is a habit, it is difficult for us NOT to do it!

How many babies (hopes) can we carry in the womb at one time? Everyone is different, but we can usually handle one or two at a time. The Lord brings a desire to the forefront, shining a light of importance and priority upon it, and we know that He is asking us to sit with it. We believe He has given it to us and asks that we stay with it until it manifests. We begin our process of brooding, and do not worry about how long the pregnancy will last. Our attitude of faith is, "Father, if it takes ten thousand years for this fruit to be born, then I can wait. I am an eternal being and I can wait as long as it takes." That is the heart of hope and faith. Allowing ten thousand years somehow releases us from all the pressures of time! It protects us from the impatience of the flesh that thinks, "If I don't see it by next month or next year then I guess it wasn't from God." The impatient flesh is without hope and will easily abort the promises of God. The spirit is full of hope; it never doubts that satisfaction awaits every desire born of God. Need and supply are as one in Christ. We feel hunger because there is food. A bird wants to fly and the sky waits. If we have an unfulfilled desire on this earth, then it is because heaven is our true home. Every earthly hope is temporary, intended to spark a greater desire for the heavenly hope that is eternal.

Maternal Instinct

A good mama dog will nurse, warm, clean, and protect her litter of pups. If a female dog lacks maternal instincts and rejects her pups, then, sadly, they may perish. If we neglect our 'hope eggs', they may perish, but Christ is the maternal instinct in us.

> Christ is the maternal instinct in us, but as His body, His hopes manifest *through* us. We look for eggs to sit on (desires to brood over) knowing His choice works through our desires. He is the Master Hen sitting on the egg; in partnership with Him, we watch, observe, and do what we see Him doing in us. We do not always get it right, which means that not every egg will hatch a chick. There are hope *exercises* in motion. Since hope often includes a refinement process, we may nurture a desire for a while only to realize that it is not our egg. That does not detract from the maternal instinct of Christ in us, nor define us as a bad hen, it is just part of the process.
>
> Relationship with Christ includes self-honesty in the light of His presence. We have to assess whether we are neglecting our hopes. We walk in the light as He is in the light, so that we can see the shadows of self-deception.
>
> SUSAN MUCKLOW

We look at where He points the spotlight, showing us where to sit and how to nurture that which He is nurturing in us. Hope is a gift from God, and Christ is the Hope of the Gospel. Every true hope and desire that we have is a reflection of heaven and has the Christ embryo.

☐ DAY 7 - REFLECTION

How are earthly hopes tied to the kingdom of heaven?

Highlights our true desires that can only be fulfilled by God in the Kingdom (Spiritual) Realm. Drink Up, Spend Time w/ Abba

☐ DAY 7 - JOURNALIZING ASSIGNMENT

Beloved, now we are children of God, and it has not appeared as yet what we will be. We know that when He appears, we will be like Him, because we will see Him just as He is. And everyone who has this hope fixed on Him purifies himself, just as He is pure.

1 JOHN 3:2,3 (NASB)

Set your minds on things above, not on earthly things. For you died, and your life is now hidden with Christ in God. When Christ, who is your life, appears, then you also will appear with him in glory.

COLOSSIANS 3:2-4 (NIV)

Lesson 1 - Heart-Work

The Heart-work is a valuable part of your inner work. Taking the time to give heartfelt responses to the following questions is beneficial for you and beneficial for sharing with others who are in your study group.

Putting it All Together

1. If you could see Christ as the sum of all you seek - if He was the name you gave to everything you desire - how do you think worry would diminish in your life?
2. Explain the 'Hope of the Gospel' as you understand it.
3. Create a story or share a testimony relating the difference between wishful thinking and hope that is based on God's word.
4. Please share your journalizing experience this week with regard to heart and frequency. How was your desire for discipline grounded in grace this week?

Note: If you are in a VI class, please include one journal from this week with the Heart-work you submit for coaching.

If not, please bring your Heart-work and a journal to share with others in your study group.

NOW TIME, TIME MANAGEMENT

Now faith is the substance of things hoped for, the evidence of things not seen.

HEBREWS 11:1 (KJV)

LESSON 2, DAY 1 - *Faith is Now*

☐ DAY 1 - READING ASSIGNMENT

The faith we will talk about is *now* faith; it isn't just faith, it's faith that is right now. God's presence is in the present moment; *now* is when and where we know the Lord. What we knew yesterday is good, but what we know today will save us now. This *now* place is the place of God's rest, for when He calls us to His rest He beckons us to His presence, now. God is the place where peace dwells; He is our dwelling place. God said His name is, "I Am." "I Am" is present tense; it is now. He did not say His name is "I Was" or "I Will Be" even though these are also true of God. No, He says, "I Am." He puts Himself in the present tense so we may always know where to find Him.

> *Then Moses said to God, "If I come to the people of Israel and say to them, 'The God of your fathers has sent me to you,' and they ask me, 'What is his name?' what shall I say to them?" God said to Moses, "I am who I am." And he said, "Say this to the people of Israel: 'I am has sent me to you.'" God also said to Moses, "Say this to the people of Israel: 'The Lord, the God of your fathers, the God of Abraham, the God of Isaac, and the God of Jacob, has sent me to you.' This is my name forever, and thus I am to be remembered throughout all generations.*
>
> EXODUS 3:13-15 (ESV)

> *And those who know your name put their trust in you, for you, O Lord, have not forsaken those who seek you.*
>
> PSALM 9:10 (ESV)

Now faith is seeing what *really is* in contrast to what *seems* to be. *Now* faith is envisioning your hopes as a reality before anyone else even knows what they are. *Now* faith is so real that your life is lived as if the promise is already manifested and the 'title deed' is in your hand.

Now faith lives from a grateful heart. It is thankful in all things and sees God in everything. It has joy overcoming and overflowing.

Now faith lives above clouds of despair. In *now* faith, we see the law of lift that supersedes the law of gravity. *Now* faith is lifted above the temporal realm where doubt and fear is heavy and despairing.

Now faith is living with substance, for anything less than *now* faith is only a shadow.

Since God calls us to live and abide in Him, and He is, "I Am," we are most at ease with Him as we look to Him in the present moment. This helps us to set a steady, moment-by-moment pace, without the push of tomorrow or the pull of the past. The flesh struggles with living in the moment; it would trade peace and rest for the fast paced, fast food, fast money society that abounds.

> *Wealth [not earned but] won in haste or unjustly or from the production of things for vain or detrimental use [such riches] will dwindle away, but he who gathers little by little will increase [his riches].*
>
> PROVERBS 13:11 (AMPC)

Jaque's Journal

Jaque, if you arrive too quickly at your desired end, by haste or by unjust means, such an end, goal, or desire, will slip away. You cannot keep the favored results that are acquired by unjust means and hasty ways. The truth works; any thing accomplished outside of truth is not lasting. But if you gather little by little you will increase your riches and maintain your results. The light dawns little by little. Each day therefore, make a contribution of time to the acquiring of light. Nothing is urgent! Nothing has to be acquired in full today; a little investment of time each day over a period of months and years works out to a full and splendid salvation that, as approached, is also maintained.

Jaque, today is the day to acquire a little more light. Don't put it off, thinking you can catch up later to your full salvation. There are no short cuts and no such thing as 'catching up.' Hope keeps faith alive, but without daily light to feed your hopes, both hope and faith die young. Having no hope equals a sick heart that casts off all restraints; it will run wild into a lack of discipline and perish because it is incapable of holding a daily vision.

Desire must be fulfilled, Jaque. I supply desire as a need in each individual, a need to be supplied by the Substance that is already present to fill it, for I never create a need without presenting a ready supply. So then, do not despise My counsel and bring destruction upon yourself, for to put Me off is to act as if I do not exist. Those who come to Me must believe that I am....

Making small daily investments in hearing God speak directly to us is what causes us to lose vagueness and to gain stability and confidence. These little investments multiply and buy up the time. Eventually, our lives are overlapped by the wisdom that is gained in the quiet times that we have spent with Him.

The Future is Least Like Eternity

C.S. Lewis said, "The present is the point at which time touches eternity."

Jaque's Journal

Jaque, freedom is only offered to you in the present moment. This is where the reality of My presence abides. Here, in what we shall call 'now time,' is where you live by faith. Here, in 'now time' is where you touch eternity. Obey My voice right now and live by faith. Bear the cross of the present moment and give thanks for the present pleasure.

Jaque, the enemy tempts you to live in the future even more than the past, for thinking constantly about the future inflames false hope and fear. Future unknowns force you to speculate and to create hollow imaginations. The future therefore, is least like eternity and most like fantasy. The future is the most illusory part of time. The past is gone, the present glows with life, and the future is not here yet.

Jaque, I want you to think of the future only as it is necessary for now, to envision and plan the acts of love which will be your duty tomorrow. The action of planning for tomorrow is a duty of today. You will loosely borrow from the future, but the duty itself is in the present. Do not give your heart to the future, do not make future plans rigid, but rather do what is required today, and when you are finished, wash your mind of the blueprint and commit the plan to Me. Return at once to the patience and gratitude that are part of living in My 'now presence.'

> *For God says, "Your cry came to me at a favorable time, when the doors of welcome were wide open. I helped you on a day when salvation was being offered." Right now God is ready to welcome you. Today he is ready to save you.*
>
> 2 CORINTHIANS 6:2 (TLB)

Each day is preparation to receive the things that God is prepared to give us. This means making 'spiritual exercise' part of each day's plan, for we do not have the strength to hold His goods until our spiritual muscles are developed.

We can see the correlation in physical exercise. By developing muscle, we become stronger and can lift more, run farther and faster, and climb mountains without fainting. Likewise, our spiritual man needs to be developed in the Word of God, that he may be equipped to *hold fast* to his salvation.

Journalizing, or writing the vision each day, is equivalent to writing a plan. Before any plan can become a clear-cut objective, different angles and strategies are gathered, thoughts and ideas are formed, so the plan can take shape. This takes time and this is exactly what God wants from us. The more quality time we give Him, the greater measure of God authored desire can return to us for completion.

We gather strategies, thoughts, and inspiration from God. We gather the thoughts of Christ and practice those thoughts in our minds. The more we think His thoughts, the more the perfect plan begins to form. We see God's perfect salvation being developed in us, from the image and likeness of Christ. Daily we are stationed in the watchtower, looking through God's eyes, gaining His perspective in our minds.

As we keep writing the vision we get from God, making the plan clear on paper, it becomes plain enough that our time has come. Though it seems to tarry, we keep writing it down. One day it will be so obvious that even skeptics won't miss it.

☐ DAY 1 - REFLECTION

Define YESTERDAY:

____

____

____

____

Define TOMORROW:

____

____

____

____

Define the PRESENT:

____

____

____

____

☐ Day 1 - Journalizing Assignment

For in the gospel the righteousness of God is revealed, both springing from faith and leading to faith [disclosed in a way that awakens more faith]. As it is written and forever remains written, "The just and upright shall live by faith."

Romans 1:17 (AMP)

LESSON 2, DAY 2 - *Yesterday, Today, and Tomorrow*

Yesterday is behind us. It is the day last passed, the day before the present. Tomorrow is the day after the present; understanding the meaning of yesterday and tomorrow is straightforward. When we look at 'now' or the 'present' moment called today, however, there is a lot to behold. The word *present* means existing or being right now, at this time, not past or future, but to be ready at hand. To be present is to be attentive in the present moment, not absentminded nor distracted. We attend to what God is saying now, as He calls us into His rest.

God's rest involves the present moment; the habit of permanent expectancy (hope) also belongs in the present moment. A habit is something we have repeated so often that it is mechanical; we can do it without thinking, so our mind can stay in the present moment. For instance, we can chew gum and ride a bike at the same time - chewing gum no longer deters our ability to pay attention to our surroundings while riding the bike. When we develop a habit, we are able to do the task and still carry on a conversation; we are able to wash the dishes, while we converse with a friend. We can drive our car and remain aware of traffic conditions. We have driven a car so many times that we no longer have to think about where the brake is, or the gas pedal, or the turn signals. We no longer have to remind ourselves to look in the rearview mirror or to use our side mirrors to help us make a safe lane change. Because these things have become mechanical, our attention can remain in the present moment, focused on what is happening around us.

Likewise, when we live in continual awareness of God, we stop doubting our choices and decisions. We are as comfortable in life as we are behind the wheel of a car.

> As the relationship between self and Spirit becomes more and more intimate, then we become less and less concerned about our own choices and find that we are making right choices - choices through association and relationship.
>
> PETER MCDANIEL

> *Do your best to present yourself to God as one approved, a worker who has no need to be ashamed, rightly handling the word of truth.*
>
> 2 TIMOTHY 2:15 (ESV)

Walking on Water

> *The boat was already a considerable distance from land, buffeted by the waves because the wind was against it. Shortly before dawn Jesus went out to them, walking on the lake. When the disciples saw him walking on the lake, they were terrified. "It's a ghost," they said, and cried out in fear. But Jesus immediately said to them: "Take courage! It is I. Don't be afraid." "Lord, if it's you," Peter replied, "tell me to come to you on the water." "Come," he said. Then Peter got down out of the boat, walked on the water and came toward Jesus. But when he saw the wind, he was afraid and, beginning to sink, cried out, "Lord, save me!" Immediately Jesus reached out his hand and caught him. "You of little faith," he said, "why did you doubt?"*
>
> MATTHEW 14:24-31 (NIV)

It was early morning, before dawn, when Jesus came walking on the water. The disciples in the boat thought He was a ghost. Jesus said, "Don't be afraid, it's Me!" Peter said, "Lord, if it is You, then bid me come." Jesus did, and Peter walked on water. The important thing to grasp is that when Peter walked on water, he was walking on the command of Jesus. Obedience to the command of Jesus allowed Peter to walk on something that most people cannot walk upon. Obedience to the command of Jesus allowed Peter to defy the laws of physics.

Peter walked on the word or command of Jesus, and only when he diverted his attention to the wind and the waves (the circumstances) did he begin to sink. When the Lord speaks to us, He is asking us to walk on water - to step out in faith and walk on His command. When we do, we are walking on the top of our circumstances. We are walking above all that is happening around us.

People will often ask, "How are you?" A common reply is, "Well, under the circumstances, I'm doing okay." We should not be *under* the circumstances; we should be walking on top of the circumstances where the Lord has invited us to come. We sink when we look at our circumstances (the wind and the waves). If we are drowning in our circumstances, it is because we are looking at the wrong subject. Walking on the water is simply walking on His command.

In this story, Jesus did not say anything to Peter about the water, the wind, or the waves. He did not point out the improbability of walking on water. He did not give Peter a pep talk about how He (Jesus) is God and therefore Peter could trust Him. Jesus did not puff Peter up by saying the he (Peter) could do this because he had more faith than the other disciples. All Jesus said was, "Come."

He just said, "Come," because it should be common understanding that anybody can walk on top of their circumstances (water, wind, and waves) if they are obeying His command. Faith in His command holds an energy that defies physics. Faith is a *substance* that makes the nature of water irrelevant. Faith in the personal word that He speaks to us will hold us up every time.

Jaque's Journal

Lord I want and need to talk to You about stewardship of my time, money, and relationship with the things that I am supposed to take care of in life.

Jaque, stewardship is for rest, it is in the intangible realm. Remember, Jaque, that I once told you that the tangibles rise up from the intangibles?

Yes, Lord, I do. You said that this was why the Israelites could not enter the Promised Land; they did not cherish the right place within them, the intangible place. Rather, they cherished time, money, relationships, and family, more than they cherished You. They did not learn to love You with all their heart, soul and being.

Jaque, rest is the Promised Land. It is the land of peace, confidence, joy, and 'knowing' without knowing how you know. The Promised Land is where you learn to possess little by little. When a little more fear is kicked out the door (regarding these externals or tangibles) then there is more peace to possess and more joy to maintain. The promised land of peace and rest is inherited a little at a time. You can only inherit a little each day; therefore, you must walk on the water of My instructions to you. Today, you must hear My Word say, "Come to Me!" Today, you must leave the boat where you feel secure and step out on My Word. Time, money, and relationships are back in the boat. They tend to make you feel more secure, especially if you have enough of what you think you need for today. They are in the boat, and now I say, "Leave them, and walk over to Me! Come to Me, abide in Me, and leave the boat behind you."

Do not worry, Jaque, about how big your boat is, or if it will be sturdy enough to contain all that you desire in this earthly life. I know that you desire to be a good steward of the goods that I have given you, and you are because of Christ in you, not because of anything that you do or do not do. What more is there, Jaque? The real stewardship is the stewardship of Christ in you, by Christ in you.

Father, my mortal mind has complicated everything, hasn't it? You say it well.

Jaque, seeing it helps you comprehend that your boat is too full of stuff and that it is sinking anyway. Leave the boat and come to Me! Walk free of all the baggage. My yoke is easy and light, and allows you to run and not be weary, to walk and not faint. Do you want to enter the land that I have promised you?

Yes, Lord, I am coming right now; as a matter of fact, I don't have anything else to do. Nothing is any longer of importance in life in the light of Your call.

When all we know to *hope* for is God, when He is all we want, we will never feel the need to ask for anything else again. *Now* is the place where God dwells, the place of His rest. When He commands us to love Him with all our 'heart, soul, strength, and being' He is saying, "Love Me with all of your attention."

> Faith never knows where it is being led, but it loves and knows the One who is leading.
>
> OSWALD CHAMBERS

☐ DAY 2 - REFLECTION

In your own words, explain how walking on water is like walking on His word.

the invisible bridge (Indiana Jones); exhillerating, but you know He is there every step.

Peter walked on the command of Christ's invitation.

☐ DAY 2 - JOURNALIZING ASSIGNMENT

Therefore, since we are surrounded by so great a cloud of witnesses [who by faith have testified to the truth of God's absolute faithfulness], stripping off every unnecessary weight and the sin which so easily and cleverly entangles us, let us run with endurance and active persistence the race that is set before us, [looking away from all that will distract us and] focusing our eyes on Jesus, who is the Author and Perfecter of faith [the first incentive for our belief and the One who brings our faith to maturity], who for the joy [of accomplishing the goal] set before Him endured the cross, disregarding the shame, and sat down at the right hand of the throne of God [revealing His deity, His authority, and the completion of His work].

HEBREWS 12:1,2 (AMP)

LESSON 2, DAY 3 - *Hope and Prayer*

It is our goal to live in the present moment, but it does not come without a struggle. It will involve labor because there is an agenda pitted against us to keep us unaware. The distraction of the enemy is embedded in the system of this world. Empty entertainment and diversions of every kind try to keep us from entering in. A dear friend, Claudia, once shared her definition for the word 'entertain.' Coming from enter and detain, to be entertained is to be detained from entering in. Entertainment keeps us from entering in. In the hands of the enemy, it is a hidden agenda. The world is full of entertainment; if we are not aware, it will keep us from entering in to where God has called us to be.

God is calling us to peace for our soul, and rest in the finished work of Christ. God wants our attention in the present moment. Hope incubates God until a revelation is born. All we ever need is a revelation of God. We feel the need for many things, but under the surface, all we need is a revelation of God. Other things do not distract hope; hope stays with the pregnancy until faith brings the baby home. Hope is not going anywhere; it is waiting for faith to bring the baby home - and faith *will* bring the baby home as long as hope stays with the pregnancy.

Jaque's Journal

> *Jaque, an earnest prayer life means remaining alert and aware. Expectation has its eyes open at all times. A mother hen is jealous over her eggs. Wild animals guard their eggs; they are prepared to fight to the death with any predator who would come to steal this treasure of potential from them. This is a picture of an earnest prayer life, a hen interceding for the potential of her unborn chicks. Prayer and hope work together. Hope intercedes; it comes in between to guard a goal from any would be predator. The potential of each goal and desire is that it grows for the glory of God. Hope protects it from that which would seek to destroy its hopeful expectations.*

Intercession means to stand in the gap; it is standing between two things. On one side is the potential of all that we are meant to be in Christ, on the other side is anything that opposes the formation of Christ in us. As long as we live in these bodies, there is still a residue of the false nature that prefers the flesh, the things of this world, and the indulgence of selfishness in every form. It is at enmity with God and will never be at peace with God. Thus, the spirit must rise up and put the flesh in its place; the new creation must take control of this city!

Predators

Fear is a big predator, so are anger and despair; we must strain, struggle, and slay these enemies. We fight until every fear has fallen at our feet. We clear the way for our hope to be born. We guard the seed like the hen guards her eggs - against anything that would want them crushed.

My friend, Kim, and I ended up at an ostrich farm one weekend. I was preparing to teach the subject of hope, so I thought I might get to observe the behavior of a mother 'hen' guarding her eggs. Instead, I saw these ostrich mamas running all around practically trampling their eggs underfoot! We wanted to pick up some feathers, and had to wait for the ostriches to let us have those feathers because, we discovered, ostriches are a little mean and somewhat aggressive! Even in the Bible, a mother ostrich seems a little vilified, until the parenting role of the ostrich is understood. Mother ostrich will abandon her eggs, or even trample them underfoot - and at this farm, we certainly had this concern. While a female ostrich may not *seem* to have good instincts as a mother, it is important to note that among ostriches, the *male* primarily protects the eggs and guards the young. We learn something new everyday!

So, we got our feathers, no eggs were squashed, but we did not have the object lesson we were expecting! Nonetheless, and ostriches aside, *we* must fight off the predators that want to crush our eggs and guard our babies until they can stand on their own. We must buy every opportunity to carry our potential beneath our wings and to slay the enemies of hope.

We grow in the faith to live this way. We get strength and ability to guard our eggs as we practice His presence. We hold fast to the confession of our hope, and stir one another up to love and good works. We cultivate the habit of genuine Christian fellowship, and encourage one another in faith. We protect the potential He has put within us.

> *Let us hold fast the confession of our hope without wavering, for he who promised is faithful. And let us consider how to stir up one another to love and good works, not neglecting to meet together, as is the habit of some, but encouraging one another, and all the more as you see the Day drawing near.*
>
> HEBREWS 10:23-25 (ESV)

Jaque's Journal

> *Jaque, I am here right now and to hear Me, you must enter the atmosphere of the present moment with greater awareness. To be more aware of Me and My presence, you must decrease your sense of self. There is much detaching to be done, for it is attachments that make the false self feel alive. Attachments to people, places and things, to money, or addictive substances, cause distraction and become forms of empty entertainment.*

Distractions keep us from entering the places that God wants to take us; they cause our false self to feel alive. The false sense of self will not die on its own; it will do anything it can to deceive us, to keep us attached to our favorite distractions. The more alive it feels through our attachment to distractions, the more fear will surface - making us afraid of losing anything at all. The more attached we are to something, the more fear we experience.

We tremble at the thought of losing that to which we are attached. Fear keeps us out of the presence of God. Fear makes us afraid to leave the boat that is filled with our creature comforts. At about the time we are ready to step out of the boat and to walk on the water, we remember something in the boat that we really like. There are things our flesh is attached to that keep us out of the present awareness of God. The more we have to be attached to, the longer we struggle with fear. The fear continues while hopes and opportunities pass us by.

The key to buying up opportunities (seeing opportunity, seizing it, fulfilling its potential) is detaching from that which is counterproductive to the life of Christ. Our attachments distract us. As long as we refuse to detach, fear stays alive. Fear feeds on attachments and makes us feel that, if we lost that thing, its absence would make us miserable.

Little by little, we learn to detach. Little by little, we come alive in the presence of God. *Today* is the day to acquire a little more light. When we get up in the morning, we can get up with a prayer in our heart that says, "Holy Spirit, good morning. What are You going to show me today? What are You going to teach me today? What are You going to dictate in my journal today? What new bird am I going to see, or new song am I going to hear? How will the sunrise look today? It is a new day, a day that has never been before." Do we wake up with that kind of expectation? We should, because God is here today!

A Prayer of Hope

> Lord, what do You want to show us today? We will do a little of whatever command You give us today, we are going to step out of the boat and walk onto the water. We are going to plan and think about tomorrow only as it is our duty in today. And we are going to prepare to receive all the things You have prepared for us to receive today. Only in *this* day can we receive certain things. Today is all we have, tomorrow is not promised, and yesterday is behind us. Today…what are You going to show us, *today*? We will plan little acts of kindness as You show us who You are in us. We will live out of Your integrity and create a great future, right now. Right now, we know everything is going to be all right in all of our tomorrows.

What would our days be like if, every day upon waking, we knew that everything was all right, right now, for always? What if we did not have to live in the fear of what is yet to come? Oh, happy day!

☐ DAY 3 - REFLECTION

What is one distraction in your life that you would feel reluctant to give up?

____

____

____

____

What is God showing you about your true purpose?

To share the character & ♡ of God with others through intimate relationships.

____

☐ DAY 3 - JOURNALIZING ASSIGNMENT

Love must be sincere. Hate what is evil; cling to what is good. Be devoted to one another in love. Honor one another above yourselves. Never be lacking in zeal, but keep your spiritual fervor, serving the Lord. Be joyful in hope, patient in affliction, faithful in prayer.

ROMANS 12:9-12 (NIV)

For this reason, ever since I heard about your faith in the Lord Jesus and your love for all God's people, I have not stopped giving thanks for you, remembering you in my prayers. I keep asking that the God of our Lord Jesus Christ, the glorious Father, may give you the Spirit of wisdom and revelation, so that you may know him better. [I pray that the eyes of your heart may be enlightened in order that you may know the hope to which he has called you, the riches of his glorious inheritance in his holy people, and his incomparably great power for us who believe]

EPHESIANS 1:15-19 (NIV)

LESSON 2, DAY 4 - *Planning for Tomorrow is Today's Duty*

Planning for tomorrow is today's duty because "as now, so then." I used to keep this motto on my desk. We can flip the order of the words and they still work - "as now, so then" or "as then, so now." What we do today sets the stage for tomorrow and what we did yesterday set the stage for today. Everything we do, think, and say today contributes to the quality of our tomorrow. It is not specifically about having all the ducks in a row on our calendar; it is about how we prepare to be who we are each day. Who are we going to be today? Will we be people of integrity who meet their deadlines, act responsibly, do what is necessary? Will we handle money wisely, be kind and generous? Will we change our plans for His whisper in our heart? Will we talk to God today? Will we listen to what He has to say today? The answers determine our future.

Some may think, "I am not going to do it today, but I will do it tomorrow." No, they will not! The good and right that we will not do today *in some measure,* we will not do tomorrow. To think otherwise is to deceive ourselves. Our character today is determining our future. We cannot put off being true to the character of Christ in us, or delay answering His command. Baby steps and little by little is all that is being asked of us. The pain we create by avoiding hard work is worse than the pain caused by the work itself. If we will not apply a measure of effort toward the hope that God is authoring, then the dream will deteriorate. The deterioration of dreams is painful. We may seem fine on the outside, but on the inside, the delay is causing disease. The path to wellness is a willingness to 'baby step' our way to progress.

Little acts of kindness and integrity today create a great future. If we are true, and living from His character right now, we already know tomorrow is going to be just fine. We have a great peace. If we walk on water today, we are not concerned about sinking tomorrow. The mechanics of scheduling and keeping a calendar fall into the integrity category.

The Bride of Christ

In the book of Proverbs chapter thirty-one, we see the virtuous woman, a type of Christ and His Bride. As His Bride, we are people of integrity who use whatever strategy is necessary to remind us to keep our word and keep our momentum going. We order our time; we are reliable. Living by the Spirit and acknowledging that God can change our plan is not an excuse to be irresponsible any more than grace is an excuse to sin. We use a calendar - we do not expect the Holy Spirit to remind us of our appointments!

As people of integrity, we acquire the skill and practice we need in such disciplines because we are awake, and building a righteous bank account from which others can draw. We see ourselves as a rich resource for the glory of God, for we have skillfully practiced seeing with the eyes of God. Strength and Dignity are our clothing, our position is strong and secure. We rejoice over the future knowing that we are ready. We planned yesterday, so today is cared for. We plan today, so tomorrow is cared for. We plan for integrity every day.

We do not just *happen* to remember an appointment, or to pay the mortgage. Because we live with integrity, we schedule things today that must be done tomorrow. We use strategies because we are people of integrity. We open our mouth in skillful and Godly wisdom and on our tongue is the law of kindness, giving counsel and instruction. This is not just happenstance…we plan to be wise tomorrow by spending time in His presence today. We look well to how things go in our household. We do not eat the bread of idleness, gossip, discontent and self-pity. We will have none of it because we are people of integrity. Our children rise up, call us blessed, happy, fortunate, and to be envied. Our spouse boasts saying, "Many people have done virtuously, nobly and well with the strength of character that is steadfast in goodness, but you excel them all." Charm is deceptive; beauty is vain because it is not lasting. Listen, young people, it is not lasting. It will not get us where we need to go. The day will come when we can either face growing old with charm and integrity or with some sort of sorrow and self-pity. A person who reverently and worshipfully fears the Lord shall be praised. We reap the fruit of our planning, strategic hands, and we let our works praise us in the gates of the city. Praise to Christ in us, our *hope* of such glory!

Hope Goes the Distance

Christ is our hope of glory. He is the virtue and integrity of His Bride. He is the keeper of our hope and our hope goes the distance. Just as a pregnant mother plans for her baby, we have a plan in place. When hope is ready to be born, we are ready for it. We look ahead, at tomorrow, today. We anticipate the upcoming needs of tomorrow, today. We do not spend our days wasting time, daydreaming, or pretending we have a baby. No, an actual baby is on the way and we have to prepare. We think of the future only as it is necessary for today. We are planning acts of kindness today that will be tomorrow's tasks.

The only business we have with the future is with a calendar, mechanically and practically speaking, that allows us to schedule appointments and to outline plans and timelines for the visions, hopes, and goals that God births in us. We have no business speculating or fantasizing about the future as a distraction or a way to entertain ourselves with lies. To walk away from fantasy takes conscious acts of discipline. We are going to be busy in our mind with something; if we are not going to be hearing God, fellowshipping with other believers, or having meaningful discourse, then what will we do? Likely, we will waste time with fantasies, regrets, false hopes, and vain imaginations. We will project a pretend life while real life is passing us by. We are not promised tomorrow…today is all we have.

Please remember, the only reason to go out into the future is to schedule appointments, make plans for acts of kindness, and to plan and strategize the vision and hopes that God intends to turn into tangible realities. The future belongs in God. Other than that, we do not need to use it as entertainment, or to worry or fret about it. We do not need to have imaginary conversations or to dwell in the past; we do not need to relive or rehearse wrongs. Each day is sufficient.

☐ Day 4 - Reflection

According to this lesson, what is the use of a calendar and what is our correct interaction with the future?

schedule appts & plan acts of Kindness - God is our future - Full STOP

☐ Day 4 - Journalizing Assignment

Therefore do not worry about tomorrow, for tomorrow will worry about itself. Each day has enough trouble of its own.

Matthew 6:34 (NIV)

We urge you not to receive God's grace in vain. For he says, "In the time of my favor I heard you, and in the day of salvation I helped you." I tell you, now is the time of God's favor, now is the day of salvation.

2 Corinthians 6:1,2 (NIV)

working together HNV

LESSON 2, DAY 5 - *Letting Go...Into the Present*

Jaque's Journal

Jaque, the future is vague everywhere except where it really matters - eternal security and confidence in knowing who you are matter more than all the goal setting that will ever be done to secure your little boat of life. Nothing you can do to make your little boat more secure matters when compared to your eternal security and identity in Christ. Thinking of the future in any other way is truly a waste of precious time.

Lord, I desire to be at rest in a spontaneously flowing life. I see now how Your life is eternal life, Your way the everlasting way. My goal is to let go. This is my hope. Please give me more strategy and show me how to plan for this. What is the activity to be performed?

Jaque, your greatest need and most necessary conviction is to see the path of letting go into a present focus. Attention means being here, right now. Awareness is an awakening provoked by love. Your cooperation is a decisive surrender - unpurposed, attentive surrender of your busy faculties into the present moment. You must be ready to see how you busy yourself, how the false nature controls you, and how you think that the things you are doing are so important.

The activity to be performed, is actually a strategy to slow down, on purpose, so you can see more and notice how you betray yourself with your busy schedule. Even if it is not busy anywhere else (on the outside), it is busy in here on the inside. Your mind races with, "I need to do this, I need to do that," and you compromise your own life with all such thoughts and thinking. Planning, and knowing what I really want for your tomorrows, takes focused attention today.

Writing the vision in our spiritual journals each day, just between God and ourselves, is writing a plan for believing. That is the first plan - the plan to believe. God is here, He is in the equation, and we can walk on top of the circumstances. Clear-cut objectives come to us through our journals. As we write, we see more clearly and from different angles; strategies are gathered. The greater *quality* of the time that we give Him, (we are not talking *quantity*) the greater measure of God-authored desire or hope will return to us.

We may not even know what we want or desire because we have not given Him enough quality attention. We have not really seen our own potential; we do not even realize what is in us, waiting for God to reveal. If we would leave our little boat of trouble and answer His call for us to come, we would be on the threshold of our potentials. As we leave the boat where we have hoarded things that were supposed to make us feel more secure, we would discover that those things were actually making us feel more insecure. The security that we are seeking comes to us when we do the scary thing and walk on the water.

In our journals, we are learning to walk on top of the instructions that come; we are learning to walk over the circumstances, not under the circumstances. A fresh word from Him every day will convince us that we are eternally secure, and this is the most important thing that we can know. Feeling confident about that actually puts us at ease about our earthly life.

We look for security; we ache to know that we are secure with God. We have erroneously believed that security would come from all the things that we have put in our boat. We think more money, time, friends, more of this and that, will make us secure; but the feeling of peace does not come from a heavy boat. Confidence in our eternal security only occurs in the presence of God; the relationship that we have with Him puts us at ease about our earthly life. The fears start to diminish; an absence of fear is the presence of peace. Peace of mind creates a quality of life that allows for more love and action. We have thought there were other things we had to do to get the security of peace with God, but that is fear talking. Fear continually adds to the list of things we need to do to stop feeling afraid.

We need to wake up so that we can see who is whispering in our ear. Who are we listening to? Every time we want *more* for the boat that is already too heavy and beginning to sink, we need to realize that fear is dictating false desires. Fear makes us hold on tightly to everything we have so that we do not lose anything. Letting go into the present moment, means we will need to let go of how we have interpreted past 'mistakes' and let go of our fear of history repeating itself in the future. God is in the present moment; today is where He is found. Past and future are the devil's playground. Only God can rightly handle past, present, and future. It is time to let go...into the present, which is the only place that we belong.

☐ DAY 5 - REFLECTION

Why does hearing God in your journal strengthen your confidence in your eternal security?

It reminds me whose and who I am & where I belong.

☐ DAY 5 - JOURNALIZING ASSIGNMENT

But when anything is exposed and reproved by the light, it is made visible and clear; and where everything is visible and clear there is light. Therefore He says, Awake, O sleeper, and arise from the dead, and Christ shall shine (make day dawn) upon you and give you light. Look carefully then how you walk! Live purposefully and worthily and accurately, not as the unwise and witless, but as wise (sensible, intelligent people), making the very most of the time [buying up each opportunity], because the days are evil. Therefore do not be vague and thoughtless and foolish, but understanding and firmly grasping what the will of the Lord is.

EPHESIANS 5:13-17 (AMPC)

LESSON 2, DAY 6 - *A Sinking Ship*

Jaque's Journal

Jaque, since Christ suffered in His body, arm yourself with the same attitude. Your flesh will suffer the loss of this over-burdened boat, but your spirit will soar free in the truth. The flesh does not know how to do anything but create more burdens. The burden it creates makes it feel alive. You experience condemnation when you fail to do (or not do) something the flesh has convinced you is necessary. Fear has told you what you have to put in the boat and when you fail to do it, you feel condemned. You are in conflict because you are in relationship with the false being. You are not your true self when you are in conflict and troubled. The false sense of self does not want to quit feeling alive so it creates more burdens and crises in order to have a sense of purpose. The sin principle in the flesh craves life on a sinking ship. Now stop and calmly think of that, Jaque. Notice it, Jaque, and see from your new self and then say good-bye to the boat. Say good-bye for someone new in you desires and deeply craves to live for the will of God.

Lord, Your words are powerful, they are full of life and energy. They go to the innermost part of my being where they are deeply needed. They find the diseased crevices of despairing old wounds. Your words are a healing balm, Lord. They are calming and loving me where love is most needed. Your words know me completely. They find the vowels and syllables that I need to hear and they form a salve in my own language so that I can know and receive their message. Thank You for knowing me so well, for You made me. If You had forgotten or forsaken me, I could never have been well again. I am aware of Your love for me today, I am safe right now, in Your presence right here. I know what all my hopes are, my hopes are for You, Lord.

Please understand where a crisis driven life comes from. There are those who live from one crisis to the next. If we could step away long enough, we would begin to see that we are, unconsciously, creating our own crisis because, when we do, the flesh feels alive. If we are not properly identifying with Christ, then when the flesh feels alive, *we* feel alive. Solving this problem is as simple as stepping out of the boat, and walking away from it. How can something so simple be construed as something so scary? We wonder, "Who would I be without my crisis and my problems? I have shared my problems with so many people that this is how they know me. They know my situation and I get their pity. They think I am strong, or valiant, or a victim of unfair circumstance. This is how I receive love. Who would I be without their concern for me? If I was happy, they might not give me any attention!"

If misery is our earmark, people may wonder what has made us uncharacteristically happy. They may wonder what we did with all of our problems. What a joy to be able to say, "Crisis? Oh, yes…I was in a sinking ship so I just left the boat, along with the entire crisis, and I walked away. Here is the interesting part, I realized that my flesh was creating my entire crisis driven life; it was loading up my boat and bogging down my life. The flesh was living my life and stealing my joy. The Lord said I could just walk away from it all, and so I did! I stepped out of the boat and began to walk on water. I have never been happier!"

Of course, people might think we have flipped out, but peace would be worth it. It would be great to realize that we do not need to create crisis. We do not have to identify with all the issues that we call our own. We can walk away and release them into the present moment where who we *really* are abides with Christ. We can live for the will of God. Some people would call it radical Christianity, but it should be normal Christianity. We should all be leaving burdensome boats behind and walking on the water of His word.

Letting go of the world that we thought we needed is the same as seeing who we *really* are and being released from the false self that held us in a hopeless existence. We do not need a bigger boat and we do not need more stuff in the boat. We need to walk on water, that is what we *want* to do and that is what 'living in the present moment' is about. When we step out of the boat, and let go of the past and future, we can face the reality that is here now. Living in the present moment is walking on water and hope is incubating God until faith brings the revelation; whatever revelation is needed in this moment.

☐ Day 6 - Reflection

Read Hebrews chapter three and record any insights you receive.

☐ Day 6 - Journalizing Assignment

Look at how much encouragement you've found in your relationship with the Anointed One! You are filled to overflowing with his comforting love. You have experienced a deepening friendship with the Holy Spirit and have felt his tender affection and mercy. So I'm asking you, my friends, that you be joined together in perfect unity - with one heart, one passion, and united in one love. Walk together with one harmonious purpose and you will fill my heart with unbounded joy. Be free from pride-filled opinions, for they will only harm your cherished unity. Don't allow self-promotion to hide in your hearts, but in authentic humility put others first and view others as more important than yourselves.

Philippians 2:1-3 (TPT)

My beloved ones, just like you've always listened to everything I've taught you in the past, I'm asking you now to keep following my instructions as though I were right there with you. Now you must continue to make this new life fully manifested as you live in the holy awe of God - which brings you trembling into his presence. God will continually revitalize you, implanting within you the passion to do what pleases him. Live a cheerful life, without complaining or division among yourselves. For then you will be seen as innocent, faultless, and pure children of God, even though you live in the midst of a brutal and perverse culture. For you will appear among them as shining lights in the universe, offering them the words of eternal life.

Philippians 2:12-16 (TPT)

LESSON 2, DAY 7 - *No Better Time*

There has never been a better time to spend time with God. Today is the day, now is the time. Today He has a revelation to give us about our salvation. He is in us, working it out even now. If we look for it, wait for it, hope for it, anticipate it today, then we will see it, surely it will come to us.

Notice that God called us to life, not work. When work proceeds from life it isn't troublesome or hard. God's work doesn't put us under stress, it is easy to be carried, it is light.

Every day God is saying to us,

> "Come to Me, take rest in Me...now...for I am humble and meek and easy to talk to. As you talk to Me, you will begin to see My will in a new light. You will begin to see how humble and sweet it is, you will see it like never before. It will bring a refreshing, and new joy. You will delight in it like never before. You will know My will beyond what you thought you ever could, and I will take you to new horizons, into new and exciting experiences. You will speak and command My word according to My will and results will follow. I am still the Goal, I am always your salvation. Let Me flood your soul with light and rejoicing!"

Every day we need a fresh in-filling. Just as our stomachs run empty and need refilling, so does our soul. We ask for a fresh in-filling of the Holy Spirit every day and then wait expectantly as He fills us...just like we wait at the gas pump to fill our car. Realize that there are a lot of waiting lines in the kingdom of God. Waiting is very good for us.

Sometimes we don't receive more revelations of God because we are in a hurry, but waiting men and women get the redemptive revelation because they make the time. God, in His love and wisdom, demands our time. We can give Him our money and all our earthly possessions, we may even consider it easier, but God wants our time because it measures our life, and that's precisely what He's after.

What does it mean, God wants our time? It's not that we sit in His quiet presence all day long, that's impossible, but when God reveals that He wants our time, He means He wants our ***attention***. If He doesn't have the quality attention that is filled with devotion, He really doesn't have our time, our life, or our heart for He speaks this way:

> "Be attentive to Me all the time. Expect Me to speak at any moment to give you revelation and direction. Realize that I AM. Be still and always know, I AM God.
>
> Let go of the shadows. Hold on to the substance. Expect Me to show you the differences between the shadows and the substance in your personal experiences of life."

The Shadows Are:

- ❖ What "might" have been
- ❖ What "could" have been
- ❖ "If only" this, and "if only" that
- ❖ What if? What if? What if?

The Substance Is:

- ❖ The reality that "God is"
- ❖ Christ, the Bread of Life sustaining us now
- ❖ Christ, the Vision, the forgiveness of all our days
- ❖ Christ in us, our only hope of glory
- ❖ What is! What is! What is!

Let's have hope for today. Let's expect Him to speak to us, every day. Let's anticipate that He will lead and guide us into all truth. His answers, His timing, His way, His reasons, His glory! Let's wait for His presence to stir in us, in each now moment, all the time. Our newly forming habit of hoping in God will reduce the noisy traffic in our head, protect our priorities, and help us to develop our individuality as we experience the joy of knowing Christ in us, as us.

☐ Day 7 - Reflection

Read Hebrews chapter four and record any insights you receive.

The Israelites didn't let what God (Moses) said sink deeply [from the head to ♡] They doubted so they missed the opportunity for deliverance into the promised land.

☐ Day 7 - Journalizing Assignment

Pour into me the brightness of your daybreak! Pour into me your rays of revelation-truth! Let them comfort and gently lead me onto the shining path, showing the way into your burning presence, into your many sanctuaries of holiness. Then I will come closer to your very altar until I come before you, the God of my ecstatic joy! I will praise you with the harp that plays in my heart, to you, my God, my magnificent God! Then I will say to my soul, "Don't be discouraged; don't be disturbed, for I fully expect my Savior-God to break through for me. Then I'll have plenty of reasons to praise him all over again." Yes, living before his face is my saving grace!

Psalms 43:3-5 (TPT)

Lesson 2 - Heart-Work

The Heart-work is a valuable part of your inner work. Taking the time to give heartfelt responses to the following questions is beneficial for you and beneficial for sharing with others who are in your study group.

Putting it All Together

1. How do yesterday and tomorrow relate to faith?
2. Why is planning for tomorrow todays duty?
3. Describe how a crisis driven life occurs.
4. Please share your journalizing experience this week with regard to heart and frequency. How was your desire for discipline grounded in grace this week?

Note: If you are in a VI class, please include one journal from this week with the Heart-work you submit for coaching.

If not, please bring your Heart-work and a journal to share with others in your study group.

Knowing the Purpose of God

Behold, I am doing a new thing; now it springs forth do you not perceive and know it, and will you not give heed to it? I will even make a way in the wilderness and rivers in the desert.

Isaiah 43:19 (AMPC)

Lesson 3, Day 1 - *God's New Thing*

☐ Day 1 - Reading Assignment

The Christian life begins, continues, and ends, with faith in God. We won't achieve what we don't believe. To begin anything with God, we must believe that He *is*, and that He is there *for us*. We must believe that He gives us the real desire of our heart which reflects the real desire of His heart for us.

The new covenant was an introduction of something new; God introduced His new thing, which is Christ, the first born from among the dead. God's new thing is a new creation formed from Christ in us - a species that never existed before. Christ in us, becoming flesh through individual Christians, is God's new thing. Big picture, grand scheme, overall view - a new creation in Christ is God's new thing. On a smaller scaled view, the unique and individual desires of our heart are also God's new thing. Our hopes are God's new thing.

As a quick review, our acrostic for hope is the Habit Of Permanent Expectancy. Habit is an exercise we create to help us to do something repeatedly, until it becomes mechanical, so we can give our attention to the present moment. 'Of' is defined as concerning or regarding. 'Permanent' is defined as stable, continuous, abiding, timeless, constant, and enduring. 'Expectancy' is defined as expectation, hope, anticipation, likelihood, and pregnancy. *Pregnancy* is the word that we will continue to spotlight.

We are all pregnant with the vision of God. If we belong to God, we are pregnant whether we *notice* that which is growing in us or not.

We are pregnant with all that God intends to do in and through us. We are waiting to experience the fruition of that pregnancy.

Jaque's Journal

Jaque, your way of life is anticipatory, you are pregnant all the time. You are My new dawn of hope, and I love to bring you to one high noon after another. High noon occurs every day. Through your surrender to Me, the image of Christ is being formed in you. You take on more of His qualities each day. His great quality of hope abides in you. The very fact that you hope in Christ increases your grace to carry more hope. The more you hope, the more pregnancies you will bring to term. Hoping makes more hoping possible - it creates more expectancy. Faith remains steadfast and immovable, waiting for mother hope to find the next vision, the next goal. Faith sees what is inside mother's tummy before it is exposed for all other eyes to see, and it waits like a doting father. Jaque, hope is like a mother, and faith is like a father. The substance occurs when the child is born. The mother and father possess the child with their heart long before the child appears. While 'mother hope' warms the egg, 'father faith' names the child - calling those things that are not as though they already are. Faith names the child, and in the fullness of time that which was not, suddenly is! Baby becomes! The history of faith keeps recurring.

Herein are the springs of life, Jaque, this is the way life works. The just shall live by faith. This is why you must guard your heart and keep it from empty entertainment. Empty entertainment will keep your heart sterile, causing you to abort one hope after another. The purpose of empty entertainment is to keep you from conceiving hope eggs. You turn on the television and even though it offers no message of truth for you, you watch it regardless. It keeps you from entering into pregnancy - the promised land for which true hope nests.

Jaque, your heart can either carry empty carcasses or desires of promise. Your heart is the womb of your life, guard this womb and guard it well for your bright and hopeful future depends on it. Let go of idle entertainment; remember, the chains of habit are not broken easily, especially the chains of the flesh. My word is like a hammer that breaks stubborn resistance; I will break the rocks and you will have more love, more power, and more life for your hungry heart.

> *Is not My word like fire [that consumes all that cannot endure the test]? says the Lord, and like a hammer that breaks in pieces the rock [of most stubborn resistance]?*
>
> JEREMIAH 23:29 (AMPC)

Possessing the New Creation

To possess His new creation reality we must come to understand Christ, who has been freely given to us; for we don't possess what we don't understand; that is, we don't make it our own until we see it. This is something that won't go away; it is the yearning for God's new thing to be made manifest in our lives.

He *has* authored, and *has* given us Christ, the true desire of our heart! It's an *accomplished* fact. In order for us to possess it we must comprehend the will of the Lord. This isn't learning the will of the Lord *for our lives,* it is learning the WILL OF THE LORD. Therefore our job is to seek His Kingdom, to seek out this salvation and allow it to occur on the outside as well as the inside.

Christ died to save *all* of creation so technically, all of creation is already saved, but the key is to *see* it and *receive* it. What one doesn't *see* and *receive* he doesn't **experience**. Although salvation is a free gift, we will have to work hard to *see* it because "another mind" is standing between our daily experience and the reality of God. Our desire is to possess what we may not have yet seen. The first step is believing there's a *whole lot more to see,* and then waiting on Him to show it to us. God's purpose is to wake up the hope or the desire He placed within us so He can expose His new creation within us. When we clearly see it, we can plainly *ask for it* to come from within to without, and God will answer our prayers.

Possess What We See

God wants to show us His purpose. He wants us to clearly see it, plainly ask for it, and ably act upon it. He has given us grace, God-given ability. We can conceive His plans and give birth to His desire. Each of us has Christ and He is our ability to possess what we see. The question becomes, "What are we seeing?" If we do not like what we are possessing then we need to see something new. If we do not know what we want, we need to spend more time in His presence. We must see the desire. If we take a desire to Him, He will confirm or deny its legitimacy.

I will tell you a secret from the Lord, and you can take this to Him to see if it is true - the true desire of every heart is to *be* someone new. We all want to be different, better, more mature. We want to feel differently about ourselves, about our life. The self-improvement industry relies on this fact. We try to acquire more things to fill the void, hoping we will feel differently. We put on a different persona, or try a new approach, hoping we will feel differently about our identity.

There is something in us grasping and groping for identity. It is the deepest desire of our being. Some disguise their longing in other things, some are in denial, but everybody is craving the same thing. Unhappy people try to fill their lives with 'happy.' The only thing that can ease the hollowness is God's new creation.

Everyone has a hole inside that was made for God. We think God is what we need, but here's another secret - we need God, but the longing to be someone new is satisfied only through death (new life) in Christ. Christ in us is a new creation in us and He is going to manifest *His* life through us. He does not make a new creation to fulfill the selfish desires of the old creation - God comes with a completely new identity. To fall short of knowing this is to be ignorant and run amiss.

God wants to show us He has made a new creation on the inside of every believer. We are pregnant with that reality. We desire the new creation because we were *made* to desire the new creation. This is a fast look at God's predetermination. God predestined us to desire a new creation, to desire to be someone new. It is not voluntary. It is a desire that He has put in us...and God will give us the desires of our heart.

☐ Day 1 - Reflection

Define DESIRE:

internal act which influences the will to action, passion, prayer to obtain, pleasure is expected or wanted, appetite & longing

To delight yourself satisfy

Define GOD'S NEW THING:

Christ, the 1st born alive in us New Creation, christ becoming flesh again through each of us

☐ Day 1 - Journalizing Assignment

Behold, the former things have come to pass, Now I declare new things; before they spring forth I proclaim them to you.

Isaiah 42:9 (NASB)

And He who sits on the throne said, "Behold, I am making all things new," and He said, "Write, for these words are faithful and true."

Revelation 21:5 (NASB)

← Here & Now statement individual acceptance?

Therefore if anyone is in Christ, he is a new creature; the old things passed away; behold, new things have come.

2 Corinthians 5:17 (NASB)

LESSON 3, DAY 2 - *The New Creation Leaves the Boat*

☐ DAY 2 - READING ASSIGNMENT

The Lord put the need and the desire for the new creation inside of us, and then He gave us the supply to meet the need. He gave us Christ, our 'someone new'. When need and supply meet, we experience fulfillment. God created us to be 'need' for His supply. We are designed to be the negative for His corresponding positive.

As new creations, we learn to embrace our need and to expect His supply. We learn to let go of the former way of life. We discover that the safest place for a new creation is not in the boat that is sinking, but rather walking on the water without any concern for the boat. This is an aspect of every new creation; we walk on water. In Christ, we are pregnant with a vision to walk on water. We hear His command for us to 'come' and we continue to hear that same command until, at some point, we are able to step out of the boat. It is natural; it is who we are and what we do.

A new creation is not worried about the boat - ever. Who we *really* are finds walking on water appealing. The concern for leaving behind what the boat represents does not stem from the new creation. The false nature is stressed and concerned, but the new creation walks in delight of God's command to walk on water.

The new creation has integrity; he or she does not have to try to have integrity, it is part of who we are. We do not have to try to be someone new; we *are* someone new. Recognition needs to occur, but it is the truth of our identity. We have to believe in our position in Christ, start living from His position in us, and listen as He speaks in us *before* we will grasp our identity in Christ.

When we dialogue with the Lord in our journals, we are not talking to a far away God, we are talking to God who is here, manifesting in our individuality. Christ is manifesting as a unique new creation in and through us. This new creation is our true self.

To a new creation, truth and security is the same thing. Formerly, we were so concerned with security that we would shun the truth. Concerned for security, we would stay in dismal little boats in fear of loss. Our blind quest for security kept us looking for more money, more time, more love. Rarely would we search for truth because the false self has always known that truth would set us free…from the false self! Only truth can set us free and only freedom can create security.

The new creature is home to Christ, the Truth. With Truth abiding *in* us, we begin to see that security is taken care of. We no longer feel the need to be afraid to lose sight of our boat and all that it contains. We are ready to say, "The boat no longer troubles me, I am no longer anxious about the size of my boat or how much stuff it contains. I am secure being light as a feather and walking on water. I walk on top of the circumstances, because I am not afraid of sinking anymore."

This is union life, a seamless unity, and the reality we rehearse in relationship with God. In one form or another, every word He speaks to us is an invitation to 'come to Me.' His will, our desire, and our lifelong goal is fulfilled each time we come to Him. Sometimes we wonder what His will is for our lives, as though it will be different in each of us. In actuality, it is not different for me than it is for you.

The *will* of the Lord for each of His children is the same. The *specifics*, however, are worked out in the individuality of Christ in us. We do not need to worry about the specifics; He reveals details in personal relationship. However, the *will* of the Lord for each of our lives is the same. We desire His will, and desire to know His will, because we are His new creation. His new creation thrives on His will.

When we see Him, we will be like Him. When we manifest, we are the manifestation of the sons of God, for whom the whole of creation waits and groans (Romans 8:19). His Kingdom, on earth as it is in heaven, is His will for our lives. So, when He commands us to seek His Kingdom, seek it we must. It is not truly optional. "Seek first My Kingdom and My righteousness," is more than a suggestion; it is a directive with pivotal importance. We can try to disregard it, but as children of God, it is more likely that we will adhere to it - especially when we realize that life works better when we do. It will never be as good for His body if one adheres, but not another. While it is still called today, His children are being asked to seek His Kingdom. That is His command; when we step out of the boat and walk on the water of that command, then the concern for everything else is left behind us.

> *"So then, forsake your worries! Why would you say, 'What will we eat?' or 'What will we drink?' or 'What will we wear?' For that is what the unbelievers chase after. Doesn't your heavenly Father already know the things your bodies require? So above all, constantly chase after the realm of God's kingdom and the righteousness that proceeds from him. Then all these less important things will be given to you abundantly. Refuse to worry about tomorrow, but deal with each challenge that comes your way, one day at a time. Tomorrow will take care of itself."*
>
> MATTHEW 6:31-34 (TPT)

All these other things will be taken care of, as we step out of the boat in response to His command. Abandon fear, and let the boat sink. Christ is a better boat than the boat that is sinking. As Christians, His Kingdom is our life's pursuit. If we have not begun to seek His Kingdom, then we are miserable.

If all I know is that you are a Christian, and that you are not actively pursuing His Kingdom and His righteousness, then I need not see your face or know your name to know that you are unhappy. If the seed of Christ is within you, then it aches to grow in you. If you are not seeking Him and His Kingdom, then you have a thousand unanswered questions and you are miserable. I know that about you, because this quest is written in the spiritual DNA of every new creation in Christ.

> *O God of my life, I'm lovesick for you in this weary wilderness. I thirst with the deepest longings to love you more, with cravings in my heart that can't be described. Such yearning grips my soul for you, my God! I'm energized every time I enter your heavenly sanctuary to seek more of your power and drink in more of your glory. For your tender mercies mean more to me than life itself. How I love and praise you, God! Daily I will worship you passionately and with all my heart. My arms will wave to you like banners of praise. I overflow with praise when I come before you, for the anointing of your presence satisfies me like nothing else. You are such a rich banquet of pleasure to my soul.*
>
> PSALM 63:1-5 (TPT)

☐ DAY 2 - REFLECTION

According to today's reading, what is God's will for your life?

To be in God's Will by seeking the Kingdom first and expecting or Knowing that it is on earth as it is in heaven. I Expect signs, miracles & wonders

☐ DAY 2 - JOURNALIZING ASSIGNMENT

For I know the plans I have for you," declares the Lord, "plans to prosper you and not to harm you, plans to give you hope and a future. Then you will call on me and come and pray to me, and I will listen to you. You will seek me and find me when you seek me with all your heart. I will be found by you," declares the Lord, "and will bring you back from captivity I will gather you from all the nations and places where I have banished you," declares the Lord, "and will bring you back to the place from which I carried you into exile."

JEREMIAH 29:11-14 (NIV)

But godliness with contentment is great gain. For we brought nothing into the world, and we can take nothing out of it.

1 TIMOTHY 6:6,7 (NIV)

I sought the Lord and He heard me and delivered me from all of my fears.

PSALMS 34:4 (KJV)

O Lord God of hosts, who is mighty as you are, O Lord, with your faithfulness all around you? You rule the raging of the sea; when its waves rise, you still them.

PSALM 89:8,9 (ESV)

Lesson 3, Day 3 - *We Need to Define*

☐ Day 3 - Reading Assignment

Jaque's Journal

Jaque, never forget My foreknowledge; I foreknew and fore-loved you. Before you were a thought in your parent's mind, you were predestined in Mine. Before you were formed in your mother's womb, it was My will that you would be formed into the image of Christ and inwardly share in His likeness. Christ is being born from out of the midst of you. He is forever the firstborn from amongst the dead. The resurrection experience is just that - it is Christ being born in you, even while you still co-exist in the deadness of the old sin-laden, selfish, dung heap of the past, and the manure piles of days gone by. Christ is the flower growing up from the center of your soul. Regardless of your history, I fit you into My plan and call it good. It is a plan for good and not for evil, for you are called according to My design and to My wise purpose.

Jaque, My purpose is the glue, the strength of your mutual harmony and destiny with others within your community of believers. My purpose is Christ in the midst of the congregation, deferring to and loving one another, and believing the best of one another. This Spirit in your midst is the highest potential for good among you. If it is of Christ, then it can be done, together, in the Spirit. Any miracle can be performed here; any healing can occur. Anything that Christ did in His earthly life in flesh can be done again in the midst of His congregation. He leaves nothing out; He has taken nothing with Him, He did not leave His people with a void. He is here, in His 'All-ness' in the variety of people and members that He puts together. Begin to see the potential of a group, the hope of a group, the hope of a

> *community, as it begins to form one mind together. Each member has different personalities, but you all have one mind. One mind is being formed; it is the mind of Christ. Intercede, Jaque, for each member to see and to desire it.*
>
> Lord, I will, for this is what I want. You have said it. I want the group that is called into community right here to see the potential in our numbers, in our mass, in our midst. I pray for the coming out of the whole, that each one would begin to participate and give their gifts in the character of Christ. I pray that Christ would be formed in each one until only Christ rises out of our midst. Let it be, let Christ be fully formed in us. That is my prayer and my hope.

There is potential in every community that God forms. There are groups of people that He puts together, and in every case, He has a plan. Individual members must surrender with commitment, not interest. It is not good enough to be interested, because if you are just interested, you will only be involved when it is convenient. You will only be in fellowship when it is convenient. On the other hand, when you are *committed*, you will accept no excuses, because in your heart you say: "This is my spiritual community, this is where God has placed me and only He can plant me elsewhere. God is acting out of the midst of His people in this place, accomplishing His purpose. He is not operating through one or two individuals; He is functioning through the group. Everybody has a part and everybody is learning to see, desire, and hope for it. We come together, not just to receive, but also to give. We give to one another in order to make up the body of Christ. This is a full body, right here, present in Christ. Hallelujah."

Faith takes hold of this attitude because it is clearly cut, clearly defined, clearly seen, and therefore easy to grab onto.

> Hope warms a vision, writes a vision, until it is plain to see. Then, faith takes hold because it has finally become clear that we know what we want. Faith sees that our vision has been clearly defined through the patient process of hope. Hope filters and refines a potential desire. Faith does not go after vague hopes or desires. If we are uncertain of God's will for us, if we cannot say with absolute assurance that *this* is the goal of our faith, then faith keeps waiting for our certainty to manifest. When we are certain, faith *will* reach into the unseen realm and make it a tangible reality.
>
> SUSAN MUCKLOW

If faith manifested indefinite hopes, we would not recognize them when they appeared. If we are never able to *name* the desire, it remains too vague for faith to apprehend. If all we can say is, "I think I want this or that..." but by tomorrow it shifts, then we have not sat long enough with our own heart in the presence of hope.

Jaque's Example

In my journal, I began naming a desire for my personal community in Christ. I was naming what I saw for my group in the Spirit. I saw the group forming the body of Christ and completing His desires. A vision of what community should look like was taking shape. God put the desire in my heart, and was encouraging me to ask Him for that desire. We have certain desires because He plants that desire, and we ask Him for it! It is a God story; it is not about us, it is about Him. He requires therefore, that we are able to repeat back to Him (clearly) that which He is placing in our heart. As we *continue* to journalize the subject, the desire takes on more detail and shape begins to emerge.

In time, the desire for my personal community became a desire for other communities to form. I wanted others to experience what we were experiencing. From this small beginning, and as His potential in each member of my community emerged, a ministry to help *duplicate* community was created. It took many hands, many hearts, many expressions, many perspectives...and one mind - Christ!

☐ DAY 3 - REFLECTION

In your own words, how does hope refine the vision so that faith can grab onto it?

It makes our desires clear when we sit in the Presence of The Living Hope by giving Strategy, direction, focus, tools, skills & Knowledge to manifest those desires that He has given us.

☐ DAY 3 - JOURNALIZING ASSIGNMENT

Trust in the Lord and do good; dwell in the land and cultivate faithfulness. Delight yourself in the Lord; and He will give you the desires of your heart. Commit your way to the Lord, trust also in Him, and He will do it.

PSALM 37:3-5 (NASB)

Trust in the Lord with all your heart and do not lean on your own understanding. In all your ways acknowledge Him, and He will make your paths straight. Do not be wise in your own eyes; fear the Lord and turn away from evil. It will be healing to your body and refreshment to your bones.

PROVERBS 3:5-8 (NASB)

revere, awe, honor,

(navel, umbilical cord)

essence, substance, self

acknowledge - (Yada) to Know (by experience), perceive, find out & discern, distinguish, recognize, confess, consider, understand

confess → announce, indicate, narrate

[To see Him & verbally announce] talk to Him

LESSON 3, DAY 4 - *Blind Bartimaeus*

☐ DAY 4 - READING ASSIGNMENT

Nothing about our life in Christ should remain vague. In Mark chapter ten, as Jesus and His disciples were leaving Jericho, a blind man named Bartimaeus cried out, "Jesus, Son of David, have mercy on me!" Jesus asked him, "What do you want me to do for you?" The answer to that question seems obvious. He is blind, surely he wants to see. Jesus knew he was blind, but please notice He doesn't *assume* that 'healing his blindness' is what the man wants. Jesus wants us to make *specific* requests, that's why He asked Bartimaeus the question.

To ask for what we want, we need to know precisely what desires we want fulfilled and then trust that faith in Him will make us whole. Hearing God speak to us will stir up those desires so we can get better acquainted with them and get a clear cut definition of them. We may not know what we want in the beginning; our aim may not always complement the *true* desire of our heart. It is imperative to possess ourselves and our desires in God. Without the real goal, the one that only God can interpret, many of us languish in hopelessness.

Hopefulness, on the other hand, invites us to live a life knowing exactly what we want and where we belong. Vagueness causes us to despair in life, to feel lonely and disconnected from a sense of purpose, and to never quite know where we belong. It keeps us dissatisfied with what we are doing. We were meant to *know*. We were intended to know who we are and where we belong through an ongoing, inner revelation of God's new thing in us.

Jesus wants us to name our desires. He already knows what they are, but we still need to ask. Our ability to ask shows Him that *we* know what He already knows. He wants to see that our hope has grown, that we can name our desire, and that we are unwilling to live without our need being met. The only needs we are unwilling to live without are the ones that have been clearly defined and incubated in His presence. What do we want? Faith states its desire and names the baby before it is born.

Even in other relationships, we tend to expect others to read our mind. We assume people know who we are or what we want. We lack the boldness to state our needs clearly and thus expect them to guess. This does not work in *any* relationship. It is healthy self-awareness to know ourselves well enough to state our needs, wants, and desires to God and to others. People do not know what we think they know. What if we were blind and a great healer assumed we wanted our sight when what we really wanted was healing in our marriage.

Even Jesus, who really does know our heart, will ask us what we want. We need to be able to name it. Perhaps we are not ready to receive sight for our blind eyes. Perhaps we stubbed our toe and that is the pain we want alleviated. He will heal our little toe. We can only receive answers to that which we can name.

We must be able to name what is in the 'womb' so that we can identify it when it appears. If it has no name, no description, no definition, then how will we know that what has appeared is God's answer for us? Things appear all the time that we cannot lay claim to because we do not recognize that it belongs to us. It is like a package arriving on our doorstep when we did not order anything. We naturally assume it belongs to a neighbor.

We restrict God authored hopes when we are unable to name our desires. We close the womb to countless 'babies' that could be ours. Vagueness is spiritual slumber that makes God unrecognizable as God. He comes, He knocks, but we do not recognize Him. More than angels, we have entertained God and have been completely unaware that He was in our midst. God is ready to speak vision along with blueprints for that vision. Spiritual slumber keeps us vague; lack of vision will cause us to stumble around. Faith sees God's goal in us and attends to the details He unveils. Faith is married to an expectant mother named Hope. There is a father and a mother, and the child's name is Desire.

> *If people can't see what God is doing, they stumble all over themselves; but when they attend to what he reveals, they are most blessed.*
>
> PROVERBS 29:18 (MSG)

In Christ there's no need to despair further, for when we participate in abiding fellowship with Him, it all comes out in the open! We can know, we were foreordained to know, and it is our right and heritage in Christ to live in the fulfillment of God's purposes in us.

There is a true seminary for the saint of God, and it's the teaching we receive in our heart from the Holy Spirit. Scripture reveals that anyone who desires to do His will, will know what His will is.

> *If any man desires to do His will (God's pleasure) he will know (have the needed illumination to recognize, and can tell for himself) whether the teaching is from God or whether I am speaking from Myself and of My own accord and on My own authority.*
>
> JOHN 7:17 (AMPC)

Jesus was assuring us that if we desire to *do* God's will, then we will *know* His will. We will be able to discern the true from the false. When we say in our heart, "Lord, I want to do Your will," then He is more than willing to give us the necessary illumination to do His will. As new creations, who does *not* say that in their heart? When we are ready to do it, we are ready to see it.

> We complicate the issue of knowing and doing God's will because we do not trust ourselves. We do not trust ourselves because we are not identifying with our *true* selves in Christ. We listen to the accuser who says that we do *not* want to do God's will. It is an accusation that is simply not true of a new creation in Christ. There is an inborn desire within us to do His will. He shines a spotlight as we commune with Him, and we begin to recognize that our true hopes, goals, and desires are actually His will for our lives.
>
> SUSAN MUCKLOW

It is simple, but we make it complicated. We simply need to enter the process of naming our desires in the presence of the Lord. He will filter them, sift them, and sort them. True desires will rise to the top; the false will be tossed away.

☐ Day 4 - Reflection

If God already knows our desires, why do we need to be able to name them, and then ask for them?

To remove the vagueness
Name & claim the desire He placed
in us. Our spoken words hold power
to unlock heavenly blessings

☐ Day 4 - Journalizing Assignment

Lord, you know everything there is to know about me. You perceive every movement of my heart and soul, and you understand my every thought before it even enters my mind. You are so intimately aware of me, Lord. You read my heart like an open book and you know all the words I'm about to speak before I even start a sentence! You know every step I will take before my journey even begins. You've gone into my future to prepare the way, and in kindness you follow behind me to spare me from the harm of my past. With your hand of love upon my life, you impart a blessing to me. This is just too wonderful, deep, and incomprehensible! Your understanding of me brings me wonder and strength.

Psalm 139:1-6 (TPT)

Lesson 3, Day 5 - *Press In With Passion*

☐ Day 5 - Reading Assignment

Jaque's Journal

Lord, I want the letting go, I want the less of me, and more of You. I want Christ to be fully formed in me, and I trust You for how that will be in me, how it will appear, how it will manifest. I want less of my opinions of what the future should be. I want to see life as it is, and not as I would *instruct* it to be. I want to conform to Christ and not to the conformists. I want to let go and to let God be in me as He already is. This is gaining Christ.

I want to live where Christ in me wants to live. I want to stay where I am until it is His time to move. I want to move along with Him until it is His time to stay. I want all of my boasting to be in Him. I want a God story to be told here, not a Jaque story. I want to know Your hopes and passions. I want to see the glory of You coming forth in all Your power and majesty.

I do not want any more of Jaque's suffering, the kind that invokes pity. I want to share in Christ's suffering, the kind that transforms lives into His likeness and glory. I want to experience the resurrection of Christ, Him rising in me and lifting me up and out from among the dead, even though I am still physically present on the earth.

Jaque, press into this with passion, keep stating your desires like this. Call out what you want, and incubate it until it is your reality, hold fast to these convictions. Walk and order your life by them. For these are the very desires for which I have made you My own. You are waking up, and you are hearing My love as it calls out to these desires in you. You hear the sound of eternal life, the eternal purpose in you. You are asking for reality, and believe Me, it is My delight to give you My Kingdom. State what you want clearly, ask for it daily and make it your prayer, and see it coming in you, as you.

Five Steps to Help Us Define True Desires

Let's look at five steps for defining our inner desires.

1. Faith is the substance of 'clear cut' things hoped for. Make a list of goals and desires that currently fill you with hope.
2. If you believe these hopes are true, adopt a hopeful *attitude* toward them. Hope with all your heart. Stir these hopes in your journals. The more you talk to God about it, the hotter it becomes; and the truth He speaks back to you will keep it blazing in your heart. Faithfully stay with it; if this vision is from God, it will take on definition. Do not despair if it seems slow in coming to pass. Keep it hot! (Sit on it!)
3. Thank God for the substance of this thing (the title deed). Commune with Him until you are certain you are pregnant in your soul. It is one thing to *want* to have a baby, it's quite another to be pregnant with a baby! In this step, we are praying for a spiritual pregnancy. After becoming pregnant with His vision, we have the assurance we are *going to have* a baby! We are going to give birth to the vision!
4. Show the evidence of faith. Reveal your pregnancy; speak the Word of God over your vision and desire. Guard your heart with all vigilance, for your vision is not built in the external world but in the eternal realm, inside the mind of your heart where God dwells in Spirit and Truth. Give faith something to do; call things that be not (to the human senses) as though they already are. Your standing will be firm and immovable because of what you know that you know.
5. Allow God to define, redefine, and modify the shape of the vision as His sovereign right. In the end, it will be a perfect fit!

Christ, the Resource is within us, so we can make our faith usable through the process of incubation. In our heart, when we incubate (meditate) on the vision, we will see:

- ❖ Who we really are
- ❖ Why we are really here
- ❖ What we are to do
- ❖ Where we are to do it

Hearing God Defines Hope

Defining our hopes rests in hearing God. It sits at the heart of that which we already enjoy - hearing Him as He speaks to us in the quiet recesses of our heart and mind. Hearing the Holy Spirit as He speaks God's word is the refinement process of our hopes and dreams. Every day, when we hear His voice speaking to us, and we take the time to write down His words, just a few of them, just a little journal, short as it might be - our desires become more defined. Our conversations with the Lord are lengthy at times, other times they are short. Whether we hear His voice in a journal, another person, nature, or in the innocence of a newborn baby - hearing God fans the flame of our desire.

Every time we hear His voice, hope gets hotter and hotter. Why must we continue to hear His voice? His voice is the sperm that fertilizes the egg. If we do not hear, crave, come to, and keep coming to His voice, then the flame starts to diminish and the fire goes out. We return to empty entertainment - and what is the purpose of empty entertainment? Empty entertainment keeps us from getting pregnant.

Therefore, hearing the Lord is what gives us hope. Incubating His words as He speaks to us provides assurance. When we grow weary, or begin to doubt that a baby is growing, hearing His voice rekindles our expectations. His voice has allowed us to see into the unseen realm; we almost forgot that His promises were golden, and we almost stopped warming our eggs…but we heard His voice again and all is well. Our pregnancy is intact. We see evidence of the future; our hope has a name. God has a purpose, and His purpose is for souls.

☐ Day 5 - Reflection

Use the five steps to begin the process of naming one of your hopes.

☐ Day 5 - Journalizing Assignment

Many plans are in a man's heart, but the counsel of the Lord will stand.

Proverbs 19:21 (NASB)

Prepare plans by consultation, and make war by wise guidance.

Proverbs 20:18 (NASB)

Wise people are builders - they build families, businesses, communities. And through intelligence and insight their enterprises are established and endure. Because of their skilled leadership the hearts of people are filled with the treasures of wisdom and the pleasures of spiritual wealth. Wisdom can make anyone into a mighty warrior, and revelation-knowledge increases strength. Wise strategy is necessary to wage war, and with many astute advisers you'll see the path to victory more clearly.

Proverbs 24:3-6 (TPT)

LESSON 3, DAY 6 - *Delighting in the Lord*

☐ DAY 6 - READING ASSIGNMENT

Jaque's Journal

Jaque, you cannot delight in what you do not trust. To take pleasure in me you must first trust me, then you can lean on Me and I will hold you up. When Jonah sat down in the hot sun after delivering My message to Nineveh, I caused a shade gourd to grow above Jonah. And he delighted in the shade of the gourd.

He was exceedingly glad under the protection of the gourd. The next day, I sent a cutworm to eat away the gourd and the gourd withered up. When the sun arose, the wind came up; it beat upon the head of Jonah, he fainted and wanted to die. He was no longer delighted or glad.

Then I asked Jonah, "Is it right for you to be mad about the loss of the gourd?" Jaque, you can fill in the blanks here so that it applies to your life! No matter what your gourd is called, is it right for you to be mad about the loss of the gourd? Jonah was angry enough to want to die! You see, Jaque, Jonah did not trust My ways, for Jonah was very opinionated and judgmental. He did not think that Nineveh deserved mercy, but I gave them mercy after they repented. That really made him mad. Although Jonah was angry that I showed mercy to a repentant nation, he was even angrier over the loss of a simple gourd (over the loss of his own comfort). Jonah could not see that the loss of the people of Nineveh would have been a much greater loss.

Jaque, I am a God of the people, and I will allow any gourd, boat, hope, dream, or material loss to take place in order to put the right values back into the hearts of the people. I come for souls; but men and women come for houses, lands, cars, lovers, spouses, offspring, and all sorts of things that belong to the cosmos. They love the gourds more than the souls of the people, and I will send a cutworm, if necessary, repeatedly.

Can you delight in this? Can you lean hard into Me because you trust the sovereign purposes of your God? There is much to detach from, Jaque, even if the gourd does not die. I am making you a lover of souls and a woman of God's purpose. If you care less and less for gourds then you will care more and more for My creation. Jonah was not being generous in his heart towards others, but you decide to be, Jaque. Your desires can be righteous, making you rich in mercy and grace.

Jaque, it is My desire for you to see many people turn to Me, exceedingly more than you can think. I want you to know the delight that those who are rich in God possess.

Delighting in the Lord will make us feel rich. We may know people with a lot of money who can travel and vacation all over the world. However, if people are troubled, fear the loss of gourds, are weighed down by their own opinions, or have judgments about what the people of Nineveh deserve, then they are not rich. True prosperity occurs when we trust God and trust that Christ is being formed in us. It cannot be bought or sold, and it cannot be taken away from us.

Knowing His Purpose, Personally

Knowing the purpose of God means finding the desires He has placed within us. We know His purpose *personally* by trusting the integrity of Christ, who is being formed in us. When we trust Him, we no longer doubt ourselves. Therefore, to find, comprehend and incubate those desires is to discover first hand the will of God for our life. God is actively at work in us, waking us up to the discovery of our true desires. As we recognize Christ in us, as us, awakening occurs. As we awaken from our sleep, our eyes are still shut (like baby kittens). If our eyes are going to open, we have to be willing to detach from the comfort of our slumber so that we can be children of the day. To be a child of the day is to be a child of resurrection in Christ. We keep rising…like bread dough. We rise until we reach the full stature of Christ; He is our leaven, and the true Bread of Life.

Christ is the firstborn from the dead of night. The slumber we have known all our life has no more rights to keep us in darkness. The purpose of Christ has come - He is establishing His Kingdom within us. His Kingdom is a place in us where Truth is glorified through all the proven principles of His character. Our Father has drawn us to Himself, and calls for Christ to come up and out of us. This is resurrection from the dead, and we experience it, day in and day out. Our surrender encompasses the discipline to stay where the Kingdom is. We are learning to live and abide in the present moment, for it is from there that His Kingdom is released.

The more we seek and find the desires of our own heart, the more we love the Kingdom…for it is written and built into our own desires. What a gift we have received from God in the form of these desires!

If we are Christians, we do not have an option. God's purpose for us is that we seek the Kingdom of God and His righteousness. We are to seek it, and to seek it well, because that is our work. We are pregnant with His Christ, and we will not be happy until we are in a seamless unity with Him.

Clouds

As we seek His Kingdom, clouds will block our view - clouds of anger or jealously, or clouds of doubt and fear. They will pass by, if we will *let them pass by* without giving them much attention. We lend our strength to our focus. Our strength and energy will give the clouds greater substance - enough to form yet another false identity - unless we wake up to their ploy. We no longer need to resist the clouds, for they do not belong to us. We can let them go; they have nothing of substance in us to hold on to. We are someone new now and are fulfilling the purpose of God simply for the self-surrender that accepts His Sacrifice.

The wisdom of God compels us to seek His Kingdom and to know our own desires. His wisdom is many-sided; there are many ways to see and to express it. His wisdom, as expressed through His body, has infinite variety and innumerable aspects. Let us accept that God's wisdom takes many forms, and let go of judging what we do not understand as His will is manifested and spoken with such diversity.

> *[The purpose is] that through the church the complicated, many-sided wisdom of God in all its infinite variety and innumerable aspects might now be made known to the angelic rulers and authorities (principalities and powers) in the heavenly sphere. This is in accordance with the terms of the eternal and timeless purpose which He has realized and carried into effect in [the person of] Christ Jesus our Lord, in Whom, because of our faith in Him, we dare to have the boldness (courage and confidence) of free access (an unreserved approach to God with freedom and without fear).*
>
> EPHESIANS 3:10-12 (AMPC)

DAY 6 - REFLECTION

According to the notes on Day 2, why is seeking God's Kingdom not truly optional for a child of God?

We can only be in relationship with, to gain understanding & wisdom from the Father when we see the many faceted ways He is speaking to us in His Kingdom & in us as heirs

☐ DAY 6 - JOURNALIZING ASSIGNMENT

> *His delight is not in the strength of the horse, nor his pleasure in the legs of a man, but the Lord takes pleasure in those who fear him, in those who hope in his steadfast love.*
>
> PSALM 147:10,11 (ESV)

LESSON 3, DAY 7 - *The Number One Reason*

☐ DAY 7 - READING ASSIGNMENT

Jaque's Journal

Jaque, I have a purpose for you, a reason for which you were created to exist in this time frame, in this location...as a woman...in this temperament...with this people. The number one reason for your existence is to receive My love for you - for My own Name's sake. You were created for love. You serve love's purpose through our intimate fellowship. You and Me Jaque, coming together in love.

Committed to Me in love, all your plans shall succeed.

I know why you do everything you do. As you commit your motives (your heart) to Me, I cause all your motives to become agreeable to Mine. This is why you succeed in your plans...you act in harmony with My will.

Jaque, our relationship feeds your desires. It is My Spirit that adds passion to your hopes for, without passion, hope lies dormant and you remain in doubt or ignorance. Hope is full of desire and our relationship feeds your hopes. Passion then comes alive because passion (faith) is the substance of things hoped for.

Oh how I love to bring your hopes to pass, for they are our children, and they glorify Me, making Me known to many others. Oh how I delight in your happiness and fruitfulness, oh how I love My creation!

Father, when hope is alive, planning takes place! When hope is alive, I number my days and buy up the opportunities. You are my hope dear Father. I find all the resources I need in you. I am so grateful that I don't need to search in a thousand different places for materials to accomplish my dreams. You are everything, and You have accomplished Your work in me. I am in the delightful process pre-ordained for me and I am loving every minute of it. Thank You, oh God of hope!

Seeds of Hope

The manifestation of our desires is important because they are the manifestation of our purpose in God. Our desires are His desires, and until they bear fruit, there is no glory. What is the glory of a seed that goes into the ground and dies if it stays in the ground and never becomes the oak tree? The manifestation of desire is the manifestation of the children of God. Therefore, something *must* happen to each seed that goes into the ground and dies. That which dies, leaves death behind it, and that which escapes death is resurrection life! This is what must happen to each of our seeds of hope. As they are incubated in the darkness, all that is not life is being turned back into ashes so that the true desires can escape death and shoot up out of the ground to sing praises to God forevermore. Thus, those desires, which are Christ in us, must come forth just as Lazarus walked out of the tomb. They will live and bear fruit for God forevermore.

We state our objectives clearly because this is how a 'Lazarus' is raised. The life within our seeds of hope has gone into the ground along with those parts that have to die. The 'life' needs to be resurrected. When Jesus raised Lazarus from the dead, He did not say, "Hey! You in there, whoever you are…come out!" No, He called for Lazarus by name. Otherwise, who knows what else would have come out of the tomb!

Likewise, God is calling our desires to the forefront, by name. We need to discern which aspects of our desires are meant to die and which parts are meant to live. This discernment is developed through purifying prayer. It occurs as Christ prays from within us. What a great day when Christ in us calls things that are not, as though they are - creating new life within us.

We not only have the right to our true desires, we have the calling to manifest them. God intends to reproduce Himself in a dead and fallen race. Then He calls Himself forth! Christ is the Life in every dead seed; He shakes off death, and lives again. For this we were created; to die and live again to the praise and eternal glory of God.

All that we do on earth is meant to come from the seed of *being*. Knowing who we are, *being* who we are in Christ, is never a selfish endeavor. It is the calling of God upon our life. An old and dead man does what death is, but a new species does what life is. We are someone new - someone who has escaped out of the ground and become what never existed before! Knowing ourselves from the inner Christ is what His purpose and intention has always been for you and me.

Hope, an Overview

Hope is the weight that anchors us to God; to how things *really* are. Hope is confident expectation in the unchanging God; it is expectation that always keeps its focus on the object of its desire. Hope is desire for God that envisions His true image inwardly. When that image transcends thought, it gives birth to action, otherwise known as faith. To hope is to envision with pure desire. God is the object of our desire and the author of our vision. The whole purpose of the imagination is to hope in the unseen Christ until He comes into full view. He is the reality, and our imaginations exist to make Him manifest. The fact that 'God is' is the beginning of hope. To *see* God is the meaning of clarity and hope.

Pure hope must be fed good spiritual food, which is nourishment from the word of God. Whoever eats from God's word will have plenty of hope to keep him or her hopeful. Hope keeps a clear view of God knowing that junk food clouds reality. Hope inflames the passion of faith until faith goes into action bringing back the thing hoped for. Faith goes after God until it gets Him, so hope will never be disappointed.

☐ DAY 7 - REFLECTION

Why is the manifestation of your hopes and goals the same thing as your calling in life?

God planted the seed of His True desires & purpose for our individual & unique lives into us so asking for them, expecting them, & envisioning them (focus) is building up, equipping & preparing us to walk into our destiny.

☐ DAY 7 - JOURNALIZING ASSIGNMENT

So we are convinced that every detail of our lives is continually woven together to fit into God's perfect plan of bringing good into our lives, for we are his lovers who have been called to fulfill his designed purpose.

ROMANS 8:28 (TPT)

Set your gaze on the path before you. With fixed purpose, looking straight ahead, ignore life's distractions.

PROVERBS 4:25 (TPT)

Can you not discern this new day of destiny breaking forth around you? The early signs of my purposes and plans are bursting forth. The budding vines of new life are now blooming everywhere. The fragrance of their flowers whispers, "There is change in the air." Arise, my love, my beautiful companion, and run with me to the higher place. For now is the time to arise and come away with me.

SONG OF SONGS 2:13 (TPT)

Lesson 3 - Heart-Work

The Heart-work is a valuable part of your inner work. Taking the time to give heartfelt responses to the following questions is beneficial for you and beneficial for sharing with others who are in your study group.

Putting it All Together

1. What is your number one goal today?
2. Why is it so important that we can clearly state our desires to God?
3. How are our desires clarified in us?
4. Please share your journalizing experience this week with regard to heart and frequency. How was your desire for discipline grounded in grace this week?

Note: If you are in a VI class, please include one journal from this week with the Heart-work you submit for coaching.

If not, please bring your Heart-work and a journal to share with others in your study group.

SETTING GOALS, MAKING PLANS

Where there is no vision [no redemptive revelation of God], the people perish...

PROVERBS 29:18A (AMPC)

LESSON 4, DAY 1 - *Potency and the Birth of Vision*

☐ DAY 1 - READING ASSIGNMENT

Direction comes to those who move consistently along the path of vision; they know what to do *as they go* because they keep hoping in the God of all vision. Strategies that work long into the future work through those with potent vision (goals) and potent vision belongs to those who fellowship intimately with a potent God. Until our vision hatches, we keep seeking His kingdom, knowing that all these other things will be added. We seek Him, and He unfolds the strategy that will be needed in order to act on the vision that hatches.

Procrastination is hope deferred. It makes the heart sick; it has no potent goal, thus it lacks strategy and sees no need for a calendar or a plan. It isn't so much that people are lazy as that they have impotent goals, that is - goals that don't inspire them. God's word *stirs* desire in our hearts until it becomes potent enough to move us.

Potent: something powerful, having great influence, authority, control, or dominion.

When God gives us a vision it has to be potent; it has to have authority. If it does not have authority, it will not get us to move. It has to have enough influence to motivate us into action. If hope does not lead to action, we have to question whether we have hoped.

In this study, we are looking at what it means to be pregnant with the visions of God. Pregnancy means that we have *received* something that was potent enough to impregnate us. Conception occurs when potent sperm and egg unite. When God imparts hope, it is potent. It is important, at that point, to incubate the developing 'hope baby.'

What habits are we creating to help us continually hope in God? What habits are we creating to help us inherit His Kingdom? Even a fertilized egg is not enough if we are not going to brood over it until it can be born.

Jaque's Journal

Jaque, see to it that the goals you set in this earthly life are not to save or secure your earthly life. As a woman of integrity, you are a good steward of earthly things while you need them here. However, earthly things are secondary aids to the spiritual goal of inheriting the inner Kingdom. The physical things that people make their primary goals, are like majoring in the minors. They try to make secondary matters first priority. The secondary goals are valid, but they are intended to support the primary purpose of inheriting My Kingdom and My character.

Learn to use a calendar so that you can safeguard time for incubating your hopes. Learn to plan and strategize so that you can manifest My Kingdom on earth as it is in heaven. Learn to create boundaries that protect true hopes and desires. Learn to strategize and to prioritize to facilitate your goals. These are secondary aids to the first priority - the emergence of Christ in His Jaque form.

> *I need to emphasize, friends, that our natural, earthy lives don't in themselves lead us by their very nature into the kingdom of God. Their very "nature" is to die, so how could they "naturally" end up in the Life kingdom?*
>
> 1 Corinthians 15:50 (MSG)

It is not the goal of the natural flesh to inherit the Kingdom of God. The natural, earthy man would focus on food, clothing, and shelter. It is unnatural, to the natural man, to seek God's Kingdom before all these other things. The natural man *naturally* worries. God keeps pointing us to the spiritual man, to our new selves in Christ, but we keep getting our priorities mixed up.

We often feel we do not achieve the things we want in life because we do not have enough discipline. I have done it, I am sure you have too. We think, "If I just had stronger willpower, I could reach my goals." The problem is never a lack of discipline; we fail to bring vision to full term because it is not *potent* enough. Our desires are lukewarm.

God wants us to possess true vision for our lives. This vision is not something we acquire by thinking, scheming, or planning, or from ideas or information we have acquired on our own; it is something that comes from His Spirit to ours by the way of 'unknowing.' It must be received by waiting in His presence; there is no other way. And when it comes from Him, we know that we know without knowing how we know. This is deeper than thought; it is Spirit.

To keep God-authored vision hot, we must fan the flame, stir the pot, and incubate hope in the fire of His word.

Day 1 - Reflection

Define STRATEGY:

plan or scheme for deceiving an enemy, device to obtain an advantage, resource, means to an end

Define CALENDAR:

A register of the year orderly table, or numeration of persons or things press Forward into the future

☐ DAY 1 - JOURNALIZING ASSIGNMENT

Praise be to the God and Father of our Lord Jesus Christ! In his great mercy he has given us new birth into a living hope through the resurrection of Jesus Christ from the dead, and into an inheritance that can never perish, spoil or fade. This inheritance is kept in heaven for you, who through faith are shielded by God's power until the coming of the salvation that is ready to be revealed in the last time. In all this you greatly rejoice, though now for a little while you may have had to suffer grief in all kinds of trials. These have come so that the proven genuineness of your faith - of greater worth than gold, which perishes even though refined by fire - may result in praise, glory and honor when Jesus Christ is revealed. Though you have not seen him, you love him; and even though you do not see him now, you believe in him and are filled with an inexpressible and glorious joy, for you are receiving the end result of your faith, the salvation of your souls.

1 PETER 1:3-9 (NIV)

LESSON 4, DAY 2 - *Burning Desire*

☐ DAY 2 - READING ASSIGNMENT

A burning desire keeps vision alive. Incubating hope in the fire of His word is the component often neglected. In my early twenties, I read, *Think and Grow Rich*, by Napoleon Hill. What I remember was that he said that we could do anything in life that we want to do as long as we have a burning desire. I did not have a relationship with the Lord yet, but I knew that I needed a burning desire and that I did not have one.

When I came to Christ with the absolute surrender and dedication of my life, I knew I still did not have a burning desire. Something in me yearned to be someone new and wanted to do something meaningful. However, I did not know how to get a burning desire. I had little dreams, tiny flickers of desire, and there were things that I *thought* I wanted...but nothing was a burning desire.

In retrospect, one sentence in one book had a huge impact on how I came to the Lord. The need for a burning desire was the impetus behind my boldness before the Lord. The need to hear His voice directly, the desire for the knowledge of His word and for the intimacy of His presence, were all born from this angst for God to give me a burning desire. Journalizing was the personal habit that the Lord inspired me to practice. He was teaching me, and then I was teaching, preaching, and speaking to groups wherever I was invited to speak. My own private studies became study manuals. In the end, a ministry to help others to have a burning desire was developed. Anything I have accomplished has been the result of God faithfully showing me what it means to have a burning desire.

I learned that a burning desire is nothing less than a potent goal. It is potent enough to get us to act. In those early years, I may have felt like God was partial and showed favoritism. Some people had a burning desire and others did not. Not only did I not have one, but also I had no clue how to get one. When I was a young Christian, I attended a bible study. I decided to ask the pastor how to get a burning desire. I had just handed him a cup of coffee, and he said, "Like this," as he proceeded to stir cream and sugar into his coffee. He said, "If you want a burning desire, Jaque, you have to stir it up. God has put His will in the form of *desires* on the inside of each of us. They are dormant until we stir them up." This wise pastor also told me, "Jaque, read the word of God and the word of God will stir you."

Our hopes are desires that need to be stirred until they become our burning desire. This is the process of incubation. We recognize a desire, and by faith, we take it into the presence of the Lord and speak life over it. My first burning desire was the desire for a burning desire. God met that desire with Himself, taught me what it meant, and then gave me instruction for how to get one.

From the counsel of that pastor, journalizing took form in my life. God whispered an unfamiliar word and it became an instruction that required my action. It became a goal, a potent desire, and was forever used by God to stir every other desire my heart has ever conceived.

Journalizing was God's solution to my quest for a burning desire. It came with vision; writing down the words He would speak to me from His scriptures, day in and day out, would stir every desire that He had placed within me. He promised me that, although I did not know my own desires yet, He did - and He would teach me how to turn latent potential into potent goals.

Every vision or goal that God gives includes the strategy to bring it to pass.

> *"All this," David said, "I have in writing as a result of the Lord's hand on me, and he enabled me to understand all the details of the plan."*
>
> 1 CHRONICLES 28:19 (NIV)

When my son was four years old, I remember saying to him, "Eric, what do you want for your birthday?" He said, "I want a brother." Of course, that was *not* going to happen! Then Eric said, "But he has to bring his own toys!" I pictured myself in labor, having this little brother just for Eric, and coming out behind the little baby were a baseball bat, toy piano, stuffed animals, and building blocks. I have a vivid imagination; I also give names to purple onions!

My son stirred an imagination in me when he innocently expected a baby to come, toys included. As silly as that visualization is, it is not so fantastic in God. When God gives us a vision, all the 'toys' come with it. The vision includes instructions *and* the batteries are included. What are we supposed to do with this thing, what is it here for, where is it going to lead, what is next? A plan to address every question will eventually follow. The details and strategy arrive on time.

We incubate the vision, we wait for it to be born, and then details unwrap one step at a time. Energy, grace, and gumption (the batteries) are part of the package. If we do not exercise grace and patience, we run the risk of miscarriage. We abort the pregnancy because we do not believe in the reality of the vision.

We often pin a timeframe to the goals and plans of God, and assume He is in a hurry, just like us. Incubating the ideas that God deposits in us is an important step, and it requires us to slow down, unpin the timeframe, and to develop patience. When I began my public speaking ministry, a particular female speaker had something that I knew that I wanted. She knew the word of God like nobody I had ever seen. She knew how to pray the word, to skillfully handle it, and to apply it in her message with great proficiency. Each time I attended one of her seminars, her example would fan a fire inside of me. I prayed to know the word like she knew the word. I wanted to know Him, the way she seemed to know Him. At first, I thought I could just ask and receive it - like a gift. I did not realize the time this woman of faith had dedicated to the study of God's word. Thankfully, I wanted to know God's word enough that I became willing to spend time in His word, and to incubate the words I read. This woman's example in my life was a log on the fire; it was generating a burning desire.

When a desire is ignited today, it will manifest on some tomorrow if we sit on the nest and incubate the egg for as long as it takes. Stay with it; do what He says, and expect the manifestation. The baby will come, and with it, there will be more 'toys' than we can imagine. That is the thing about a baby or a vision - they grow, they change, they evolve, they develop, they become multi-dimensional.

Where do we start? First, we know our priorities. If priorities are out of order, and we put earthly things first, then we are off the mark. God gave us the correct order - *first*, seek His Kingdom and righteousness, and *then*… all these other things. This is God's order. As I continued on my journey with the Lord, I realized that my desire for a burning desire was also the desire for God's order. We all want our lives to be in order; discovering God's priority is discovering the correct order of our steps. To know what comes *first* is monumentally important to receiving step number two, and three, and four.

☐ Day 2 - Reflection

Why is it important to have a burning desire?

Fan the flame, seek God for vision, passion strategy & steps, Keep seeking & stirring

☐ Day 2 - Journalizing Assignment

Whom have I in heaven but you? And there is nothing on earth that I desire besides you. My flesh and my heart may fail, but God is the strength of my heart and my portion forever.

Psalm 73:25,26 (ESV)

In the path of your judgments, O Lord, we wait for you; your name and remembrance are the desire of our soul. My soul yearns for you in the night; my spirit within me earnestly seeks you. For when your judgments are in the earth, the inhabitants of the world learn righteousness.

Isaiah 26:8,9 (ESV)

One thing have I asked of the Lord, that will I seek after: that I may dwell in the house of the Lord all the days of my life, to gaze upon the beauty of the Lord and to inquire in his temple.

Psalm 27:4 (ESV)

Lesson 4, Day 3 - *God's Divine Order, the New Creation*

☐ Day 3 - Reading Assignment

But seek first the kingdom of God and his righteousness, and all these things will be added to you.

Matthew 6:33 (ESV)

Our goals must be prioritized. God gives us the correct action with the word *seek*. He gives the correct priority with the word *first*. He gives us the correct goal with the words *His Kingdom* and *His righteousness*. First…we seek…His Kingdom and His righteousness. It seems simple enough, but our heads have a hard time accepting this as the most important beginning for our time. This is why we need a cross in our lives; the cross is here to crucify any false authority that would question His authority about what comes first.

Following His priority comes with incredible promise - *all these things shall be added*. What are all these things? He had already named forgiveness, answered prayer, reward, heavenly treasure, revelation, light, value and worth, peace, food, drink, clothing, rest, and shelter. However, *all these things*, means *all* these things. We cannot think of a thing that we need that is not included in this promise.

Jaque's Journal

Jaque, the goals you set and plans you design should have as their ultimate (God ordained) purpose, the salvation of your soul. You live each day with ordinary things set before you, but as you learn to work 'from' Life and Truth, your goals and plans start to change. They change as your focus and motive changes. Changing self-centered motives to Christ-centered motives, changes everything. It is good to learn how to set goals and make plans, but what prompts you to set particular goals and plans is more important.

A living hope is within you because you are a new creation. The new creation will prompt new goals and plans. I did not put My living hope in the old man - him, I crucified. Do not plan to find anything worth resurrecting in the old man, for him, it is over. Jaque, all the conversations I have with you are between Me and My new creation. Hope is for My new creation, not for the old man.

The branch that is connected to the Vine needs to receive the Vine's sap - the Spirit of Christ, the mind of Christ, the Life of Christ - rather than trying to use the head of a dead man. New wine (the Spirit) must enter the new wineskin (the mind of Christ). My Spirit does not function in old wineskins (the mind of the flesh), for the life of the Spirit will tear the skins (thoughts) and leak out through the tears of despair. Old wineskins are useless, Jaque. So make plans and set goals for the new creation, the true self, and start perceiving them with the mind of Christ

Lord, this instruction turns my head around. I must realize what the clear goals of a new creation are. Ah, to perceive clearly with the mind of Christ, what a relief. Someone inside me is resurrecting from the dead. I can feel her coming up! The fire and trials of former days have been burning away the chaff and the clutter around her. I can see her better now. I will consult with her and see what goals and plans she would like to set in this Kingdom that she is inheriting. Thank you for awakening the hope that once laid dormant within me, Father.

Jaque, I love My new creation; wait until you see her even better. You should plan on getting to know her; this is all you need to do.

My desire for a burning desire was also the desire for God's order. We all want our lives to be in order - even if order looks differently in each of us. Many goals that we want to set, and fail to accomplish, are centered on an innate desire to feel like our life (our very being) is in order. Finding priority is finding order; to understand what the first thing is, is to find the order for everything that follows.

> **Order**: a proper state; when bodily organs are in *order*, a person is in health; when bodily organs are out of order, a person is indisposed; regularity; settled mode of operation; managed; arranged; adjusted; prepared in a particular manner; a pattern, arrangement, or rule.

God's Divine Order is in His New Creation.

If we look for order from any source but Christ, from any part of us but the new creation, we will find nothing but chaos. There is no order with the flesh, heart, or soul. Apart from Christ, we will get frustrated, distracted, impulsive, confused, busy, complacent, lazy, and all the other things that can get us to forsake order. However, God has appointed all of us to a divine order; the divine order that is in His new creation. Within this divine order are righteousness, peace, and joy. These three things equate to health and wholeness - soundness of mind, body, and spirit.

God is in fellowship with His new creation. He is not in dialogue with the old man who was crucified, the false self or ego, the carnal mind or the flesh, the liar, or with whom we *think* we are, or *try* to be.

> *And we know that the Son of God has made our understanding come alive so that we can know by experience the One who is true. And we are in him who is true, God's Son, Jesus Christ - the true God and eternal life!*
>
> 1 JOHN 5:20 (TPT)

> *The mature children of God are those who are moved by the impulses of the Holy Spirit. And you did not receive the "spirit of religious duty," leading you back into the fear of never being good enough. But you have received the "Spirit of full acceptance," enfolding you into the family of God. And you will never feel orphaned, for as he rises up within us, our spirits join him in saying the words of tender affection, "Beloved Father!" For the Holy Spirit makes God's fatherhood real to us as he whispers into our innermost being, "You are God's beloved child!"*
>
> ROMANS 8:14-16 (TPT)

The correct order for our life is to seek Him, His Kingdom, righteousness, and His new creation in us. To find our true self is to find Christ in us, as us. In fellowship with the Father, we realize that we are His beloved children. We identify more with our newly created self than with an old crucified man. If we look for our self apart from Christ, we are out of order. Our true self leads to God's true order for our lives.

Order is in our new identity. Until we recognize our new life in Christ, until we see who we are in light of the gospel, then other details of our life will also be out of order. New wine is the Holy Spirit and He flows from a new wineskin (the mind of Christ, in a new creation).

If we try to put the new wine in an old wineskin (the mind of the flesh), it will rip and the new wine (Holy Spirit) leaks out. When we try to be disciplined or fix ourselves through the false nature, we leak. It is like going to church, feeling good, going home with new determination to be a better person, only to fail after a day or two. We were trying to hold the new wine in an old wineskin. Pumped up like a tire on the weekend, we go flat during the week. An old wineskin leaks.

Even our capacity for the new wineskin requires we be slowly stretched. We cannot contain the whole truth at once. Jesus withheld a lot of teaching, and the Holy Spirit teaches us little by little. The old wineskin is who we sometimes *think* we are; it is the false nature. Some Christians live identifying themselves by this false nature, and then wonder why they always feel the need for a fresh 'infilling.'

However, when new wine goes into new wineskins, rivers of living water flow. When we see that we are the righteousness of God in Christ, have eternal peace with God, are one with Christ, and then fellowship with God from the position of a new creation, the river flows. The Holy Spirit has the freedom to expand with the Gospel of peace and the new wineskin has the necessary elasticity. This is divine order.

> *Neither do people pour new wine into old wineskins. If they do, the skins will burst; the wine will run out and the wineskins will be ruined. No, they pour new wine into new wineskins, and both are preserved.*
>
> MATTHEW 9:17 (NIV)

☐ DAY 3 - REFLECTION

Share your current understanding of the new wine, and the new wineskin versus the old wineskin.

The recognition, understanding, knowledge and wisdom of more of who Christ is in us. The slow, life-long stretching of the soul to fit more of Him.

☐ DAY 3 - JOURNALIZING ASSIGNMENT

The Spirit searches all things, even the deep things of God. For who knows a person's thoughts except their own spirit within them? In the same way no one knows the thoughts of God except the Spirit of God. What we have received is not the spirit of the world, but the Spirit who is from God, so that we may understand what God has freely given us. This is what we speak, not in words taught us by human wisdom but in words taught by the Spirit, explaining spiritual realities with Spirit-taught words. The person without the Spirit does not accept the things that come from the Spirit of God but considers them foolishness, and cannot understand them because they are discerned only through the Spirit. The person with the Spirit makes judgments about all things, but such a person is not subject to merely human judgments, for, "Who has known the mind of the Lord so as to instruct him?" But we have the mind of Christ.

1 CORINTHIANS 2:10-16 (NIV)

G350
anakrino
[discernment]
examine
investigate
inquire
appraise

LESSON 4, DAY 4 - *David Stated Clear Objectives!*

☐ DAY 4 - READING ASSIGNMENT

New wine can flow through a new wineskin even when the old wineskin is present. At one time, I questioned why the Lord would allow the new creation to dwell alongside the flesh (like the wheat and the tares), but now, it actually excites me to see the marvel of God's wisdom in motion. For instance, Susan and I recently recorded one of our monthly conversations. I went out to her office, tired in my flesh. I was experiencing the dry cracks of the old wineskin. The body gets tired; in the flesh, neither one of us felt like recording our monthly conversation. We did not even have a topic of discussion in mind, but we were in this together. There was a grave problem weighing heavy on both of us, and we had to press through. Before we could record our talk, we prayed, "Holy Spirit, here we are, new wineskins in Christ. You are the new wine and you have not leaked out. You are still here, alive and well, even though our flesh is weak and our bodies are weary. I am going to open my mouth, Susan is going to open hers, and we trust that YOU are going to fill our mouths." I am sure you can guess the end of the story; the Holy Spirit filled our mouths!

Once we started recording, the flesh was no longer pressing us down. The new wine was there; He was ready to pour Himself out of new wineskins through vessels that were tired and weary and wrapped in flesh. He was right there, just that quickly. One second we were only aware of the fatigue in our flesh, then the recorder was turned on, and a message of hope for His people was alive and active. There was no struggle, and it was one of our best monthly messages. We had a lot of feedback from that particular month's conversation, and we were so glad that God proved His faithfulness.

When our whole life is the study of His Kingdom and His righteousness, then we do not have to 'study' every time we are going to open our mouth and speak, teach, or converse. New wine from a new wineskin is free to flow at the Lord's impulse. That is our goal; it is where we want to be and how we want to live. That is the order we crave; it is divine order. When we operate in this kind of order, we state goals and objectives with ever increasing clarity. We know the order of our steps as clearly as David did when He met Goliath on the battlefield.

David stated his objectives clearly (1 Samuel 17:45 - 47):

- I come in the name of the Lord whom you, Goliath, have defied
- Today (meaning this very day), my Lord will deliver you to me
- I will take off your head (clearly stated objective)
- Next, I will give the dead bodies of your comrades, the Philistines, to the birds of the air and the wild animals in the bush (you are *all* going down… clearly stated objective)
- Then the whole earth will know that the Lord is God.

David clearly stated whom he represented, when the plan would be executed, how it would occur, whose deaths would follow, how far the story would spread, and Who would be glorified.

David's priorities were obvious, so was His confidence and courage. He *knew* God was with Him. His encounter with Goliath was a revelation of the Kingdom of God. Centuries later, we still talk about it and sing songs of his encounter. David's purpose prevailed - he intended to show everyone that the Lord is God, and he was confident that the giant, Goliath, could not continue to stand against God.

Jaque's Journal

Jaque, David named the baby before the baby came, and when the baby arrived, everybody knew it was David's. The faith of David is still heralded today. David demonstrated the way of hope, faith and love, and he did it in My name. David also taught Solomon, his son, to be brave and courageous, knowing that I would not forsake him, either.

I am the same God speaking to you now, fanning the flames of desire with strong encouragement. You will step forward and bravely speak to the Goliaths that come to taint your faith and make you feel afraid. Continue to name your babies, Jaque, for now you recognize you are always pregnant with vision. I will show you the seedlings of desire in you that you can begin to name. As you realize and discover how to name them, you will begin to move forward with the plans to prepare for their arrival. I will give you the strategy, wait on Me.

One of the larger desires or seedlings in you, Jaque, is for worship. Can you see it? How will you name this one? Begin to define and prune this until you have a clear cut objective, then set the goal and get the nursery ready. The baby is on the way. State your desire for worship, name it, practice and incubate the subject.

Lord I want to worship freely with my family, yes. I want this vision to be born, I want music around me that honors You, and is sweet to the souls of Your creation. I want to sing and freely dance for You, just like David did. I want this freedom so deep within me, and I want it to surface. I want to tap on tambourines, march on Satan's gravestone, and to defuse the minefields of despair. I want militant worship, twirling, and piano worship, to bubble up to the surface then tinkle on black and white keys. I want to show You my love in worship, and to be mindful of no one else but You.

Naming our hopes takes courage and confidence, as David exhibited. We name our baby, for it is coming. David did it; so do we. We incubate the vision and the vision gets hot. It gets so hot, that no Goliath can stand against it. We write it down, state it clearly, and practice (like David) on a smaller scale. Remember, David had already killed a lion and a bear. Bringing down this giant with a slingshot and a rock, and then cutting off his head, was a natural progression of faith for David. When our objectives are clear, like David's, and our baby is born, everybody will know it is ours. God is revealing Himself through the desires that we can name.

Jaque's Journal

Jaque, I am preparing hearts to receive unprecedented vision. The vision of God, the vision of the King of the Kingdom, is Christ. With the vision will come access, or the way to carry on, from the first step to the next. In this, I refer to the strategy that helps you to know what action comes next. Each person will seek his or her own way, for the way for each person is within him or her. I am speaking of the vision of Christ in a million different shades, hues and dimensions.

Write the vision and cherish the inspiration. Write it on napkins, calendars, and computer forms. Write to understand what is in you, inspiring you to act, and as you do then the next step will come in due time. Only write the first step you see; do not worry about all the other steps. You only need one step, Jaque. Do the first thing, the next thing will follow. Acting on what you see to do one baby step at a time, will inspire you more and is an invitation for the next step to come. With the writing of the vision, more will come. More is given to the writer of the vision than to the memorizer. It is foolish to depend on your memory to help you manage the affairs of your house. Even to write your appointments and plans on a calendar gives you more understanding of the proper use of time.

The vision has substance that it wants to share with you. People live mindlessly because they think that is freedom. It is not freedom; without form, there is no freedom. Structure, strategy, and form is not to put people in bondage, it is put in place to set you free. When you understand how form works in your favor, it sets you free. Form creates order, and when order is working on your behalf then you are free to think about other things. When you do not have order, you are scrambling to find order - you are scrambling to figure out what comes first, second, and every other next. A maze of confusion keeps you from discovering what to do next. The vision wants to give you more, so write the vision!

Spontaneity, Jaque, is not mindlessness. Writing the vision puts what should be captured in its place so that you are free to act from inspiration that is fully secured. If people think that freedom means that they do not have to submit to form and discipline, they are deceived. They are lead into bondage not knowing what to do next or where to be. That is not spontaneous freedom. Free, and delightfully joyful, are the disciples of discipline. Disciples who know what to do next and what road to follow are full of delight.

Jaque, seeking and finding Me was the road you took to more vision. The first vision was for seeking Me, now you follow one 'vision step' after another. For you know the road to follow because you have written down all the stones along the path to the future with this very pen. I have given you the vision to capture each vision and follow the way Christ leads you within it. There is more to see. You thought you had something that was a big deal, because it was so clear. However, it is not clear enough yet, there is still more to see. You have further to go with the vision you have. The vision of journalizing Christ as He is in you will continue to give you the goals, plans, and paths that you should follow.

We have these precious promises, but we have to wake up and learn to number our days. Numbering our days will supply a heart of wisdom; it will show us where God wants us to be, one day at a time. In order to be awake, we have to let go of former days, the things gone by. The past does not equal the future.

☐ Day 4 - Reflection

What is your current understanding of the marriage between form and freedom?

Form places the vision in it's place (write it down, speak it out) So you are free to act from inspiration that is fully secured.

☐ Day 4 - Journalizing Assignment

His divine power has given us everything we need for a godly life through our knowledge of him who called us by his own glory and goodness. Through these he has given us his very great and precious promises, so that through them you may participate in the divine nature, having escaped the corruption in the world caused by evil desires. For this very reason, make every effort to add to your faith goodness; and to goodness, knowledge; and to knowledge, self-control; and to self-control, perseverance; and to perseverance, godliness; and to godliness, mutual affection; and to mutual affection, love. For if you possess these qualities in increasing measure, they will keep you from being ineffective and unproductive in your knowledge of our Lord Jesus Christ. But whoever does not have them is nearsighted and blind, forgetting that they have been cleansed from their past sins.

2 Peter 1:3-9 (NIV)

Concept

Becoming ONE

Incarnational Listening

(Emotionally Healthy Relationships)

Psychological Terminology: Active / Empathetic Listening

LESSON 4, DAY 5 - *Teach Us to Number Our Days*

☐ DAY 5 - READING ASSIGNMENT

So teach us to number our days (use our time correctly), that we may get us a heart of wisdom.

PSALM 90:12 (AMPC) (PARENTHESIS ADDED)

Learning to number our days (use a calendar) and still be governed by the movement of the Spirit requires watchfulness; we must be practiced in His presence enough to have plans, but continue to return our attention to the present moment where He might ask for a change in plan. We need to see where God wants us to be, one day at a time, but in order to do so, we have to let go of former days, and capture the future only as it pertains to today. The past does not equal the future, but God makes perfect use of yesterday, today, and tomorrow.

As we awaken to each new day, we only need to know what we need to do today - more precisely, right *now*. Our habit is to put Him first until we know that He is all we want. When He is *first*, and acknowledged as our All in all, then the other things find their proper rhythm in life. Putting things before Him creates disorder and chaos.

We have all made this mistake many times. We think we know what we want, so we run after a plan or a purpose that did not originate in Christ. It becomes an incomplete project; we lost interest, it was not satisfying. When He is our one and only thing, He discloses everything else that fills our life with meaning. We never change our 'number one' priority - Christ. We never change our 'only thing' to something else. We look to Christ; He brings every other desire into focus and fruition.

Focus is the common bond between the use of a calendar and having a strategy to support our goals. We all want to be more focused. If we live in a fog, or run into spider webs, we will wonder why everything is fuzzy. God asks us to number our days, and to write the vision until it is clear enough to act on. He has given us a vision and He will give us the accessories for that vision. I will repeat this to help you grasp its importance - we seek God (for God), He provides vision *and* a strategy; it will require focus, a calendar for managing time and mapping strategy, and time to incubate the vision, write the vision, and to allow God to continue to talk to us about this vision. He is our first and only focus; everything else falls in line behind Him. He will give us desires, hopes, and goals that provide a sense of purpose and meaning. We learn to manage and manifest the hopes that He imparts. However, we never put the cart before the horse - He is our priority, everything else is His priority to manage in us, through us, and as an expression of us, as we are in Christ.

Where is our vision? Do we want to see something happen in our family, or our community? How do we see the Kingdom of God coming to the earth? First, the Kingdom needs to come to our house. If the Kingdom is not at our house, how will we take it to the world? The Lord will spotlight the areas in our life where His Kingdom needs to come and His will be done. He may want to bring His Kingdom order to our finances. He may want to bring order to our use of time. His Kingdom may need to manifest in our marriage, or our health. There are many areas of our personal life where God wants to reveal His Kingdom. The key, as always, is that we focus on Him and allow Him to lead; we follow wherever He goes because our gaze is fixed on Him.

When God leads us to hope, we incubate the desire and He begins to impart details. The fact that vision comes with strategy helps us realize that there are steps to be revealed. We ask Him where to begin and expect Him to guide us to the starting line. A calendar is a place where a strategy can be captured. What good is strategy if we are not willing to carve out time to carry it out? A calendar is for planning and numbering our days. It helps us to buy up 'time opportunities' that are available for us to apply strategy. We use a calendar as a protection plan against urgent intruders who are always knocking at the door.

Crises will always come knocking on the door. People often say they are unable to get to a goal, strategy, or plan that God wants them to implement because of 'time goblins'. The unexpected push from urgent needs and requests that stem from outside sources create time crunches. Consider the adage, "Lack of planning on your part does not constitute an emergency on my part," which basically means that issues created by those who failed to plan do not necessarily need to fall in our lap. Learning to say an appropriate 'no' is helpful, while also remembering that 'plans never go as planned.' In other words, we leave room in our calendar, and grace in our heart, that allows God to navigate us through the minefield. Effective measures for reaching a goal are subject to both grace and patience. We are not obsessed with efficiency over effectiveness; we want a plan that will address specific and necessary steps, as well as the most efficient way to take the steps to accomplish the goal. In it all, we remain fluid, not rigid. We are watchful, but not dogmatic. We are careful to observe the spirit of the law, not the letter.

> *One Sabbath, when Jesus went to eat in the house of a prominent Pharisee, he was being carefully watched. There in front of him was a man suffering from abnormal swelling of his body. Jesus asked the Pharisees and experts in the law, "Is it lawful to heal on the Sabbath or not?" But they remained silent. So taking hold of the man, he healed him and sent him on his way. Then he asked them, "If one of you has a child or an ox that falls into a well on the Sabbath day, will you not immediately pull it out?" And they had nothing to say.*
>
> LUKE 14:1-6 (NIV)

We allow for the unexpected without allowing the unexpected to devour our time. We discern the rare time when a true emergency intersects our 'Sabbath' time with the Lord from the common time thieves of daily life. Crisis management is not an effective way to live, even though many do. Crises can be habit forming. Figuratively, we can be like a pyromaniac and go from one fire to the next. We crave a flame so much that we will start a fire just to watch it burn.

I used to live from crisis to crisis because the enemy had control or sway over my life. I was in Christ, but I allowed the enemy to use my authority. I did not know that it was *my* authority in Christ. When I learned that I had authority in Christ, I began to speak the word of God into my circumstances. I learned to call things that are not, as though they were. He diffused the crisis mentality as I sat and wrote His personal words to me on the pages of my journal. I am forever grateful that the first strategy He ever gave to me was: journalize.

In our journals, He will move us out of crisis living and into order. He creates strategy as we incubate vision. We pick up the pen and paper of our calendar and our journal and we wait for His plan in writing. By faith, we write; we record plans in our calendar and vision in our journal. We strategize in His presence, on paper. We set the plan in motion by first setting it in ink.

Of course, we prioritize time with God each morning, and crisis calls. We schedule an afternoon of strategizing, or implementing part of the plan (our date with destiny), and there is a knock on our door. The 'time thief' rings the bell and we have a decision to make. Will we honor the new creation or conform to the patterns of the flesh? If we honor the important, we find that the *urgent* can actually wait.

> I have two kinds of problems: the urgent and the important. The urgent are not important, and the important are never urgent.
>
> DWIGHT D. EISENHOWER

The Lord wants us to value His priorities in us, and to learn the difference between what is important and what is distraction and avoidance. Good time management is a balance between being effective and efficient. We keep a calendar with grace and patience - we leave wide margins to help reduce the stress of the unforeseen, and the epiphany of having set an unrealistic demand, deadline, or undertaking. We plan while leaving some room for the unexpected, but we do not allow the unexpected to continually spoil God's plan for us.

Usually, the important things will serve *our* goals, while urgent things often serve someone else's goals. When we can filter the important from the urgent, we can overcome the fear of disappointing others. Additionally, we will find the faith to focus on what is essential in the accomplishment of our goals in Christ, and will do so in obedience to the faithful movement of His Spirit.

Occasionally, that true emergency will arise, and God takes care. He will press us with the need to respond or to alter plans. We are not dismissing legitimate emergencies. However, too often what we call urgent is just an intruder invading the space we have carved out for God, and for setting goals and making plans.

SUSAN MUCKLOW

☐ DAY 5 - REFLECTION

What changes need to be made to make better use of your time?

putting everything on a unified calendar

☐ DAY 5 - JOURNALIZING ASSIGNMENT

I glorified you on earth, having accomplished the work that you gave me to do.

JOHN 17:4 (ESV)

Besides this you know the time, that the hour has come for you to wake from sleep. For salvation is nearer to us now than when we first believed.

ROMANS 13:11 (ESV)

It is in vain that you rise up early and go late to rest, eating the bread of anxious toil; for he gives to his beloved sleep.

PSALM 127:2 (ESV)

Lesson 4, Day 6 - *The Integrity of the New Creation*

☐ Day 6 - Reading Assignment

Jaque's Journal

Jaque, it is good to look forward to the future prophetically, to look forward to the prophetic words that I speak in your journal. Every vision that I speak gives you hope and a future. Only what I say to you should be illuminated and respected in your thoughts about the future. When you live in My presence with thoughts of tomorrow, you are full of hope. True hope reaches into the future, and faith takes what is there (in the future) and uses it for today. Faith can pull substance out of the future and bring it into today. With all the plans that you make, Jaque, keep this lesson in mind. It will mean making plans by prophetic inspiration.

Think about this, Jaque, because the superficial world makes plans according to external conditions. However, the most profound things are the things that you cannot see. Let me ask you this question, Jaque - is it more important for you to feel 'right' on the inside of yourself, or to feel good about your job performance, ministry, relationships, houses, and cars? Your life is about more than how fast you can get a job done or how nice your house looks. Walk away from the lure of being liked and admired by others based on your ability to achieve outward goals.

Let us talk about setting goals. Most people set outward goals as if they are the most important things they can have. However, this is not true. The weightier matters are always in the Spirit. Which of the following is more important? And, yes, I am talking now about important versus urgent! Thus, which is more important - the goal to finish your work, or the goal to live with integrity? The integrity of your being will direct you to accomplish true goals. How about the goal to either finish a big project (like writing a book), or the goal to know you can finish any project that comes along? Who would even see this as a goal?

Lord, I would rather know I could handle any project, than to worry about finishing a book I am writing.

Jaque, integrity is what will cause you to see to it that the mechanics get done. Integrity makes sure that, at 4 o'clock, you are where you said you would be, instead of attending to a false crisis armed with nothing more than worry and anxiety. People worry about potential emergencies and paralyze themselves; they cannot act from the integrity of the new creation because of the 'what ifs' of life. They are afraid to make commitments because 'crisis living' keeps them from being reliable. Integrity makes the commitment; integrity says, "I will be there at 4 o'clock, see you then." And things get done...

What is more important, Jaque, having a sense of safety and community or having a ministry policy on gossip? Integrity builds trust; it lets people know that you do not intend to hurt them. Our relationship is based in these absolutes, Jaque. If with integrity you love people, you will never need a policy on gossip. How about having goals for guidance, are they worthy goals? Questions for guidance arise when people do not know My voice, My purpose for their life, and therefore cannot trust their own heart and conscience.

Our questions for guidance and direction arise because we have not been incubating the will of God in our lives. It is God's will to reveal His will. He is not withholding it from us. His will comes through our own personality as we listen (in the 'incubating place' in us) to His voice and work out His strategy for our lives. If we are uncertain, we can know this - our first desire is for Him. If we will seek Him, follow His lead, and endeavor to love Him with our whole being, then 'who we want to be when we grow up' will unfold from there.

> *When you know Me, Jaque, your life is guided all the time for you know My will…as you go. You understand that My desire for you is for character, integrity, honesty, and love. My goals are already established; you cannot see them, for they are Spirit and life. However, they are set within as the desires of your heart. When you ask Me for them, you begin to see what I am after.*

We learn to ask, to consult His wisdom, and to expect His desires to surface. "What do you desire in me, Lord? Where do you want to go, what do you want to do? There is a problem infuriating me…shall we solve this problem together?" There is so much that we already know about what direction we are meant to go. Confusion comes from not making Him our one, only, and first priority. Keeping first things first keeps everything else plain and clear.

> *Jaque, do not go through life attached to people, places, and things. Do not miss life because you were too busy. Exchange wishes for desires - for I know you by your desires. Feed your desires or they will die. Incubate them. Discipline your mind or it will run you ragged. Parents and society conditioned your mind, but you must take back the land I have promised. You have the mind of Christ, use it.*

> *You have guidance in the form of My leadership. A mature faith does not need a list of other rules, for I will point the way as you go. Find your life in My requirements, for My commands hold the requirements for a fulfilling life.*

We are catching a glimpse of the lifestyle and order that we have craved. It is in us, waiting to be revealed through our fellowship with the Spirit. Order, direction, and guidance are *already* in us - it is not in heaven or in someone else's counsel. If we do not know what to do, if there is confusion in our life, then we need to spend more time with God. Confusion leaves when being with Him is our way of life.

> *Jaque, the fruit of the Spirit is in the middle of two extremes, always. A pendulum swings towards two extremes, but balance is in the middle. Truth, or the balance of life, is between the extremes. For instance, what is in the middle between stinginess and being a spendthrift? In the center is a generous person. What is in the middle between being a people pleaser and a people hater? In the center is the willingness to be unimportant. When you have to be important, Jaque, you either want people's applause or you feel disdain and want nothing from them at all. What is in the middle between perfectionism and chaos? In the center are spontaneity, freedom, and order. Jaque, you do not want perfectionism or chaos, you want order and form.*
>
> *I know you, Jaque, I hear your request. I answer you and tell you again what I have told you before. Find your life in Me and in the commands I have already given you. Find life in My character, in My integrity. Look for your life in Christ and live in harmony with what you find, and as you do, you will be blessed. I will clear you from all debt, I will cleanse this temple, and I will set you at liberty. I will call you up into My tower, you will see higher things as I reveal more of My secrets to you. I will show you what to write and you will be My mouthpiece and I will be your God.*
>
> Father, cleanse me from hidden faults; grant a continual spirit of repentance. I will not worry about anything for You have become my refuge and hiding place. All I want is more of You and less of who I think I am. Amen.

Find life in His commands, we will find divine order and we will know the strategy for our life…

☐ DAY 6 - REFLECTION

Practice seeing truth in the middle of two extremes by naming two extremes of your own and then naming the balance / truth between the two.

Pigstye

Clean house vs Peaceful Family

☐ DAY 6 - JOURNALIZING ASSIGNMENT

The integrity of the upright guides them, but the unfaithful are destroyed by their duplicity.

PROVERBS 11:3 (NIV)

Let your eyes look straight ahead; fix your gaze directly before you. Give careful thought to the paths for your feet and be steadfast in all your ways.

PROVERBS 4:25,26 (NIV)

And not only this, but we also exult in our tribulations, knowing that tribulation brings about perseverance; and perseverance, proven character; and proven character, hope; and hope does not disappoint, because the love of God has been poured out within our hearts through the Holy Spirit who was given to us.

ROMANS 5:3-5 (NASB)

LESSON 4, DAY 7 - *Purpose, Activity, and Resource*

☐ DAY 7 - READING ASSIGNMENT

Teach us to number our days and recognize how few they are; help us to spend them as we should.

PSALM 90:12 (TLB)

Learning to live from the integrity of the new creation is the safest way to know how to spend our days as we should. The new creation holds the balance between being too structured and having no structure at all. In between these two extremes are spontaneity and obedience to faith. We all face the challenge of discerning the proper use of time. We struggle with the differences between what is important, urgent, and true emergency. How many times has the phone rung, or a text message popped up, while we sit with the Lord and our journal? Rather than silence our phone, fear speaks; we worry there could real trouble and that someone may actually need our help. The Lord will often remind us that He is bigger than we are. We are not God, and God is able to do more in a crisis than we are. When we value our appointment with God, then our appointments with God become very productive. When He knows that we are serious, He seriously begins to unfold strategy for bringing goals to pass.

We have to decide that what God has to say is more important than what everybody else wants from us. The false nature loves to be everybody else's hero because it makes it feel alive. It is *not* alive, but it feels alive and so it tries to keep us away from the truth that would expose the false nature that is hijacking our goals.

When we use a calendar to set goals with God, it is a decisive act on our part; it is a deliberate statement that we will not conform to the flesh. It is a declaration that we have plans. When this is our lifestyle, crisis and urgency do not knock on our door as often as before. It is as if they receive a spiritual memo stating we officially know our true purpose now, we know what is important, and we will no longer be easily distracted. We know the order for our lives and we operate in discernment. We know what is important, and what is not. We put Him first; we see the *purpose*, the true *activity* to be performed, and the *resource* that is at our disposal. Goals are taking shape.

Our *purpose* is to seek Him and His righteousness; He is first, He is number one. After that, our purpose could be to sing a song, write a book, invent a new mousetrap, start a business, organize the house, and the list is endless. The *activity* is to create a path, strategy, or a discipline. How? We begin by picking up a calendar and a journal to receive His details in writing. We schedule His important tasks in the timeslots of a calendar and receive His important strategy for achieving His goals on the pages of a journal. We write, and we fan the flames of desire until we have hotter desire. Our resource is Christ in us. He is the One who gives the vision and the strategy that comes with it; He gives everything else that is needed, like energy, inspiration, resolve, renewal, focus, attentiveness, details, revision, desire, desire, and more desire.

The Beginning of Wisdom

The fear and reverence of the Lord is the beginning of wisdom. When we fear and reverence God, we start every day with wisdom. Taking time to seek God is always time well spent. Putting down His words on paper every day, writing with a heart full of faith, gives us an edge to success, for in this we are cherishing the prophecies of our Prophet.

Jaque's Journal

My children, take time to wait on Me. Plan on it, budget time for it, even schedule it into your life. I know that waiting is a troublesome idea to an old wineskin; I know that people dislike waiting lines, waiting in traffic, or waiting at all. An old wineskin hates waiting...period. Living in a "hurry up," insta-society makes it difficult to enjoy My waiting room; but understand it is not for the mind of the flesh to ever consent. You must then, in view of all My mercies, present your bodies to Me as a reasonable sacrifice while My Spirit transforms your minds into new wineskins.

Jesus lived slowly and quietly enough to know Me. Without car, bike, or plane, He walked where He went and had time to wait on Me. He did not have email, social media, computers, or access to the internet. He did not have a burger barn or a chicken palace to get a meal in a minute. He waited because waiting was His "lifestyle." I am not saying you can or should live in a culture like Jesus did; I am saying you can find a way to give Me time, because you must, and it is how Christ in you still lives. He spent thirty-three years waiting on Me and there was not one ounce of waste in His life. He set the example; follow Him.

Planning Is...

1. Identifying the overall *purpose* of a project.

And I continually long to know the wonders of Jesus more fully and to experience the overflowing power of his resurrection working in me.

PHILIPPIANS 3:10 (TPT)

2. Identifying what *activities* need to be performed.

So take a new grip with your tired hands and strengthen your weak knees. Mark out a straight path for your feet so that those who are weak and lame will not fall but become strong. Work at living in peace with everyone, and work at living a holy life, for those who are not holy will not see the Lord. Look after each other so that none of you fails to receive the grace of God. Watch out that no poisonous root of bitterness grows up to trouble you, corrupting many. Make sure that no one is immoral or godless like Esau, who traded his birthright as the firstborn son for a single meal.

HEBREWS 12:12-16 (NLT)

3. Identifying the *resources* needed to complete the project.

Living within you is the Christ who floods you with the expectation of glory! This mystery of Christ, embedded within us, becomes a heavenly treasure chest of hope filled with the riches of glory for his people, and God wants everyone to know it!

COLOSSIANS 1:27 (TPT)

True prosperity is the progressive attainment of God's goals for our lives; it's the ability of God in us to meet the needs of mankind, whatever those needs may be. Poverty is simply the lack of vision for God's purpose and plans. Be prepared to spend time with the Lord in a calendar and journal to: practice incubating hopes, goals, and purposes in God; practice identifying the activities and strategies necessary to manifest them; to identify the resources available to help bring those purposes to full fruition.

☐ DAY 7 - REFLECTION

What is your number one purpose today?

What activity needs to be performed to attain this purpose?

What are the resources available to you?

☐ DAY 7 - JOURNALIZING ASSIGNMENT

Not that I have already obtained all this, or have already arrived at my goal, but I press on to take hold of that for which Christ Jesus took hold of me. Brothers and sisters, I do not consider myself yet to have taken hold of it. But one thing I do: Forgetting what is behind and straining toward what is ahead, I press on toward the goal to win the prize for which God has called me heavenward in Christ Jesus.

PHILIPPIANS 3: 12-14 (NIV)

Therefore, since we are surrounded by such a great cloud of witnesses, let us throw off everything that hinders and the sin that so easily entangles. And let us run with perseverance the race marked out for us, fixing our eyes on Jesus, the pioneer and perfecter of faith. For the joy set before him he endured the cross, scorning its shame, and sat down at the right hand of the throne of God. Consider him who endured such opposition from sinners, so that you will not grow weary and lose heart.

HEBREWS 12:1-3 (NIV)

LESSON 4 - HEART-WORK

The Heart-work is a valuable part of your inner work. Taking the time to give heartfelt responses to the following questions is beneficial for you and beneficial for sharing with others who are in your study group.

PUTTING IT ALL TOGETHER

1. How does time with the Lord in both a journal and a calendar help hone the strategy and details of His plans for your life?
2. What is your current understanding of what is important, urgent, and a true emergency? How will you know the difference between them when they arise?
3. Why is waiting (incubating) not a waste of time?
4. Please share your journalizing experience this week with regard to heart and frequency. How was your desire for discipline grounded in grace this week?

Note: If you are in a VI class, please include one journal from this week with the Heart-work you submit for coaching.

If not, please bring your Heart-work and a journal to share with others in your study group.

Identifying the Activity to Be Performed

And we desire for each one of you to show the same diligence [all the way through] so as to realize and enjoy the full assurance of hope until the end, so that you will not be [spiritually] sluggish, but [will instead be] imitators of those who through faith [lean on God with absolute trust and confidence in Him and in His power] and by patient endurance [even when suffering] are [now] inheriting the promises.

HEBREWS 6:11,12 (AMP)

Lesson 5, Day 1 - *High Noon*

☐ Day 1 - Reading Assignment

The means of coming to the end of a thing is also the key to keeping it. Hope knows the way to a goal, and how to keep the goal. Hope is God's kind of expectancy - the expectancy of excellence. Excellence is Jesus Christ - alive in His people. Hope puts a demand on this Christ-excellence inside of us. We expect *Him* because we know He is here, and we are not about to settle for less! It would displease God if we were to expect less than all that He has given us in Christ. We want the whole portion. Therefore, we will not shift from our resolve to know God and the knowledge of His will. Our mistakes may be many, but they do not frighten us away, for we still anticipate the achievement of every goal that is ours in Christ Jesus. We have God's word on it, and His word is the announcement of His will. The marvelous truth about God is that His will is one with His action. He speaks a word and it is done! His power is one with His purpose. Our hope is based on, and is in fact, full of His words. Hope knows that the means to the end is God's word on the thing, and the way of keeping, grasping, and continuing to hold the promise is the same as the means, it is the word of God. I knew that my goals in Christ must continually inspire me, therefore I continued to journalize the word of God.

The activity is remaining permanently in His Presence

> *[Oh, I know, I have been rash to talk out plainly this way to God!] I will [in my thinking] stand upon my post of observation and station myself on the tower or fortress, and will watch to see what He will say within me and what answer I will make [as His mouthpiece] to the perplexities of my complaint against Him. And the Lord answered me and said, Write the vision and engrave it so plainly upon tablets that everyone who passes may [be able to] read [it easily and quickly] as he hastens by, for the vision is yet for an appointed time and it hastens to the end [fulfillment]; it will not deceive or disappoint. Though it tarry, wait [earnestly] for it, because it will surely come; it will not be behindhand on its appointed day.*
>
> HABAKKUK 2:1-3 (AMPC)

Jaque's Journal

Jaque, you don't just suddenly have high noon after midnight. First comes the dawn of day as the ever increasing light brings the full brightness of the day. This is how it is with My answers. I speak truth to you and as the truth dawns on you, you progressively come into the fullness of the wholeness that the truth brings. The truth doesn't develop... you develop in the truth. And this is why you continue to develop: because you place yourself in the sunrise. If you sleep through it, you will never see it, but when you are available to it, you see it from start to finish.

The noon day is like the vision, Jaque, it is for an appointed time. Though it tarry, wait for it. Don't go back to sleep, for it will not deceive or delay. High noon will surely come and it will not be behindhand, it will not be late! So wait on Me in the passing hours. Like the sun dawns the horizon and progressively moves upward in the sky, so does every grace and freedom come to you as you behold your God. Stay for the whole show! Don't go to sleep before the ending or you will miss receiving the desires of your heart. 'I' am writing Jaque! I am writing the dawn on your heart and high noon is coming! My writings dawn the truth in you and make you understand. I pen the truth in these journals, and Christ appears.

There are many facets of beauty in the sunrise Jaque, and the truth is dawning in all its many glories through these words I write to you. Tell others this: "If you have the faith to write, then write...and God Himself will dawn on you."

Oh yes, there will always be skeptics, but faith overrides skepticism. Faith writes, so keep writing. Write all the words I tell you in a book. It will be the book of dawnings and at full noon, you will understand how you got from there to here. These writings are a deep form of your prayer life, Jaque, they are exhibitions of faith and as high noon is coming, it will reveal the substance of your faith.

Everything you believe for has its high noon. There is a high noon for every darkness, for every trouble, for every desire, and for every 'awake' believer.

Jaque, if I know clearly and concisely what you want, then why is it so important that you know it as clearly? And if I know, why don't I just write it in the sky, telling you plainly instead of waiting while you discover it for yourself? Isn't it a great waste of time for Me to wait for you to get it? Are not these some of the questions trafficking through your mind?

Yes Lord, I admit I have thought these thoughts.

But now that you have heard My voice, do you understand the answer?

Yes Father, I do, and so I will give You an answer. Now I know that You are not waiting for me to figure things out, or to discover things on my own. No, you **are** telling me. This is what our daily fellowship is about. I write by Your Spirit, I write and write the words You say. You always say the words that will condition me to receive the clear concise focus, the full light of day, for alone I can't see. It's sort of like waking up before dawn when it's still dark, but gradually You bring the light...not all at once, else the brightness would blind me, but first the dawn, then the morning light, until at last I reach the full light of day at high noon.

At the dawn it seems as though the light tarries, but actually, it hastens to the end fulfillment because You have appointed high noon to come precisely on time. For this reason, I wait expectantly, for I know noon is coming.

Writing the words You say to me is the same as watching the gradual changes in the light. You have planted desires in me. Desires You knew I would like because of who I am, because of who You made me to be. And You planned to carry them out to full noon, each and every one, because it delights You to fulfill my desires. The desires You planted in me are the means by which You will accomplish Your purpose on earth in Your Jaque form. My wants, therefore, are Your wants. This is union reality, the understanding of who I am.

In the dark morning before dawn, I don't really understand this yet, but as You write and write Your truths on my heart, little by little the light approaches. I stay awake and keep writing. You give me words that prepare my heart, and understanding comes gradually. Truths begin to dawn on me, line upon line, precept upon precept. Every day Your Word conditions me for a little more truth. Eventually high noon arrives, absolutely guaranteed by Your infallible Word, and I comprehend the wants and the desires that I have. They are clear and concise, and with confidence I am sure they are from You, that they are one with Your desires, and that by Your power they **will** come to pass.

But the path of the [uncompromisingly] just and righteous is like the light of dawn, that shines more and more (brighter and clearer) until [it reaches its full strength and glory in] the perfect day [to be prepared].

PROVERBS 4:18 (AMPC)

☐ DAY 1 - REFLECTION

Define PROGRESSIVE:

Define EVALUATE:

Define INSPIRATION:

☐ DAY 1 - JOURNALIZING ASSIGNMENT

Keep trusting in the Lord and do what is right in his eyes. Fix your heart on the promises of God and you will be secure, feasting on his faithfulness. Make God the utmost delight and pleasure of your life, and he will provide for you what you desire the most. Give God the right to direct your life, and as you trust him along the way you'll find he pulled it off perfectly! He will appear as your righteousness, as sure as the dawning of a new day. He will manifest as your justice, as sure and strong as the noonday sun. Quiet your heart in his presence and pray; keep hope alive as you long for God to come through for you.

PSALM 37:3-7 (TPT)

LESSON 5, DAY 2 - *Investment, Roll Overs, and Increase*

☐ DAY 2 - READING ASSIGNMENT

Every hope we have is another new dawn and it has a high noon of fulfillment. Each new hope has a new hope that will follow. God never stops supplying fresh hopes as an investment in our hope-filled life in Christ. Faith, hope, and love, work together; we watch their continuous harmony as part of our continuous activity. Our habit is to repeatedly return to the Lord, looking for our next new hope. Which 'hope' does He want us to invest purpose, activity, and resource into today? What is today's new dawn? What will *dawn* on us today that never *dawned* on us before?

Little by Little

> *Hope deferred makes the heart sick, but desire fulfilled is a tree of life.*
>
> PROVERBS 13:12 (NASB)

Hope deferred makes the heart sick. God does not defer (put off) hope; His mercies are new every morning, and His word (like manna) is a daily portion. He admonishes us to gather His divine counsel a little every day, for whoever gathers a little at a time will increase his riches. Christians value the important things enough to make a little investment in them each day. A little bit every day makes a great big difference at the end of each month, each year, each decade. The law of use teaches us to learn to invest. It's important to form the habit of doing so, for habits form destinies. Our habit of permanent expectancy is developed because we invest a little time hearing God each day...time to sit still and really take His word in, giving it a good deal of thought and study, for whatever measure we give is the measure of light that comes back to us. The activity of faith advocates the principle of gathering little by little.

> *Dishonest money dwindles away, but whoever gathers money little by little makes it grow.*
>
> PROVERBS 13:11 (NIV)

[gaining wealth of joy, peace, love, integrity/Character, the ♡ & mind of Christ is True wealth]

Jaque's Journal

Jaque, roll and repose each of your cares on Me. Seek Me as you roll over every care and burden onto Me. After you roll over an IRA from one account to another, you relax, trusting that your previous evaluation has brought you to a better decision about where to invest your money. You move on then to think about other things. Well, when you roll over your cares to Me, it is because you have evaluated that I am a better place for them. I am the best place for causing them to disappear - for these are not investments that you want to increase, but decrease. When it comes to cares and burdens, you put them in Me and they will follow the law of diminishing returns. Worry will decrease, and your trust account will increase. To put or invest your burdens in Me is to cease from thinking about them.

Jaque, do not evaluate cares and burdens; evaluate Me as the better investment for your time and energy. When you are no longer worried about 'something,' I can show you the truth about 'something' in the twinkling of an eye. But when you keep the care and concern, your mind is burdened because you do not have what it takes to figure 'something' out. This is why you must receive your life in Me. Your desire for Me is My constant goal in you. I will accomplish My purpose in you as you pursue Me - your goal.

Seek Me, and ask Me questions. My answers are your profits; invest time in seeking Me, making withdrawals anytime you need them. Make it a habit to get everything you need from Me, this habit forms your destiny. For all things are destined to belong to you from the use of this habit. In this way, you establish your heart in grace and find more delight in believing.

To believe on the Son, and to *continue* to believe on the Son, is our primary activity. Hope is always full of God's Word. If our hope does not have the influx of His word, then it has no motivation or potency. Without God's word, there is nothing to give hope its passion. Hope is based on the word of God because His word is our only source of absolute assurance. Our goals must continually inspire us; therefore, we continue to journalize His word. We have to go from hope to hope, inspiration to inspiration. We have to be impassioned by what we see. We continue to journalize because we have created a habit that allows us to lean into it; we are *prone* to journalize. Fellowship with His word has become like needing air. We need to capture His word because it inspires our hope to go on to the next new dawning.

The word of God becomes our very breath. Without it, we gasp. Our hope (our life) would belabor for lack of oxygen. We need another word from the Lord like our lungs need to take in more air. If we are winded, we need to catch our breath; we need to catch our vision, our hope. To lose sight of Him in His word is to lose sight of our meaning and purpose. It would feel like the air was knocked out of our lungs. It feels scary when we cannot catch our breath. We need to slow down, take a deep breath and inhale His word. If breathing were not a habit, we would die. So also, if we lost sight of our purpose, we would lose our zest for living.

To believe on the Son is to believe that He is here, as breath for our lungs, circulating His life like oxygen in our bloodstream. He is here, helping us to incubate our hopes as we think about, ponder, meditate, and write His words to us on paper. We capture His words in writing - in our journal, calendar, budget, or any other method He supplies. Whatever vision He is providing this day, He will provide a way for us to make contact with paper so that we can write the vision and make it plain (Habakkuk 2:2).

Writing the vision is incubating the vision. If we discontinue, the inspiration we once held will evaporate. The inspiration will disappear into thin air; it will be like a vapor or a wisp. We will have only a faint memory of how that hope once inspired us, but we will not remember why or how. With the mind of Christ, we will stay inspired for His mind will drive us to the word of God - to hope's assurance. Without the mind of Christ as the 'known constant' within us, our hope would be an endless cycle of inspirational starts and stops, but never able to retain, store up, and then pour itself out into a tangible reality.

☐ DAY 2 - REFLECTION

What is our primary activity?

To believe on the Son
an Stay in His Presence

☐ DAY 2 - JOURNALIZING ASSIGNMENT

I will stand my watch and set myself on the rampart, and watch to see what He will say to me, and what I will answer when I am corrected. Then the Lord answered me and said: "Write the vision and make it plain on tablets, that he may run who reads it. For the vision is yet for an appointed time; but at the end it will speak, and it will not lie. Though it tarries, wait for it; because it will surely come, it will not tarry. Behold the proud, his soul is not upright in him; but the just shall live by his faith.

HABAKKUK 2:1-4 (NKJV)

LESSON 5, DAY 3 - *Constant Work*

☐ DAY 3 - READING ASSIGNMENT

Eventually, the cycle that allows hope's inspiration to leak or evaporate must end. The cracks must be mended; the mending occurs as we learn to identify ourselves as new creations. We continue hearing the Holy Spirit speak, and gradually give up who we thought we were; we lose hope (rightfully so) in this false identity that makes false promises for false improvement. We gain hope in the life of Christ operating through His new creation.

To continue to believe on the Son denotes a constant work. Finding our true self in Christ is a true work. Christ is the core of the new creation. We are growing up and learning to put on the mind of Christ. Part of the practice is writing the vision of Christ as He appears in each area of our life. We read and reread, see and re-see, write and rewrite the vision of Christ in us. His Spirit continually inspires us, breathes in us, and keeps us awake and aware that God has many things to bring to the earth through us. We need His goals (through our uniqueness) to continually inspire us in order to stay awake.

It can be shocking how often the false self lulls us back to sleep. Nonetheless, over the course of time we stay awake for longer intervals. As we bask in God's presence, the light of His word dawns on us. We do not interpret the truth; the truth interprets us. Christ, the Truth will show us who we are. As we discern the difference between His role and ours, we stay teachable. When we form our own opinions, interpretations, or doctrines apart from Truth, we return to slumber.

The truth will show us something we did not know before. We have to be ready for it. If we are not ready to be shown something new, then we remain arrogant. The book of Habakkuk reveals that a proud heart is not 'right' within us. A proud heart does not live by faith. Living by faith is the willingness to see the truth, and to allow the truth to show us what it is instead of what we *think* it is. We cannot tell the truth what we *want* it to be - the truth is what it is.

We need to notice how much we want things to go *our* way. We have expectations of particular outcomes. When things do not work out as we imagined, we are disappointed and upset. Life will take every opportunity to show us that we do not get to tell life what it should be - it tells us what it is. How we respond to life determines our ability to learn, to be grateful, and to relinquish pride in favor of humility.

We all have people in our lives about whom we believe we understand who they are to us; that is, what we mean to them, and what they mean to us. We believe we have the relationship figured out. We think we know how he or she thinks of us, usually based on how we think of them. We rest on what we *think* we know, and assume that everything is 'good.' We build up our own ideas of what the relationship means to each other. Then one day, the relationship comes crashing to the ground and life shows us that our relationship was not what we thought it was or what we wanted it to be. In that moment, we want to be angry with the other person, but there is no one and nothing to blame except our own interpretation. We feel incensed and say, "Well, they certainly were not who I thought they were!" *They* are not the problem; if we place expectations or interpretations on people (spoken or unspoken), or ask them to change, then we are asking them to lie to us. We have codependent relationships that require us to lie to one another. We 'put on' the persona they expect and vice-versa. It is a false self in relationship with another false self.

Once we begin to wake up, the truth comes out as it always does. We see and accept our true self and allow others to be their true selves. We receive people as a whole package. We may not be who we thought we were, but we will be real. I believe that we would rather have the truth than a movie reel in our head that is projecting a false image. Our fantasy is our deception, and it is destroying the potential for real relationships.

I pray we will allow the truth to make us real. The 'truth' is having a relationship with us; let us allow it to have a relationship with others through us. We will never be able to dictate what the truth needs to be. As we sit and reflect in God's word (as in a mirror), the truth will mirror itself, others, and ourselves in the light of His love.

Every high noon we have is an illustration, another revelation, and another unfolding of the truth showing us what it really is. At first, truth will make us feel angry. It is not the new creation, but rather the sin principle that is rattled. The truth has to uproot the lie, shake off deception, and awaken the sleeper, before we can begin to see the love that the truth has for us. The truth always loves us. Jesus said, I am the Way, the Truth and the Life, and that He loves us. We are all deceived about something; we have been sleeping for a long time and there is darkness in different areas of our life. We must invite the truth to set us free. We must look truth in the face and receive its love for us. Where else can we go but to the truth? We have lived deceiving ourselves for long enough. It is time for things to change. We can start to get free when we are ready for change. The truth always has grace with it. Truth is full of grace.

☐ DAY 3 - REFLECTION

What does remaining teachable mean to you?

Receive, shift, pull off the layers of the old self & seek the truth in His presence, then walk out whatever He gives us

☐ DAY 3 - JOURNALIZING ASSIGNMENT

These things I have written to you who believe in the name of the Son of God, that you may know that you have eternal life, and that you may continue to believe in the name of the Son of God.

1 JOHN 5:13 (NKJV)

Brethren, I do not count myself to have apprehended; but one thing I do, forgetting those things which are behind and reaching forward to those things which are ahead, I press toward the goal for the prize of the upward call of God in Christ Jesus.

PHILIPPIANS 3:13, 14 (NKJV)

Your hands have made me and established me; give me understanding and a teachable heart, that I may learn Your commandments.

PSALM 119:73 (AMP)

LESSON 5, DAY 4 - *Nuts and Bolts*

☐ DAY 4 - READING ASSIGNMENT

Jaque's Journal

Jaque, grace is a life of refreshment and ease lived in the strength and the will of God. You are simply resting in a boat as you glide down the river. You hold the oars, you move your arms, but the current of My River does the work; as you float downstream you actually enjoy doing your part. What a delight, what satisfaction you derive from living on My boat. What joy you experience when you can be with Me without feeling you need to get 'back to work' to toil for My gifts or approval. Whether My gifts are food, shelter, peace, character, or anything else, your awareness of grace allows you to rest. The activity to be performed is to be done in grace, and that means rest. Once you are in this place of grace, you can tackle anything because activity then stems from love's motive. It is no longer your responsibility to guarantee the results. You are ready to take on anything because, through it all, you are still gliding down the river. You know that you are the right person for the job. You no longer wonder, "Is this job right for me?" because you know that you are the right person for any job. After all, you are just gliding while My River of grace does the work.

Jaque, when you understand that Christ is the goal of every plan, structure, and method, then you are ready to move ahead and to be successful in every endeavor. In the vision I give you of Christ, acting out His life in your form, there is a seemingly secret door. Behind that door are keys that open all the other doors, which contain the answers to questions like, "How shall I implement this vision? What should I do first? How do I keep from getting ahead of it or lagging behind it? How much time will it require? Where should I write these things down? Will there be obstacles in my way and how will I overcome them?" Jaque, apart from grace, life feels like something you buy and take home in a box to assemble. You have a hard time with assembly instructions. You want somebody else to assemble it because all the parts overwhelm you. You don't know where to start. When you open the box, everything is included, but without grace (help) you give up.

Jaque, when I impart vision, I supply the grace that puts the pieces together for you. I have included strategy, plans, and parts for assembly. If you have trusted Me for the vision, then trust Me for the parts needed, directions to make them fit, and grace for full assembly. There is much work to be done, do it in grace. All the parts are included, nothing is lacking. The activity and work is to stay in rest, believing nothing is missing from the box. All of Christ, and all He is intended to be in you, is here. Take one little part you see, pick up the nut or bolt and add it to the project to connect the pieces. Each day you will see a little more and nut-by-nut, bolt-by-bolt, you will watch this vision come together.

Jaque, the greatest activity is faith working to keep the soul believing that each new goal will come together. Hope puts a picture on the wall of the project before it is complete so that faith can see what this project will look like when it is finished. An instruction manual includes a picture that shows how the fully assembled widget looks. Hope takes the picture, hangs it on the wall or keeps it right in front of its face, and faith goes about the assembly process with the picture in view.

The picture of Christ keeps faith faithful in His work. Jaque, what does the vision tell you about the strategy today?

Father, it is telling me to keep going, to believe, to pick up the next nut and the next bolt. The vision is telling me that the picture on hope's wall is Christ and that faith keeps looking unto Jesus, the Author and Finisher of my faith. The goal shapes the plan, the plan sets the action, the action achieves the result, and the result brings the glory of God.

Jaque, the goal to sit at My feet is the plan. The strategy to keep hearing My voice, no matter what, comes forth through action. The fact that there is a goal determines the necessary action to achieve the resulting glory. Never fear the activity, for it is always accomplished one nut at a time.

We have a tendency to want to see the finished product all at once. We unpack the vision by taking everything out of the box, and then we give ourselves five minutes to try to force it into its proper form. I call this 'big elephant syndrome' because, at first, I am overwhelmed by the sheer enormity of the project, and then, when I finally tackle it, I feel frustration when it takes too long. This universal problem is known as impatience. We are busy either avoiding the inevitable or rushing our way through the assembly process because we want to move on to the next elephant. What are we going to do with a herd of elephants in our boat? Our boat is already too heavy.

We take on more than we need in the boat called 'life.' We take on too many roles, wear too many hats, assume too much responsibility, and end up measuring our accomplishments by the exhaustion we feel. Sadly, we often think that God is putting these demands on us; He is not.

There is an old adage that says, "Take the first step and the next one will be revealed." We do not need to know what the next step is until we have taken the step before. If our instruction manual says to attach point A to point B, then that is all we need to do right now. By taking one step at a time, we learn to live in the moment, enjoy the moment, and realize that today matters. Tomorrow is not promised. What is the right thing to do today? In all that we do, the Lord wants us to experience the joy and enjoyment of the moment. We need to repent for reducing our life to 'a work for God.' If we have 'big elephant syndrome,' it is stealing the joy to which we are called.

☐ DAY 4 - REFLECTION

What is your understanding of how Christ is the goal of every plan?

The goal is to seek & be present w/ God moment by moment and everything else we need to plan, strategize, schedule & do becomes joyful & effortless.

☐ DAY 4 - JOURNALIZING ASSIGNMENT

"All this," said David, "the Lord made me understand in writing by His hand upon me, all the work and details [to be done] according to this plan."

1 CHRONICLES 28:19 (AMP)

The Lord makes firm the steps of the one who delights in him; though he may stumble, he will not fall, for the Lord upholds him with his hand.

PSALM 37:23,24 (NIV)

Righteousness goes before him and prepares the way for his steps.

PSALM 85:13 (NIV)

For I know the plans I have for you," declares the Lord, "plans to prosper you and not to harm you, plans to give you hope and a future.

JEREMIAH 29:11 (NIV)

LESSON 5, DAY 5 - *Waiting Is the Activity of Faith*

☐ DAY 5 - READING ASSIGNMENT

I am going to share a response from Susan Mucklow when she was asked about the importance of learning to wait:

> Waiting is the activity of faith; impulsiveness is the action of self-reliance. Waiting says, "I believe God is moving on my behalf." Impulsiveness says, "I've got to *do* something about this situation." Waiting is alive with the vibrancy of hope and expectation in another's ability to give birth to solid steady steps on my behalf. Impulsiveness is driven and it is drained by wasted steps, it mistakes motion for progress and wonders why it is always tired. We think if we are busy we are progressing, we are moving ahead, it is not so. Waiting knows itself to be the precursor to true physical action that is executed in rest and peace. It is never a waste of time. It saves time to carve straight paths for our feet, whereas impulsiveness runs around in circles and finds itself continuously starting over.
>
> SUSAN MUCKLOW

Have you ever felt like you are continually starting over? Sometimes we feel we messed up so badly and there is nothing to do but begin again. Impulsive actions are akin to big elephant syndrome. In haste, we lose key components of our 'assembly package' and have to buy replacements. Haste makes waste, and now the project costs more that it would have and takes longer than it should have. This kind of frantic activity is the opposite of God's rest.

We spend far too much time doing what we think *ought* to be done rather than waiting for deliberate, specific instructions. We watch the clock too closely, and complain about God's timetable. If we feel He is slack, then we take matters into our own hand - even if that means trying to force a square peg into a round hole. God is ready and waiting patiently to provide us with instructions, but we cannot hear because we are so occupied by the thoughts whirling around our own head. We cannot hear God's direction because we are spinning our wheels like a hamster going nowhere.

Pride is a source of impatience. We want fast results because it impresses others and ourselves. Habakkuk said, "I will *wait* to see what God will say within me." Waiting to hear what He is saying is never a waste of time. Listening to other misguided voices *is* a waste of time. God does not ask for our opinions and we do well to let them go. The heaviest load in our boat is our opinions. We *think* we know something that we do not yet know. We may have *some* light, a little squeak of dawn may have come over the horizon, but we are a long way from high noon. It is not high noon until we have His full revelation; it is not high noon until God says it is.

Mary and Martha

> *As Jesus and his disciples were on their way, he came to a village where a woman named Martha opened her home to him. She had a sister called Mary, who sat at the Lord's feet listening to what he said. But Martha was distracted by all the preparations that had to be made. She came to him and asked, "Lord, don't you care that my sister has left me to do the work by myself? Tell her to help me!" "Martha, Martha," the Lord answered, "you are worried and upset about many things, but few things are needed - or indeed only one. Mary has chosen what is better, and it will not be taken away from her."*
>
> LUKE 10:38-42 (NIV)

When we decide that we are willing to sit and wait for the voice of the Lord, then we are ready to perform 'Mary' activity instead of 'Martha' activity. Martha's activity has its place, but only when received as a directive after waiting for the Lord to speak. Metaphorically, Martha steps up and out of Mary and says, "Okay, I know what to *do* because I heard what He *said*." We are all Mary and Martha, and both of them are God's beloveds. Mary and Martha are opposites in a sense, but they are two halves that make a whole. The key is in the correct priority that Mary set; Mary chose to wait upon the Lord before doing anything else. Martha thought the work was more important, but Mary recognized that Jesus had the words of life.

When we learn to put first things first, to consider hearing His voice as the most important thing, then that which Jesus gives to us will not be taken away. We will hear *and* retain His words. The 'Mary' in us sits at His feet and listens, and then the 'Martha' in us steps up, out, and onto the instruction He provided. When Martha acts after Mary has listened, then Martha's action is not frantic or begrudging. When Martha steps out of Mary, necessary tasks are gracefully accomplished. We see each step in grace and rest, and we take the next step in ease. We are called to a beautiful *resting* life, accomplishing the will of the Lord through the love of the Lord.

Sitting at the feet of Jesus and preparing food to serve guests are both activities to be performed, and both are the *right* activity, but it is a matter of proper priority. When our service proceeds from the love we hear in His voice, then it comes with the empowerment of His grace. We have confident joy that our acts of service are acts of love, not obligatory duties or efforts to win approval or to gain His affection.

To sit at the feet of Jesus is to learn of Him; it is to ask questions of Him and to be prepared to receive those answers from His Word. We evaluate the words He speaks to us. To evaluate is to ask more questions. Life is a series of questions, and prosperity is an equal succession of answers. To know God is to ask of Him, to learn of Him. Hope expects answers and cannot be put off. To know God is to know we will get the answers we need!

If God told us everything before we asked, we would not need to learn anything; we learn because we evaluate. We concentrate, not just on hearing His answers, but on *understanding* His answers.

Martha heard God's Word. She was a follower of Christ, she loved Him and really wanted to serve Him. She had so much in mind that she planned to do for Him, and she felt that what she wanted to do was so important, so inspiring, so impressive, that others would want to come along and help her do it. Then she saw Mary just sitting there! Mary wanted something different. Martha's love caused her to want to do something *for* Jesus, Mary's love caused her to want to receive something *from* Jesus. Jesus was not condemning Martha, He was simply noting that Mary had the correct order. Mary wanted to evaluate, to take the time necessary to come to understanding. Mary wanted fullness, excellence of faith. Mary became an example to us all so that we could understand that a better way is available. Mary was no more redeemed than Martha, but she was more aware in the moment that her great Salvation was present. Thus, Jesus made a point of helping us understand the wisdom of hearing Him first, and letting every other action be in response to Him.

☐ Day 5 - Reflection

Why is it important to wait and to listen to His voice for wise and loving instruction?

He offers New mercy, grace, wisdom, strategy & hope every morning for the right now task of the minute to prepare us for the future

☐ Day 5 - Journalizing Assignment

I instruct you in the way of wisdom and lead you along straight paths. When you walk, your steps will not be hampered; when you run, you will not stumble. Hold on to instruction, do not let it go; guard it well, for it is your life.

Proverbs 4:11-13 (NIV)

Lord, direct me throughout my journey so I can experience your plans for my life. Reveal the life-paths that are pleasing to you. Escort me along the way; take me by the hand and teach me. For you are the God of my increasing salvation; I have wrapped my heart into yours!

?

Psalm 25:4,5 (TPT)

LESSON 5, DAY 6 - *Learning to Evaluate*

☐ DAY 6 - READING ASSIGNMENT

Learning to evaluate things in the presence of the Lord is important. In yesterday's reading assignment, I mentioned that evaluation includes asking questions. Asking questions, or evaluating, is part of the learning process.

Have you ever fasted? When we fast solid food, we may find that we miss chewing. We can get nutrients by drinking liquids, but much of the pleasure we take in eating comes from the taste buds on our tongue. Drinking a liquid diet bypasses those taste buds. We do not eat just to fill our belly; we eat for the sensational tastes that we experience as we chew our food. Eating is natural; we enjoy different textures and flavors. All truth originates in the spiritual realm. If we look at a truth in the natural, we can find its spiritual form.

In the natural, we like to eat because we like to chew; in the spiritual, we also like to eat because we like to chew. Evaluating is like chewing on the words that God speaks. We could take it in liquid form, but we would miss the rich flavor that we experience by chewing our food. To evaluate the truth is to taste and see that the Lord is good. Once we know what truth tastes like, we could be blindfolded and still name its flavor. We chew on God's truth, we ask questions, we receive insight, we meditate and ponder, and then we use our evaluation to help us make decisions and to commit to Christ in us. When deciding, we are able to taste the flavor of peace that gives us confidence in the choices we need to make. We evaluate God's word until our spiritual taste buds are delighted by its flavor. Chewing is a part of digestion, and digestion facilitates nourishment and energy.

God is establishing our hearts in grace. As we chew on His message of grace, we move away from trying to change ourselves and move toward trusting Him with necessary change. God's forgiveness means that all we need to do is to see, notice, and acknowledge the areas in our lives that He intends to correct. There is both beauty and rest when we stop trying to fix ourselves. We experience a spiritual awakening that allows us to see what He is changing so that we are ready to receive it. Our heart is steady and ready. Why does God show us something that needs to change in our disposition? In the past, we thought He was asking us to modify displeasing behaviors. Now, we realize that He shows us what *He* is going to change so that we can marvel in His ability to perfect what concerns us. He says, "See that? Notice it, for that is what I am working on right now. That is what I am changing in you."

There is a full picture in view, a partnership in motion. When we plant a seed, God makes it grow. When we chew on His word, He turns it into substance that can make a difference in our lives. Nothing we can do (apart from Christ in us) will make a difference, we are living a 'God story' not a 'you or me' story.

Be Specific

We form habits because they form destinies. When something becomes a burning desire, other things in our life have to move over and get out of the way. We have to be willing to see how our time is currently being used. We may have to take time from something less important and use it for something that is more meaningful to us. Lily Tomlin once quipped, "I always wanted to be somebody but I should have been more specific." We can chuckle, because we relate!

When it comes to defining our path, we must be specific. What is it we want when we look down the road five years from now? How does the picture of Christ in us look? How serious are we about assembling the pieces that represent His image in us? When God asked me to journalize His word, He provided a strategy for journalizing His word, one nut and bolt at a time. I saw that in order for this to become a habit, I would have to make room in my heart, my mind, and my calendar. I had to make room for something that I did not have room for before. It was like moving a new piece of furniture into a small house. If a new sofa was coming in, something old had to go out! I had not carved space in my mornings for this kind of focus. God was faithful to teach me how to make better, more meaningful use of my time.

Jaque's Journal

> *Jaque, faith fills up an upright heart but there is no faith for the proud who think they have all the answers. Faith receives - that is one of its activities. Faith looks at the image of Christ imprinted on your heart and it receives a vision it has never seen before of becoming someone that you never were before. Faith receives because it is not proud. Proud people have proud faith - they think they know Me because they go to church. Full of what they think they know about Me, they have no room to learn from Me.*
>
> *Jaque, there is something in the image of Christ in you that you have not yet seen. I want to present it to you, but your faith must be humble faith that is willing to make room to receive and to believe something new. Faith can inherit My kingdom because it has made room to receive it; faith makes room on the inside and then asks Me to fill that room with My own treasures. Faith can write the vision, it can see things pride would never see or find. Pride would never look at the picture of Christ and see everything faith can see. The humble will inherit the earth, Jaque, because they can learn.*
>
> *There is much to learn, Jaque, about the proud versus the faithful. To be able to say, "I make a lot of mistakes, but I can learn," is the start of humility. Do not be afraid to look at your mistakes, or to look the truth in the face when it tells you, "Jaque, that is the wrong attitude, disposition, or the wrong way to treat people." Be willing to say, "Yes, Lord, you are right, I am wrong. No matter what I think, You are the truth. You teach me, I do not teach You." Jaque, that is what an open, teachable heart looks like.*

There is so much opinion floating in the boats of My people. Opinion and judgment will only weigh down your life and disparage your relationships. People are unable to walk on the water, light as a feather, because prideful opinions crowd out the truth I would speak.

Jaque, to be able to evaluate is the gift of learning. When you know that you do not know, then you are a prime candidate for My inheritance. When you evaluate, you ask Me for something you don't know. You are ready for My answers because you haven't pre-decided what they will be. With pen in hand, you are like a journalist, on a most exclusive interview with a person of highest regard, who intends to capture every word. You are intent to capture each word knowing that you will publish what you write after you evaluate what form will dress it best. These words I speak to you, Jaque, are like precious jewels to the journalist. What will you do with them? Will you address them in obedient responses or bury them in another volume of journals you have written. They are beautiful words no doubt, but just like the talents, I gave you words so that you can make them grow. What will you do with the words I gave you? If they are put away on the bookshelf, not carried out through your heart to accomplish an end result, then they are like the talent that got buried in the ground. There they are, beautiful words in volumes of journals, but there will be no increase if you do not faithfully invest these words into acts of kindness towards others. But if you do invest these words with heartfelt obedience, you will reap grace for yourself, and you will have established your heart in grace that will abound in multiple acts of kindness towards others.

Jaque, it is great that you got into the journal, but did the journal get into you?

> Lord, this is what I want to be rich in...acts of kindness towards others. I want to be rich in Your feelings and sufferings towards others. I want to spend myself out for them. This is nothing to my credit, it isn't about me. This is me feeling You, finding You, oh, I am rich! I want to give, to invest these words in people's lives. Give me more vision, Lord, tell me what to do next as I sit and wait on You. For these, my desires, will present themselves in a form that is right for Jaque.

Our lives are about hearing and cherishing the word of the Lord because He is giving us talents, treasure, and asking us to do something with this treasure. We must invest in what He says through our obedient responses; otherwise, it is an exercise in futility.

What is our unique vision of Christ? We must see the image of Christ as He is in us so that we have hope for the future. We must pick up one nut or bolt at a time, refer back to the picture of the goal, read the directions, and assemble our life, one step at a time. Everything we need is in the box. The activity to perform is to believe on the Son. Hope puts the picture on the wall everyday - it keeps the goal in front of its face. When we wake up in the morning, hope says, "Have you looked at Him, the Author and Finisher of your faith?" We start each day as Mary, and allow Martha to emerge in grace and confidence.

☐ Day 6 - Reflection

What are a few of the acts of kindness toward others that you would like to be rich in?

☐ Day 6 - Journalizing Assignment

Yet all of the accomplishments that I once took credit for, I've now forsaken them and I regard it all as nothing compared to the delight of experiencing Jesus Christ as my Lord! To truly know him meant letting go of everything from my past and throwing all my boasting on the garbage heap. It's all like a pile of manure to me now, so that I may be enriched in the reality of knowing Jesus Christ and embrace him as Lord in all of his greatness. My passion is to be consumed with him and not clinging to my own "righteousness" based in keeping the written Law. My "righteousness" will be his, based on the faithfulness of Jesus Christ—the very righteousness that comes from God.

Philippians 3:7-9 (TPT)

Listen carefully, my dear child, to everything that I teach you, and pay attention to all that I have to say. Fill your thoughts with my words until they penetrate deep into your spirit. Then, as you unwrap my words, they will impart true life and radiant health into the very core of your being.

Proverbs 4:20-22 (TPT)

Set your gaze on the path before you. With fixed purpose, looking straight ahead, ignore life's distractions. Watch where you're going! Stick to the path of truth, and the road will be safe and smooth before you. Don't allow yourself to be sidetracked for even a moment or take the detour that leads to darkness.

Proverbs 4:25-27 (TPT)

LESSON 5, DAY 7 – *Habits Form Destinies*

☐ DAY 7 - READING ASSIGNMENT

Habits form destiny; the basic *law of use* means that if we do not use something (like a muscle) we will eventually lose the *ability* to use it. To have something infers that we will make use of what we have. Jesus touched this law in one of His parables when He said, "to him that hath, shall more be given…" (Mark 4:25). The law of use teaches us to take what we have been given, invest (or use) it, and cause it to increase. Habits form destiny because they *exercise* what we have been given.

Our desires are the means by which God will communicate His goals in us. We establish our heart in grace by continuing to evaluate and to act on (make use of) the words that He gives us. Through the law of use, we incubate the vision of Christ every day because there is not another picture on the wall that takes precedence over His. Whether it is our job, ministry, or marriage, it does not trump Christ. Every other vision or necessary insight will come from the vision of Him. That is what He meant when He said, "Seek Me first, for everything else is hidden in Me."

Jaque's Journal

> I begin to name my baby again, Lord, I desire to bring forth God's Kingdom. I desire to write the vision of God into the fabric of my life. I desire to be His will on the earth. I desire to invest time, money, prayer, faith, love, everything for the sake of Him and others. I desire to be a good steward of earthly gifts. I desire to live spontaneously in the medium between all extremes. I desire to be generous, to have order in my life. I desire to enjoy every moment in His presence. Now, as I state the desired objectives, I can see what I need to do. The activity that I need to perform is to first get Your strategy, Lord, from each vision. I will take all the nuts and bolts out of the box with the vision, put it forth in a plan, put it out on the

floor and commit to what I can put together each day. Two nuts, one nut, five bolts, but everyday I can give a portion of my time to the assembly of this vision. You are in me, to put it together. In some areas of my life, Lord, I see I have only been interested; therefore, I only assemble at my convenience. Now I desire to commit and to accept no excuses. In order to commit like this I will need potency. To get potency, I will need to incubate so I can get pregnant. I will incubate in the Spirit, I will write to see what you will say within me.

Jaque, you can write to see and then actually see because your heart is right within you. No pride, you do not know what you think you know. You must put aside all past assumptions, I have a strategy and a plan for you. As you work within them, My potency will bring on the commitment.

Sometimes you don't feel committed, Jaque. Stay in My presence and My potency will bring on the commitment. I make it grow, remember? You do not fix it; you do not make it happen, I make it grow. Begin to work within your new habits for, indeed, habits form destinies. As your habit of learning and writing the vision has formed the destiny to inherit My Kingdom, so there are other habits within this habit still to be formed. Seek Me for the plan and I will make it clear and plain for you. Work it out, work it out, work it out. Do not go back to sleep, write it down, find the form that works for you. Write, write and write the vision on the form. Is the form a journal? Is the form a calendar? Is the form a budget? Is the form a meal plan? Is the form a grocery plan? Is the form any other kind of form? What is it you want? Create the form and work it out.

You can talk about it until you are blue in the face, but you will never have it until you find a form and create the habit. Consider the ant, Jaque, she follows a plan, the instinctive way. I have put My ways in you and they are there. Seek them, make your commitment. Be it a seemingly weak commitment, I will add My authority to it and you will have potent commitment.

Thank you, Lord, I am ready for conviction and potency. What is the next hope? I am ready to be pregnant again. Amen.

The Inner Voice

The little-by-little message, or assembling our hope-filled life one nut or bolt at a time, is a message that is meant to envelop us. If we let it, it will teach us to live in obedience to our conscience. As we live from Christ, moment by moment, we find that He is a safe place in us, which makes our conscience a safe compass. We learn to trust that He is authoring our desires, hopes, dreams, strategies, and plans. We forget all of our self-doubting questions and learn to dance to the melody of our own conscience.

When we commit to hearing Him (and trusting Him as the voice of conscience) then we realize that we must not ignore or stifle that voice any longer. When we commit to this inner voice, we are committing to our true selves in Christ. Christ is the true self in us! We listen for our conscience with the intent to hear the truest wisdom that is written on our heart *and* to the courageous act of obeying it.

Our conscience is the voice of God, the voice of vision, and the *knowing* place within us. What we see there is genuine to us; it *fits* us because it is the truth that is written on *our* heart. We listen and set goals and make plans, and then take action because *intention* is fully alive in us. All that we desire is *mysteriously* hidden in the action. When we act, we SEE it. This is why we must take the first step, because only then will the next step be revealed.

It is here in our conscience that we can confidently call that which we see into existence. Our good conscience is that which gives us the boldness and the confidence to act in a brand new way as a brand new person! As we walk, as we act, the *grace* to *keep* acting appears. Our foot goes into the water and the sea parts for us. It is from this source, that true hopes are conceived.

☐ DAY 7 - REFLECTION

Take some time to start 'naming your baby.' Allow your desires to flow freely. Do not censor them during this exercise. Refinement will come later. For now, just write the vision of Christ as He is in you. The space provided here would not be enough, so please, use a journal book.

To have a deeply unified, spiritual connection with my husband.

☐ DAY 7 - JOURNALIZING ASSIGNMENT

When you're feeling lazy, come and learn a lesson from this tale of the tiny ant. Yes, all you lazybones, come learn from the example of the ant and enter into wisdom. The ants have no chief, no boss, no manager - no one has to tell them what to do. You'll see them working and toiling all summer long, stockpiling their food in preparation for winter. So wake up, sleepyhead. How long will you lie there? When will you wake up and get out of bed? If you keep nodding off and thinking, "I'll do it later," or say to yourself, "I'll just sit back awhile and take it easy," just watch how the future unfolds! By making excuses you'll learn what it means to go without. Poverty will pounce on you like a bandit and move in as your roommate for life.

PROVERBS 6:6-11 (TPT)

Abilene Cares Get Ahead

LESSON 5 - HEART-WORK

The Heart-work is a valuable part of your inner work. Taking the time to give heartfelt responses to the following questions is beneficial for you and beneficial for sharing with others who are in your study group.

PUTTING IT ALL TOGETHER

1. Why must our goals continually inspire us and what gives us continual inspiration?
2. Share your understanding of how, metaphorically, we are both Mary and Martha.
3. Summarize in a paragraph what you understand about the activity you are being held accountable for by God.
4. Please share your journalizing experience this week with regard to heart and frequency. How was your desire for discipline grounded in grace this week?

Note: If you are in a VI class, please include one journal from this week with the Heart-work you submit for coaching.

If not, please bring your Heart-work and a journal to share with others in your study group.

Drawing From the Resource

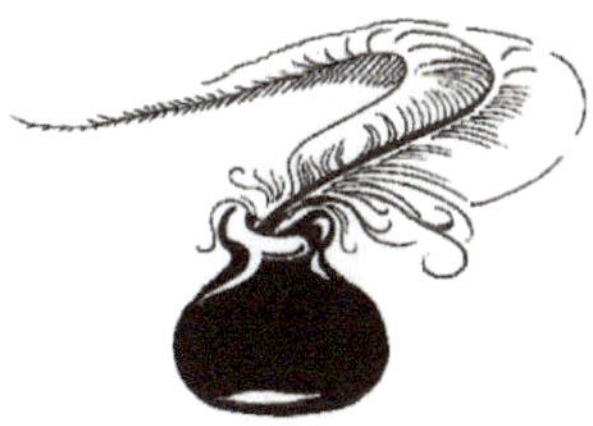

He has put all things under His feet and has appointed Him the universal and supreme Head of the church [a headship exercised throughout the church], which is His body, the fullness of Him Who fills all in all [for in that body lives the full measure of Him Who makes everything complete, and Who fills everything everywhere with Himself].

Ephesians 1:22,23 (AMPC)

Lesson 6, Day 1 - *Christ, Our Resource*

☐ Day 1 - Reading Assignment

Christ is the resource of the Church, in Him all the treasures of divine wisdom and riches of spiritual knowledge exist. The resource is in Christ, which means the resource is Christ *in us*! We have the mind of Christ (1 Corinthians 2:16) and we are learning to resource His mind. We put on the mind of Christ as we would put on a coat. He intends we wear it, not cast it aside. To wear the mind of Christ is to be dressed in the right mindset. To put on the mind of Christ is to put on the right mental posture and to step into His awareness of the present moment.

> *For God has not given us a spirit of fear, but of power and of love and of a sound mind.*
>
> 2 Timothy 1:7 (NKJV)

We have not been given a spirit of fear, but of power, love, and a sound mind. The sound mind we have been given is the mind of Christ. As our resource, His mind is our aid and support. Every time we wear *His* thinking cap, we are supported through whatever troubles we think we have. The mind of Christ is our success - it helps produce the favorable result or outcome we desire. Only through the mind of Christ will we experience fruit or profit from our labor. The profit from a peach tree is peaches. Peaches are a good result for having dug a hole, planted a seed, watered the ground, and for the exercise of so much patience while waiting for it to grow.

The profit from the mind of Christ is the successful delivery and execution of our hopes and goals. The mind of Christ unveils the strategies we need to actualize our hopes and dreams. His mind unfolds the plan and all the details that will bring our goals to fruition. The mind of Christ is our greatest resource, richest reserve, and premier means to an end - and it is within us, like a storehouse ready to access.

Hidden For Us

> *In Him all the treasures of [divine] wisdom (comprehensive insight into the ways and purposes of God) and all the riches of spiritual] knowledge and enlightenment are stored up and lie hidden.*
>
> COLOSSIANS 2:3 (AMPC)

All the treasures of divine wisdom and spiritual knowledge are stored and lie hidden in Christ. Unseen, they are mysterious and held in a place of secrecy. The true nature of our newly created selves is also hidden in Christ. There are great mysteries to be discovered and when we see Him, we shall be like Him (1 John 3:2). When we see ourselves, with the mind of Christ and by the revelation of His Spirit, we shall be like Him. All the mysteries and secret caves of hidden desire within us, are revealed in Christ.

Christ is the cave, and everything is hidden in Him. The wonderful thing about Christ is the knowledge that He is everything we have ever wanted. Every desire we have, and those we cannot even name yet, lie hidden in Him. Our very being is a mystery hidden in us in Christ. When are we going to start looking for the mysteries, the desires of our heart, the things that will make us our truest version of ourselves?

Hope is the habit of going into the cave and looking for the secrets, fully expecting the mystery to unfold. Once we enter the cave, we find treasure, and we keep going back to the dark cave because each treasure promises more treasure. His promise is guaranteed; so, we keep coming back because the Kingdom of God is hidden in that secret place. His Kingdom is hidden in clouds and shrouds of darkness, mysteriously calling us to come deeper.

The spiritual insight of Christ is hidden *for* us, not from us. It is hidden for our benefit, not our detriment. He is calling us to the joy of personal relationship and self-discovery. If we complain about a lack of understanding, then we likely believe that God is purposefully withholding His insight from us. He is not; it is being held in reserve for us, waiting for desire for His presence to lead us deeper into the cave.

When we understand that God has hidden everything in Christ for us (not from us), then we trust His reason for hiding everything in Christ. He wants us to seek it out. He wants us to find it for ourselves. He does not want us to take somebody else's word about the glorious mystery of Christ in us, He wants us to discover the truth for ourselves. He hid something for us - and He wants us to be enlivened by the prospect of finding it, finding Him, finding ourselves.

When we were children, our parents may have hidden 'eggs' for us to find in a scavenger hunt. They hid the eggs, candy, or prizes *for* us, but not *from* us. There is a difference - to hide the eggs for us meant that they fully expected and wanted us to find the eggs. In fact, when we were very young, they hid them in the easiest possible places! As we grew older, the hiding spots got more mysterious to keep our interest piqued. The challenge was part of the fun. Still, the eggs were not hidden from us. Loving parents do not bury the eggs so deep that they are impossible to find. In fact, if we had difficulty, they would steer us in the right direction.

God is a loving parent; wisdom and insight are hidden for us, not from us. He hides it deep in His bosom so that we are drawn into His loving arms. We may start with a search for answers, but in the end, we discover relationship with our Father. The treasures of divine wisdom are like a tantalizer. He lets us know that He has hidden something for us, in a secret place that is for us and us alone, like a treasure chest that has our name on it and then He says, "Will you come and find it? Will you come into the cave with Me? If so, then together we will discover precious gems. I will reveal secrets; I will show you hidden things and mysterious places that are for your eyes only. You will have great delight in the search and great reward in the discovery."

The Lord is like a parent coaxing us to come into the hidden place of Christ in us so that we can take delight in the process. If we cannot trust Him and we refuse to follow where He leads, then we are loved, but we will not know the divine secrets that He has in store.

> If God just put the eggs in our basket, requiring no participation from us, we would miss the fun of finding the eggs. Search and discovery complement each other. God invites us to search, and then discover, because we are defined and refined by the process. Our involvement teaches us to follow where He leads; we also learn that we are unique and that God relates to us uniquely. We learn things about ourselves through the specific secrets that pique our interest. We may have questions that others in our sphere of influence may never ask. As we seek for treasure, we find our value for Him and His value for us.
>
> SUSAN MUCKLOW

☐ DAY 1 - REFLECTION

Define RESOURCE:

A source of aid or support

Define HIDDEN (IN HIM):

A secret place within us, within Christ where all things can be found on the journey to becoming our truest, best self

☐ Day 1 - Journalizing Assignment

I pray that the Father of glory, the God of our Lord Jesus Christ, would impart to you the riches of the Spirit of wisdom and the Spirit of revelation to know him through your deepening intimacy with him. I pray that the light of God will illuminate the eyes of your imagination, flooding you with light, until you experience the full revelation of the hope of his calling - that is, the wealth of God's glorious inheritances that he finds in us, his holy ones!

Ephesians 1:17, 18 (TPT)

I am contending for you that your hearts will be wrapped in the comfort of heaven and woven together into love's fabric. This will give you access to all the riches of God as you experience the revelation of God's great mystery - Christ. For our spiritual wealth is in him, like hidden treasure waiting to be discovered—heaven's wisdom and endless riches of revelation knowledge.

Colossians 2:2,3 (TPT)

Lesson 6, Day 2 - *Permitted to Understand*

☐ Day 2 - Reading Assignment

In Matthew chapter thirteen, Jesus makes a distinction about what kinds of hearers we become. It becomes obvious that it is important for us to condition the soil of our heart so that we might better receive and comprehend His message. He speaks of seed that falls on different kinds of ground. His disciples asked Him why He used such hard-to-understand illustrations and He explained that only those who are *permitted* to understand the Kingdom of God will 'get it.' Those who are born of His Spirit, like you and I, are those *permitted* to understand.

> *He told many stories in the form of parables, such as this one: "Listen! A farmer went out to plant some seeds. As he scattered them across his field, some seeds fell on a footpath, and the birds came and ate them. Other seeds fell on shallow soil with underlying rock. The seeds sprouted quickly because the soil was shallow. But the plants soon wilted under the hot sun, and since they didn't have deep roots, they died. Other seeds fell among thorns that grew up and choked out the tender plants. Still other seeds fell on fertile soil, and they produced a crop that was thirty, sixty, and even a hundred times as much as had been planted! Anyone with ears to hear should listen and understand." His disciples came and asked him, "Why do you use parables when you talk to the people?" He replied, "You are permitted to understand the secrets of the Kingdom of Heaven, but others are not. To those who listen to my teaching, more understanding will be given, and they will have an abundance of knowledge. But for those who are not listening, even what little understanding they have will be taken away from them. That is why I use these parables, 'For they look, but they don't really see. They hear, but they don't really listen or understand.'*
>
> Matthew 13:3-13 (NLT)

Further along in this chapter, when Jesus offers His disciples an explanation of the parable, He refers to our need for deep roots. According to Strong's Exhaustive Concordance, if we do not have deep roots in our life then we do not hold enough divine counsel in our heart. God's insight is hidden and is beyond man's scrutiny; through His *divine* counsel we gain wisdom. This counsel comes from spending time in His presence while receiving His Words to us. Going deep does not mean it is hard to find His hidden treasure, it just means we are asked to dig for it. We are permitted to understand, which means that we are permitted to seek His face, hear His divine counsel, and to enter His presence. Taking advantage of what we are permitted to do conditions our 'heart soil,' making it easier for His word to take root.

Why does God want us to search for His treasure? He hides His pearls because He wants us to seek Him - they are hidden so we can learn to live by faith by relying on Him. To live by faith is to abide in Him. It does not mean that we try to perform good deeds to gain His approval, for we already have His approval; to *live by faith* means we accept this fact and learn to *receive* the benefits that He offers.

Christ wants to *be* our life, which is not possible if we will not let Him live His life through us. For this grace to occur, we need divine counsel in our hearts. Christians should not spend time trying to be *like* Christ but should live with faith that proclaims, "Christ can be *Himself* through me, He does not need my help, only my faithful surrender." He is our resource; our surrender is rewarded as we hunt for His insights like hidden treasure. We provide depth for the seeds that are planted by being thoroughly grounded in the Living Word of God. Acts of ministry like evangelism, teaching, preaching, or caring for others in any way, become the *spontaneous* life of Christ in us. He Himself is doing 'His own thing' through us. This is union reality. This is the branch bearing fruit, not from the branch, but from the Vine!

Repentance, Humility, and Understanding

> **Understanding**: the faculty of the human mind by which it apprehends the real state of things presented to it or by which it receives or comprehends the ideas others express and intend to communicate. It is the intellectual faculty by which we obtain knowledge. It relates to *possessing* our resources as the mind *comprehends* its resources. We *own* something only to the degree that our mind comprehends.

> *But it is the spirit in a person, the breath of the Almighty, that gives them understanding.*
>
> JOB 32:8 (NIV)

We breathe; we inhale and exhale, but the breath of the Almighty gives understanding. The agreement of our mind with His, or the unison of our sentiments, is a conformity that only God can accomplish.

We can only possess what our mind actually comprehends. We cannot own what we cannot grasp. We may hold it in our hand, but we will not *own* it until we understand its purpose. For instance, we could have an incredible technological resource readily available in the form of a cellphone. If we do not *understand* its capability, we may just use it as a paperweight. In a crisis, we may wish we had a way to call for help or to access information, but all we have is a useless paperweight. Help is in our hands, but we do not *own* the help since we do not comprehend it.

Likewise, we give mental assent to things we are told are true. We believe they are true, because the pastor told us they were true. However, if we have not tested the truth for ourselves, then mentally agreeing is quite different than owning the truth. If we understood the truth, it could set us free, but if we do not, then it is like a millstone around our neck. Mental assent is as useless as a paperweight in a crisis.

If the soil condition of our heart is poor, then we will lack understanding and yet, ironically, understanding softens the heart. Repentance and humility will also condition the soil, making us good ground as we make our return to the Father. Understanding means that we are humble enough to let go of old mindsets and to search, embrace, and draw life from the truth that is hidden within us. We have to go to the place where Truth abides, receive His correction, and experience His breath of reproof. Eventually, the ground of our heart softens, understanding takes root, and we experience the rescue that it contains.

In this same way, hopes become spiritual babies. When we understand what we are hoping for, we can give birth to that which we have envisioned. We *know* our hope, and our hope *knows* us - there is *mutual* understanding. The inspiration of God comes as a little seed, a little something that we wanted to meditate on, a little secret that He whispered in our ear. Then, He breathed life upon it. We carried it in the womb of our heart until it was time to be born.

Whether we talk about the fall of mankind, or the slippery slope we slide down when we fail to recognize Christ as our life, we have no idea how far we have fallen. Imagine if we fell into a well - a deep, dark hole. We hit the bottom and must find our way out of this darkness. We start to climb, grabbing for the sides, hoping to grab onto a root, a rock, or a ledge. We look up and see the light, but it is like a pinhole. It feels like we have already been climbing for a year. We keep climbing. We see a little more light. We climb for what seems like another year and the pinhole of light is only slightly broader. We think to ourselves, "My God, I cannot believe that I fell this far. It just did not seem like I was falling for very long. To be this far down I must have fallen asleep as I was falling - floating down into this abyss for decades! I had no idea that I was this far from the light." We keep climbing and crying out for God. His light becomes our hope at the end of this tunnel. We keep climbing and realize that repentance becomes a rock we can grab onto and humility forms a ledge. Each time we let go of pride, we find a root that we can climb like a rope. Little by little, we see progress. As we keep climbing, the light increases our understanding of the depth of our fall.

We realize that we have barely scratched the surface with the light that we have today. We hardly see the light that is yet to be revealed. We must hold on to every ray of divine counsel, and never entertain the notion that we have enough light. We can keep climbing our way closer to the light for the next twenty, thirty, or one hundred years, and our pinhole of light would only be four inches wide. What is four inches in the light of infinity with God? It is nothing. We will experience God forever. So let us each hold on to what we have, keep searching His depths, and never feel like we have *arrived*. In one sense, we have arrived; we have arrived in Christ and because we have reached Him, we now have eternity to explore the wonders of His love and to discover all the things that He has hidden in Himself for our pleasure and His.

☐ DAY 2 - REFLECTION

What does the statement 'we can only possess what our mind comprehends' mean to you?

The roots of a thought, belief, dream, vision or idea have to go deep to become a part of who we are, To be our truth.

☐ DAY 2 - JOURNALIZING ASSIGNMENT

My response is to get down on my knees before the Father, this magnificent Father who parcels out all heaven and earth. I ask him to strengthen you by his Spirit - not a brute strength but a glorious inner strength - that Christ will live in you as you open the door and invite him in. And I ask him that with both feet planted firmly on love, you'll be able to take in with all followers of Jesus the extravagant dimensions of Christ's love. Reach out and experience the breadth! Test its length! Plumb the depths! Rise to the heights! Live full lives, full in the fullness of God.

EPHESIANS 3:14-19 (MSG)

The entrance of Your words gives light; it gives understanding to the simple.

PSALM 119:130 (NKJV)

I have heard the rebuke that reproaches me, and the spirit of my understanding causes me to answer.

JOB 20:3 (NKJV)

And we know that the Son of God has come and has given us an understanding, that we may know Him who is true; and we are in Him who is true, in His Son Jesus Christ. This is the true God and eternal life.

1 JOHN 5:20 (NKJV)

LESSON 6, DAY 3 - *Four Kinds of Soil*

☐ DAY 3 - READING ASSIGNMENT

Hard Soil

> *"Now listen to the explanation of the parable about the farmer planting seeds: The seed that fell on the footpath represents those who hear the message about the Kingdom and don't understand it. Then the evil one comes and snatches away the seed that was planted in their hearts. The seed on the rocky soil represents those who hear the message and immediately receive it with joy. But since they don't have deep roots, they don't last long. They fall away as soon as they have problems or are persecuted for believing God's word. The seed that fell among the thorns represents those who hear God's word, but all too quickly the message is crowded out by the worries of this life and the lure of wealth, so no fruit is produced. The seed that fell on good soil represents those who truly hear and understand God's word and produce a harvest of thirty, sixty, or even a hundred times as much as had been planted!"*
>
> MATTHEW 13:18-23 (NLT)

As we continue with this parable from yesterday's reading, we see that Jesus is talking about four kinds of soil to represent four kinds of hearers. The *first* hearer has no root at all. The seed lands on top of the footpath. The footpath is hard ground, beaten down by traffic; the seed cannot penetrate the surface. The birds of the air can snatch the seed right off the ground. A hard heart will not *understand* the message since it has no way to sink roots. Words are heard, but hardness of heart makes the ground fallow, thorny at best, and in need of conditioning.

Fallow ground is tilled as we return to the Lord; we walk away from lies, stop trusting our own strength, and repent our way to a softer heart. We sow something new until He rains righteousness upon us.

> *Sow for yourselves righteousness; reap in mercy; break up your fallow ground, for it is time to seek the Lord, till He comes and rains righteousness on you. You have plowed wickedness; you have reaped iniquity. You have eaten the fruit of lies, because you trusted in your own way, in the multitude of your mighty men.*
>
> HOSEA 10:12-13 (NKJV)

Fallow ground is a hard place to sow seeds. Between a rock hard surface and the thorns, understanding cannot take root.

Rocky Soil

> *"The seed on the rocky soil represents those who hear the message and immediately receive it with joy. But since they don't have deep roots, they don't last long. They fall away as soon as they have problems or are persecuted for believing God's word."*
>
> MATTHEW 13:20,21 (NLT)

The *second* soil type is rocky. The seed lands, tries to take root, but hits a rocky layer just below the surface; it cannot survive with such a shallow root system. This person hears the message, receives it with joy, but problems and hardship allow it to slip away. The roots are too shallow and so they are easily uprooted.

Too many Christians fall into this category. It is important that shallow teaching does not fill our personal lives, or the church at large. Believers in Christ must know how to hold fast during hard times. God is calling for diggers; He wants disciples of His word. He wants us to meditate, chew, and to journalize to *internalize* His word. He wants us to discuss His word, to go back and study more, be challenged by each other, chew even more, find our voice, impart His personal treasures in and through us, and to dig ever deeper.

It will never be enough to just receive the word with joy or even to memorize scriptures. We must be able, from the heart, to live out His word, to walk the talk, and to sink our roots down deep.

I once thought that the root system of a tree was as deep as the tree was tall. Although that is not true, there are still interesting facts surrounding trees and their root systems. For instance, the deeper the tree's root system then the more drought resistant the tree will be. That should inspire us to want to condition the soil of our heart. In addition, even though the roots of a tree may not be as *deep* as the above ground portion, a healthy tree does have a root system that is as *wide* as the tree is tall; and the *quality* of the soil determines the depth and the width of the root system; so again, conditioning our 'heart soil' is key.

How tall do we want to be in the Lord? We would naturally want to be tall, tall is impressive; but it is better to want a healthy root system. I remember hearing a story about a particular kind of bamboo tree. The

Chinese Bamboo Tree begins as a hard nut, about the size of a walnut. The nut has to be planted in soil and then watered and fertilized *every day* for 5 years before it finally breaks through the ground. If at any time the watering or fertilizing process is stopped, the Chinese Bamboo Tree will die in the ground. But, if the process continues, then in that fifth year, the Chinese Bamboo Tree will break through the ground and in six weeks it will grow nearly ninety feet tall! Now, the question is, did it grow ninety feet in six weeks or 5 years? The answer, of course, is that it took five years - five years of watering and fertilizing everyday, five years of no visual progress in order to make it happen.

The Chinese Bamboo Tree embodies a principle in nature and in people. It may seem, at times, like we like are not growing, but if we are watering and fertilizing our soil everyday then we are sending down roots. One day we are going to shoot up and stand tall in the Lord.

Thorny Soil

> *The seed that fell among the thorns represents those who hear God's word, but all too quickly the message is crowded out by the worries of this life and the lure of wealth, so no fruit is produced.*
>
> MATTHEW 13:22 (NLT)

The *third* kind of soil is thorny; it is taken over by weeds that choke out the word of God. This kind of hearer is busy, crowded by busy thoughts and the myriad cares of this world such as finances, career, ministry, service, or any good thing that turns into 'busy work' that yields no fruit. When a good life becomes a busy life, then the crowdedness chokes the life out of the root system and fruit is no longer being produced. Busy-ness in the body of Christ is a trap. Our concerns grow thorns; thorns come up and choke the seeds of truth that were beginning to prosper. Weeds grow fast in a busy person.

Good Soil

> *The seed that fell on good soil represents those who truly hear and understand God's word and produce a harvest of thirty, sixty, or even a hundred times as much as had been planted!"*
>
> MATTHEW 13:23 (NLT)

The *fourth* soil type is our goal for it is good. This person is able to hear, has room in their life to understand God's word, and has roots that are strong enough to retain that which they hear. This is *a contemplative hearer*; their soil is conditioned, well soaked and properly fertilized. They are able to listen quietly and to continually retreat into the hidden place to find more secrets from God. He or she meditates on the hidden treasure until they can own the truth as a resource. A contemplative person is one who listens and says, "Hush now and be quiet. I know I have been listening for a while, but something is still going on…the Lord is still whispering His wisdom and every other voice must be silenced."

The whale hears the call of the deep, the oil digger hears the call of the oil, and the water diviner hears the call of the water source. When a contemplative is sitting quietly before the Lord, they hear the call of the hidden cave, the call of Christ in them. "Quiet now, something down there is speaking to me, I hear it." We do not want to be interrupted when we are in that place.

I love being with people; but I feel I am almost equal parts introvert and extrovert. If I stayed quiet and alone all the time, I would go crazy without people. However, if I have had too much 'people time,' then after a while I must say, "Good-bye, everybody, I hear the call of my secret place and I have got to go away and listen. I must hear what my Father is saying so that I can do what I see my Father doing." Sometimes my return is thirty, sixty, or a hundred-fold. As I have mellowed and matured, my return has been greater - I am becoming a contemplative hearer; my soil is improving.

We all get busy sometimes, and we may experience hardness or shallowness, but we are learning how to get water and fertilizer, and how to pull weeds. We are motivated to do so because the things that lie hidden, God's mysterious secrets, set us free when we make time to cherish their value. We shall know the truth and the truth shall make us free - the word of God says it, the mind of Christ echoes it, and our heart of flesh knows it is true. Who will believe His report? Who will come to the hidden place, to receive His hope, and to give birth to Christ as He is in each of us individually? When we draw from Christ, our Resource, we will intimately know that deep calls unto deep.

> *Who has believed our report? And to whom has the arm of the Lord been revealed?*
>
> ISAIAH 53:1 (NKJV)

Just as we have all been Martha and Mary, and will be again, we all grow in and out of these soil conditions. We have all been hard, and rocky, and thorny, and good soil. We will be again. Through it all, we press into Christ, our only hope of glory.

☐ DAY 3 - REFLECTION

What is the present condition of your 'heart soil' and what could you do to improve its condition?

I AM good soil, I still see areas of my land that are hard and arrid, or thorny or rocky, but I recognize them & walk in the garden as Papa shows me where to prune or plant.

☐ DAY 3 - JOURNALIZING ASSIGNMENT

> *Your spiritual roots go deeply into his life as you are continually infused with strength, encouraged in every way. For you are established in the faith you have absorbed and enriched by your devotion to him!*
>
> COLOSSIANS 2:7 (TPT)

Contemplative Hearer hears the call of the hidden.

50/50 introvert / extrovert

Falling into the deep well, keep climbing towards the light. Hold on to what you've got & continue to look for more.

Lesson 6, Day 4 – *Wait On the Lord*

☐ Day 4 - Reading Assignment

As we enter the inner sanctuary, searching for His treasure, our hearts must be prepared to hear. Learning to wait on God is central. God is not appealing to our carnal mind when He seeks to impart divine counsel, but to our spiritual mind. From the soul, we make the choice to receive what He has deposited into our spirits. The carnal mind is not an active participator in this because *that* mind hates to wait. The carnal mind wants to be in control, busy, involved, and taking credit for whatever is going on! It is selfish, aggressive and foolish when left to itself. The hardest part of waiting on God is that we have to come to His altar in a restless flesh, offering that flesh as a sacrifice to God.

We live by faith, as one who is alive from the dead. Therefore, we must bring the flesh into submission to the obedience of Christ. Once we have done so, we wait on Him. In the Greek language, to *wait* has the same meaning as making a braid. The idea is that we braid ourselves together with God, entwined with all He has to say to us. Our Resource is ready to impart divine revelation if we could only receive it. We have access to the Spirit of wisdom as the unseen means to every prosperous end we could hope for. We begin to pray like this,

> *Lord, open the eyes of my heart that I may understand the hope to which You have called me. I am rich, let me comprehend this richness. I want my roots more deeply planted in Christ. Grant me the grace to receive it, Lord, I choose to wait on You. The Holy Spirit is alive in me, may I desire fellowship with Him above all else.*

Direction from the Director

I remember a time when I experienced His direction in a simple, yet profound way. I asked which way I was heading. I wanted to know specifics like, "Where will I be in five years and what will I be doing?" I guess I wanted a fortune teller instead of a word from God. I learned from this experience that God stands by His word, and that alone, because He posed His answer to me as a question. He said, "Who are you following, Jaque?" to which I replied, "Well, you know Lord, I am following Jesus." Then He replied, "Then that is where you will be and that is what you will be doing!"

This is *resource* my friend, true direction from God. In His answer I understood *again* that I live by faith. I may not know which way I will turn until I get to the corner - but I know that wherever I end up, I will be in Him and He will be in me. Our resource is never depleted; He is ready at any moment, any location, and any circumstance.

We Wait for More

Our job is always the same; we wait for more. There is always more to see. We use any strategy and plan that God has given, we design a new one, lay out a new budget, or make a new plan for a new lifestyle. We use whatever is at our disposal to wait on Him with our attention, our focus, and with our strength. We give God all of our being and we wait to see what He will reveal in the hidden, secret places.

Jaque's Journal

Jaque, the secret to prayer and peace is in making Me a part of your everyday consciousness. I will keep you in perfect peace when your mind is stayed on Me. Rehearse My word to combat fear. When you awake at night and feel afraid, remember My word. Use night seasons to practice returning your mind to Me. Remember that truth is hidden in you and you are to rest in Me. I will never leave you or forsake you, Jaque. With the mind of Christ, rehearse the scripture. Know that which is true and trust that which I speak to you.

If there is one missing link in the chain of peaceful living, it is the deliberate practice of becoming consciously aware of My word and My indwelling presence. My presence and My word are your source of comfort. To be consciously aware of something, Jaque, you must be mentally present with it -

you must be thinking about it, singing, writing, and praying about it. When you meditate on My word, you take in substance for the inner man, and the manna of true life. My word is bread, wine, water, and meat. My word is spiritual food and, when you digest it, then it becomes strength in your present circumstances. My word is digested through our communion and in no other way. Abide in Me; this is the inner work of receiving that which sustains you.

Jaque, the power of My word is in proportion to how alive it is kept in your consciousness. Let My word abide in you until it bears fruit; allow My word, in all its forms (meat, water, wine, or bread) to nourish your ground so fruit can grow on your branches. Food for the tree comes from My life in you; it does not come from the outside. I will prune the tree; you will understand the pruning process through the challenges you face that you wish would go away. The natural self, the carnal mind, the flesh, does not like My pruning because they are what is being trimmed away. The discomfort they exude help you to see what you could not see before - that there are many more dead branches that need to be removed. Once you see what I am pruning, you will understand that it must occur to protect the fruit. Abide in Me, Jaque, and you will find rest - even in pruning.

God grooms His trees, His fruit-bearers, by pruning dead branches. It is painful when He cuts off a branch of pride or a limb that revealed that we did not know what we thought we knew. When there is a part of us that we thought should stay and He says, "Here, let Me take care of that!" and then He cuts it off…it hurts…but it is for the good of the tree. God will prune every aspect of our life that does not conform to His image. He will cut every branch that will not bear fruit. As our trust for His goodness grows, we stop suspecting His intention. We find the humility to say, "Cut or prune the tree as you see fit, Lord, for I want to bear Your fruit." We begin to cooperate with His plan.

Jaque's Journal

> *Jaque, pruning a branch is cutting it off, while discipline is bending a branch to grow in a certain direction. My words both 'cut and bend' for they reveal where you need to let go (cut), and where you need to conform (bend). Cling to Me in the process and you will bear fruit to the praise of My glory.*

We learn to hold on to the truth and hold it fast. We hear the truth repeatedly so that it is there in a crisis. It comes in the moment that we need it. Then what do we do? We spend the rest of our lives waiting for more. We keep digging and then we realize that God is our vocation. We see that we are rich, because we are inheriting the Kingdom. There is so much resource in Christ - in us and in each other.

☐ DAY 4 - REFLECTION

How does knowing what the Lord is pruning affect how you receive His discipline?

You lean into Him more so your flesh doesn't fight it. We loosen or grasp or let it go as needed & nudged

☐ Day 4 - Journalizing Assignment

The work of righteousness is peace, and the result of righteousness is quietness and confidence forever. My people will live free from worry in secure, quiet homes of peace. No matter if hail destroys the forest and the city is leveled, you will be happy and blessed as you sow your seed beside every stream and loose your ox and donkey to graze freely.

Isaiah 32:17,18 (TPT)

For whom the Lord loves He corrects, just as a father the son in whom he delights.

Proverbs 3:12 (NKJV)

Now no chastening seems to be joyful for the present, but painful; nevertheless, afterward it yields the peaceable fruit of righteousness to those who have been trained by it. Therefore strengthen the hands which hang down, and the feeble knees, and make straight paths for your feet, so that what is lame may not be dislocated, but rather be healed.

Hebrews 12:11-13 (NKJV)

LESSON 6, DAY 5 - *Mama's Apron*

☐ DAY 5 - READING ASSIGNMENT

I remember hearing the story of Susanna Wesley, who had given birth to nineteen children, ten of whom survived infancy. It is said that when she needed time alone with God, she simply stood in her kitchen and pulled her apron over her head. When the children saw the apron go over her head, forming a small but private tent, they knew not to disturb her. There, under the privacy of her apron, she would intercede, read her bible, and experience the depths of God.

Certainly, Susanna could have made excuses for herself. It was a challenge, to say the least, to find privacy in a house filled with so many children. She had known great hardship and loss. However, early in her life she vowed to reserve two hours each day for prayer and study. When Susanna was under her apron, she was with God. No amount of distraction could keep her away and her life produced great fruit.

In addition to spending two hours a day under her apron with God, she also spent thirty minutes of one-on-one time with each of her ten children every week. She also ran her household and taught her children to read using the Bible as her only textbook.

Her son, John Wesley, is estimated to have preached to nearly a million people in his lifetime and his theology formed the foundation of Pentecostalism worldwide.

Charles Wesley wrote more than six thousand hymns, many of which are still in hymnals today.

Charles and John Wesley were the key leaders in the great spiritual awakening of the eighteenth century. Many historians believe that this great awakening was the primary reason England was spared a bloody revolution like the one that occurred in France. Susanna Wesley's children literally changed the course of a nation, and influenced the destiny of countless lives.

When mama's apron went over her head, mama was in her cave. The children had respect and knew that all their questions and squabbles would wait until the apron came down. It is a picture of dedication and determination. Anytime I need a break in the middle of a little chaos, I think of Susanna Wesley's apron. If she can do it with ten children, then I can do it when my life gets hectic. I can say, "Friends, family, my apron is going up and over my head. When the apron is up, I am not available. I will not answer a phone, door, email, text, or anything else." When the apron goes up, I am with the Lord receiving secrets from His heart to mine, praying and interceding on behalf of those I love." If we will honor our time under the apron, then we will come out from the apron with peace and joy. We should never try to live without the peace that comes from time in His presence. We need a sound mind. No matter what it takes, we need to stop and throw the apron over our head. We need to know what our apron is and how to get it over our head each day. If *we* will respect our apron, others will too.

Respecting Our Own Apron

The things that lie hidden are God's mysterious secrets that would set us free if we would find them and cherish their value. To respect our apron means we will create a habit that carves time and space dedicated to God. We create a habit of digging because we have hope that treasure awaits. We will lack depth in our life if we are not paying attention to Christ's words. If what He speaks to us just barely scratches the surface, it is because we have not softened the ground. We soften the ground when we give His word thought and attention.

People who are willing to pay attention are willing to wait. We wait to hear, wait to see, wait to understand. We no longer want to take things at surface level, so we dig beneath the apparent meaning of the words to find the deeper meaning of the words that are often clothed in mystery. To run deep is to run into God ON PURPOSE. We *plan* on running into God. We are conscious of the desire that we long to run into God so we act on the desire by working the plan that God has given. The habit of digging is greater than the pearls it uncovers because if we dig in a barren field, the habit will take us on until we finally reach the field filled with great treasure! Our God has more than one pearl for us so He says, "Dig deeper." In other words, "Pay more attention to My words, find the deeper wells of salvation and living water within you." We do whatever it takes to find out what our own apron looks like, and to value the practice as much, if not more, than the payout.

Digging is the vocation of true seekers. If a stranger were to ask us what we do for a living we could say, "I am an oil digger; I dig until I reach the oil of the Holy Spirit and all the riches of His wisdom." The force of patience is the beauty of wisdom and wisdom belongs to those who wait. With wisdom comes understanding but it takes time, a lot of time. We are walking in a relationship that is the journey of a lifetime. Our lives are the extension of seconds, minutes and hours that turn into days, weeks, months and years. We take this journey "one second at a time" and we are learning to wait with hope and patience for all of the future moments yet to unfold.

Our definition of success changes as we recognize wealth in the richest spiritual sense. We will never be completely successful at anything that does not give us ultimate peace with God. To have peace with God means to have absolute confidence in what we are doing from moment to moment. We find it to be a rule: NO peace, NO confidence. The dictionary says that success is the favorable completion of whatever is attempted. That is good, but it is a little shortsighted, for the favorable completion of LIFE is what we must use as the criteria of the definition. True success means a favorable conclusion to our life. There is no greater 'favorable conclusion' than to rest in righteousness, peace and joy that comes from the One who made us. His success for us is *Christ in us as us*, the only hope of ever concluding our life on earth favorably.

☐ Day 5 - Reflection

How does the story of mama's apron inspire your own ability to carve out time that is dedicated to the Lord?

I do this every minute that I can. I prioritize (learned the hardway) stopping and retreating under the apron, even if it means walking away from responsibility, conversations, etc.

☐ Day 5 - Journalizing Assignment

But when you pray, go into your [most] private room, and, closing the door, pray to your Father, Who is in secret; and your Father, Who sees in secret, will reward you in the open.

sent ahead disciples Matthew 6:6 (AMPC)

Then He directed the disciples to get into the boat and go before Him to the other side, while He sent away the crowds. And after He had dismissed the multitudes, He went up into the hills by Himself to pray. When it was evening, He was still there alone.

Matthew 14:22,23 (AMPC)

And in the morning, long before daylight, He got up and went out to a deserted place, and there He prayed.

Mark 1:35 (AMPC)

LESSON 6, DAY 6 - *Waiting for Direction*

☐ DAY 6 - READING ASSIGNMENT

Jaque's Journal

Jaque, I am teaching you more about waiting, you see more as you wait. Waiting makes for good soil, it allows roots to go deep into the ground and take hold. Wait on My word, for in it is all authority, anointing, energy, and the ability to stay on a straight and godly path. Hearing, and understanding what to do, means everything for your life. How many say, "What should I do next?" You must enter the cave, and wait for Me to tell you what comes next. When you know how to receive the next step by faith then you are on a progressive track towards freedom. It is not about understanding the whole plan, or what the exact outcomes will be, but rather it is the understanding that the next step leads to each next step. You do not need all the steps - just the next one. Let go of the false need to know the future. Hidden in Christ, you will be found in Him in each of your tomorrows.

Jaque, Christ is where you are headed. He is the next step, the insight for what to do, or of what restraint or action comes next. Christ is the path which leads to the next revelation. See, and do what you see. People inundated with questions are not pulling the apron up over their head. They are not entering the cave where treasures await. Go into the cave, Jaque, and you will see what to do. Draw from your Resource. Christ is the individual Resource in each of my children, and He is the collective Resource of My body. That is why there is safety in the multitude of counselors. Draw from the Resource in you and in one another, ask questions, do not forsake gathering together.

We come together with others who want intimacy with Him. We draw from the Resource in ourselves and in each other. We pull the apron over our head and we gather with others. We search for treasures alone and we search for treasure in each other. When Jesus said, "I only do what I see My Father doing" He was referring to His private view of the Father in Him. He went into the hidden place where His Father was and, alone in the treasure trove, He fellowshipped and received vision. Other times, He asked His disciples to come away and pray with Him, and yet at other times He broke bread and had communion with His disciples and with large crowds. Jesus knew when to be public and when to pull the apron over His head. Even Jesus had to wait with attention for His Father's words and visions.

> *Jaque, give My Words your strength and awareness. I have so much more I want to give you but you must verify and confirm your need for Me, to do this you need to see your need for Me. You are not always conscious of your need because you are so quick to just go about your business. Slow down, see what the new need is and take the next step that I want to reveal. Each step leads to more hope, greater vision, and the birth of new goals.*

When we go about our lives, doing all the familiar tasks, time seems to go by quickly. At the end of the day, we wonder where the time went and find ourselves wishing for a few more hours in the day. In contrast, when we wake up from spiritual slumber, and sit and wait in His presence, time slows down. We learn to live in the present moment with God. Then we begin to see something new; and each moment holds a new wonderment.

We sometimes experience this awareness when an event happens in life that jars us out of our normal routine. We notice things we never saw before. There is a way to deliberately practice a more focused awareness of the present moment, to slow down our world by being present with the moment.

Recently, I was spending time with my grandson and, even though I was busy, I decided to slow down and to take the time to just watch every little movement he made. The day was hot, and he was

The artist has to take time to notice each detail as she creates the ART.

jumping on my mini trampoline; then he jumped off, rolled onto the cool tile floor and lay still while letting the ceiling fan cool him off. I did many things that day, but what I remember most was my grandson's movements in those few minutes that I became present with him in the moment.

Consciously slowing down by becoming aware of our movements (almost like slow motion) is what it is like when we go into the cave with God. We have to give up that which is trying to push us out of the present moment (usually our to-do list) and surrender our attention as we wait on Him. We cannot say, "All right God, go ahead and give me a quick word because I am in a hurry. I have many things to do. I'll skim the scripture and you hustle out a good word." Sometimes we act like we just need to get this 'God part' over with so that we can get on with our 'real' day. Honestly, there have been times when I resented my need to 'do a journal' because I had so many things to do. We all are caught in the rush of daily life. The time pressure chokes our ability to enjoy our time with the Lord.

We must learn to speak to that push that says, "You have a hundred things to do today, you had better skip your quiet time. God will not mind…" When that push is badgering me, I have learned to say, "Oh, so you are going to mess with me? Okay, I will knock that list of one hundred things to do down to fifty. Now I have time for the Lord. Moreover, if you keep hassling me, the list will go to twenty-five. If you still keep it up, then guess what? I will zero out the day and do nothing else but spend the entire day with the Lord." It usually silences the push!

We are learning to put first things first. We will go into the cave, unhurried, and allow God to speak. This is not a meal in a minute, like fast food. We are here to wait on the Lord, to see His mysteries, and as we *enjoy* His presence, we do not look at our watch. We sit with Him for as long as it takes.

There is a dichotomy because He can do more in ten minutes than we can do by sitting there, frustrated, for two hours. The key is that He gets to choose the timeframe. We have to bring our body and our mind into silence before the Lord. As contemplatives we say, "No, mind, not what you think. I am here for what God has to say." We give the Lord our attention and He takes us further down, into deeper mysteries and secrets from God.

We have chosen a different way to study His word. We have chosen a method that invokes His presence and relies upon His Spirit to teach us His word and to teach us about our life in Christ. I have participated in many different bible study settings and have enjoyed so much of it. Yet, I have often left thinking, "There has got to be more." Eventually, I had to ask God what was missing. I needed more. I did not want to be a Christian and feel like it still was not enough. As I have said before, God used my angst to give birth to these studies and the tool of journalizing His word. I am thankful that He made me unwilling to settle for less.

☐ DAY 6 - REFLECTION

Take five minutes to slow down your breathing and to notice your own movements. Observe the sounds, sights, and smells that surround you. Noticing little details, multiple times throughout your day, can help you relax in general, become present in the moment, and to experience greater contentment. Now write down how the exercise made you feel.

☐ DAY 6 - JOURNALIZING ASSIGNMENT

My soul, wait only upon God and silently submit to Him; for my hope and expectation are from Him. He only is my Rock and my Salvation; He is my Defense and my Fortress, I shall not be moved. With God rests my salvation and my glory; He is my Rock of unyielding strength and impenetrable hardness, and my refuge is in God! Trust in, lean on, rely on, and have confidence in Him at all times, you people; pour out your hearts before Him. God is a refuge for us (a fortress and a high tower). Selah [pause, and calmly think of that]!

PSALM 62:5-8 (AMPC)

Lesson 6, Day 7 - *Emotions As a Resource*

☐ Day 7 - Reading Assignment

When we do not live honestly with ourselves, or do not live from the voice of conscience, then we do not truly love God in those moments. We may think that we do not love *ourselves*, but this is not true for it is *always* about God.

When we feel angry at each other, or ourselves, we are angry with God. In the midst of any emotional upset, we can ask God about the emotions and He will help us find the underlying cause. I used to hate the fact that I would get angry. When I went to the Lord in one instance, I learned the difference between righteous and unrighteous anger.

Jaque's Journal

Jaque, the anger you feel is connected to the withdrawal process; you are dying to the 'lie-life,' the 'false life,' and the 'false self' and it is fueling the anger. You feel angry because you realize that you have been giving your true life away, and the indignation fuels the anger.

Jaque, you can use this anger to do 'right' things. Anger can lead to change. It can move you to correct action on behalf of others or toward proper self-care. Anger can be fuel that drives you to get out of debt, out of obesity, or out of numbness. Anger can be a wake up call or a call to action. If you can see what this present anger is here to do, you will see it as the righteous anger of the true self. Do not fear this kind of anger, go where it wants to take you because it will not hurt you or others. It will cause you to do right things and to be bold for righteousness sake. This is not lethal, unrighteous anger, Jaque, it is life-affirming anger that is all 'gift.' It is the gift that comes to move you in the direction you need to go. It is keener awareness, it is potent and powerful and active and energizing. Let this anger get you working on your own behalf and go with it!"

This is what it means to be angry, but sin not. Rightly discerning our emotions in God, which requires us to continue to practice the habit of waiting on Him, will teach us to channel something we formerly labeled 'bad' into a force for positive change. When we allow Him to rightly divide our emotions, then we no longer condemn ourselves. Emotions are a part of God's abundant supply of resource. He uses them to supply us with passion and movement. They have a purpose in our life and we can learn how to use them as we let them be a part of the resource of Christ in us, as us, and through us.

Justice Satisfied

God had every reason to be angry. As a God of justice, He had to execute justice toward sin. His mercy triumphed, as He satisfied justice with a loving stroke of infinite finesse. God performed justice by giving us Christ. Christ is the ultimate Resource of eternal life and security. God justly satisfied His anger and we received Christ in the transaction. What more could Love give? What more could we want? Christ is the sum total of our every hope and desire. Everything we crave proceeds from His life in us, and as us.

God waited for the fullness of time so that He could bring forth Christ. On a personal level, He waits for us to see how He has waited for us to come to the end of our swiftness to do things our own way. He has waited to kill the will of what feels *incomplete* in us (the false nature) with His love. He has waited for us to search for and to find Him. He has waited for us to see Him as He is. He has waited to love us - to be gracious and to have mercy upon us.

Let us not wait any longer, we can receive mercy and grace today. A greater awareness of peace and safety in Christ is found in each present moment. We come into His presence because, when we do, He finds us and shows us who we are as a complete self in Christ. He has always known where our true self was, and yet He waits for us. He waits for us to burn out or to spin out of control, and when we do, we can thank God for it.

"Get over Your self"

"I'm at the end of my rope"

"I'm over my self"

Jaque's Journal

Jaque, you come to the end of the false self when you find out she is a fraud. For this I have waited so that I could be gracious and merciful to you. Now that you see this, keep yourself in My love, for My love will keep the will of all that is false under the waters of mercy and suppressed from all pretenses. Today you caught a glimpse of what I have waited for, and how I have ached to reveal the vision of Christ in you. Today, in the midst of silence, you have received My love, for which you have eternally hoped.

Jaque, the purpose of silence is that you may enter it and therein, let Me find you. There in the silence that you do not understand, you must wait, for only to that which you do not understand do I come; you have "no room at the inn" for things you feign to understand. The less you know the more I come.

Jaque, silence is, at last, the place where deliverance and salvation are received. I create you within My silence. You do not create Me, I create you. I initiate the movements, and so you wait in the cave of silence until I have made you ready to receive that which I will reveal. Silence is the place where your surrender is made complete. Silence is the place where 'I' am God. So wait for Me in the silence - be still and finally know what you have never known - here in the silence you will know who is God...and who is not.

☐ Day 7 - Reflection

Write down your thoughts about silence and how you imagine God's movement therein.

When we silence or die to our false self ("mindless" chatter) God can speak & reveal Himself in us as we wait there in hopeful expectation.

☐ Day 7 - Journalizing Assignment

Be silent, all flesh, before the Lord, for He is aroused from His holy habitation!

Zechariah 2:13 (NKJV)

Quiet, everyone! Shh! Silence before God. Something's afoot in his holy house. He's on the move!

Zechariah 2:13 (MSG)

Surrender your anxiety! Be silent and stop your striving and you will see that I am God. I am the God above all the nations, and I will be exalted throughout the whole earth.

Psalm 46:10 (TPT)

Lesson 6 - Heart-Work

The Heart-work is a valuable part of your inner work. Taking the time to give heartfelt responses to the following questions is beneficial for you and beneficial for sharing with others who are in your study group.

Putting it All Together

1. How is our 'heart soil' prepared for greater depth?
2. How does *understanding* relate to possessing our resources?
3. Do a study on the word *success* and allow the Holy Spirit to add spiritual insight to the true meaning of success.
4. Please share your journalizing experience this week with regard to heart and frequency. How was your desire for discipline grounded in grace this week?

Note: If you are in a VI class, please include one journal from this week with the Heart-work you submit for coaching.

If not, please bring your Heart-work and a journal to share with others in your study group.

Lesson 7 Notes

"The fruit of Self Control is tied to the principle of grace or release." Self Control being one of the fruits of the Spirit. To forgive and release My self, returning me to the goal or the hope, whole heartedly." - Jaque

*Watch: The King of Glory movie (3hrs)
(Can watch on You tube in 12minute increments)

when we release, and expect to receive.
"Clarity of Destiny"
A clear path is made

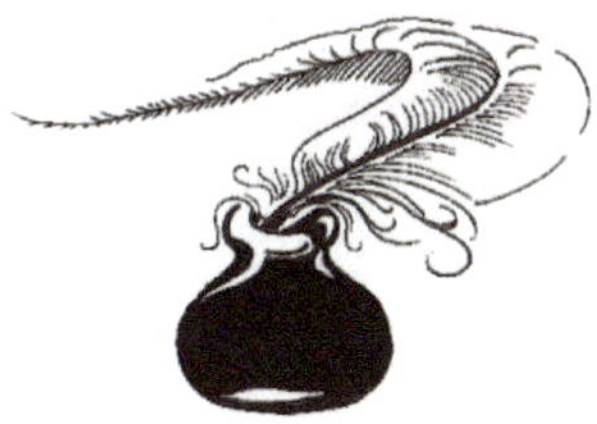

BEARING FRUIT

[Now] we have this [hope] as a sure and steadfast anchor of the soul - it cannot slip and it cannot break down under whoever steps out upon it - [a hope] that reaches farther and enters into [the very certainty of the Presence] within the veil.

HEBREWS 6:19 (AMPC)

LESSON 7, DAY 1 - *Forgiveness, Grace, and Release*

☐ DAY 1 - READING ASSIGNMENT

It is nice when God offers definition of an everyday word. If we look to a dictionary to define the word *receive* we would miss God's view. From His perspective, to receive is to *release* ourselves into His grace that is already present for our use.

God is our refuge and strength, a very present help in trouble.

PSALM 46:1 (NKJV)

Grace, like God, is not far off. It is here, right now, always ready in our time of need. Grace is our power to do all things in Christ.

If we wander away from our goals and are slack in our efforts, then grace returns us to the goal. Condemnation is not productive. We will get back on track much more quickly by releasing self-judgment. Release ties us to consistency through forgiveness. A life of bearing fruit has everything to do with forgiveness, grace, and release.

It would be impossible to apply forgiveness, grace, and release without humility. Humility is letting go of what we think we deserve and letting go of our opinions about our lapses. Humility lets go of pride, which means it aids our ability to receive wisdom and understanding from God. Humility marks the proper fear of the Lord.

The fear of the Lord is the beginning of wisdom: and the knowledge of the holy is understanding.

PROVERBS 9:10 (KJV)

Letting go of our opinions makes room to receive God's view. We cannot conceive the thoughts of God if our headspace is crowded with misnomers that we refuse to relinquish. We must continually release what we think we know so that we can receive what He *absolutely* knows.

To release is to let go, which means to forgive. Sometimes it helps to change a word or phrase, especially if we have preconceived notions about our familiar terminology. When we hear the word *forgive*, we may immediately affix more religious complication than necessary. Forgiveness is simply releasing - it is opening our hand and letting go of whatever we were holding onto.

Letting go of a resentment, grudge, hatred, or bitterness, is to open our hand and let the whole situation fall into God. Forgiveness does not mean that offence did not occur, or hurt was not experienced, it just means we are releasing the offender into God's capable hands so that we can be free.

We hold the key to freedom. Grace is already present, and it offers us the strength we need to forgive everything we harbor against others and ourselves. When we let go of that which we have held on to, then we can return to the consistent habit of brooding over our hopes and desires. When everyone is 'off the hook' then we receive clearer vision than ever before. We see God at the heart of *every* goal.

Being stuck in an offence is not worth the damage that occurs. If we cannot release others and ourselves, then the pure intention that belongs to God has been stolen - and we have let that happen. We give ourselves to that which we will not release. We become a slave to that which we will not let go of. The only way we can get free is through forgiveness. We are slaves if we will not receive grace to forgive and release others and ourselves.

What It Takes to Receive

God wants us to receive the desires of our heart because through them we know and experience Him. How could we know who we are without discovering our true desires? Our desires are the colors and hues, the textures and grains of our personality, which is really Christ in us, *as* us. To seek and to know Christ in us, *as* us, we have to receive the desires of our heart. We learn to receive through surrender and submission to the active practice of His presence.

The fruit of righteousness, peace and joy is the fruit that is coming to full bloom in our heart. Out of righteousness, comes true identification in Christ and the ability to see ourselves as we really are. Out of peace (which ensues as we see and accept our true selves), comes boldness and frankness in *being* (or acting from agreement with) our true selves. Out of the experience of righteousness and peace, comes unadulterated and abounding joy, where pleasure is derived from knowing ourselves as true beings that dwell in the presence and kingdom of God. Righteousness, peace, and joy are the fruit of our surrender to His life in us, as us.

Jaque's Journal

Jaque, if you can receive, you can have whatever you ask for. However, it takes forgiveness, grace, and release, to receive. You can receive whatever you think is available to you, and whatever seems available to you is according to your idea of what you deserve. Unforgiveness greatly alters the underlying beliefs that surround what you think you deserve. Deep in your heart, you know how much you have been forgiven, and if you withhold forgiveness from anyone (yourself included), then the injustice of that withholding makes you feel guilty and undeserving.

Your conscience must be clear; if it is not, then you will receive far less than what you deserve. People who know themselves in Christ can receive it all, but those who know themselves 'in themselves' are poverty-minded and cannot receive much from Me. Who then is the person who can receive? The one who knows Himself in Christ - for the one who knows Himself in Christ has also learned to forgive as he or she has been forgiven.

Father, this is the privilege of boldness and humility that we have when we know ourselves in Christ. When our hearts do not condemn us, then we know that whatever we ask for, we receive. How can I accomplish Your will on earth and help others if I myself am full of shame?

Jaque, it is My pleasure to give you grace to travel this path free from shame. Continue to exercise kindness and forgiveness toward yourself and others. Joy will abound, passion will increase. Each new hope will find its end fulfillment. Fulfillment breeds more hope (desire) and passion (faith) is the action that once again brings it to conclusion. It is your joy to deliver My fruit to the earth.

☐ DAY 1 - REFLECTION

Define FRUIT:

To use, to take the profit of, production of that which is produced. Fruit of Spirit offspring, advantage, everlasting enduring, perpetual

Define THE GLORY OF GOD:

Clear, open to expand & enlarge. Bright & Shining, Brilliance, magnificente, Praise, splendor, HONOR, Divine Presence, Divine Perfection or Excellence,

☐ DAY 1 - JOURNALIZING ASSIGNMENT

And never let ugly or hateful words come from your mouth, but instead let your words become beautiful gifts that encourage others; do this by speaking words of grace to help them. The Holy Spirit of God has sealed you in Jesus Christ until you experience your full salvation. So never grieve the Spirit of God or take for granted his holy influence in your life. Lay aside bitter words, temper tantrums, revenge, profanity, and insults. But instead be kind and affectionate toward one another. Has God graciously forgiven you? Then graciously forgive one another in the depths of Christ's love.

EPHESIANS 4:29-32 (TPT)

Beloved, if our heart does not condemn us, we have confidence before God; and whatever we ask we receive from Him, because we keep His commandments and do the things that are pleasing in His sight. This is His commandment, that we believe in the name of His Son Jesus Christ, and love one another, just as He commanded us. The one who keeps His commandments abides in Him, and He in him. We know by this that He abides in us, by the Spirit whom He has given us.

1 JOHN 3:21-24 (NASB)

LESSON 7, DAY 2 - *Moving to Humility*

☐ DAY 2 - READING ASSIGNMENT

We bear fruit consistent with repentance (Matthew 3:8) as we continually release, let go, and forgive others and ourselves. We will not forgive others until we learn to forgive ourselves. When we exercise grace upon ourselves, then we can exercise it upon others. If we will not forgive and embrace ourselves, we will never outgrow the things that we hold against ourselves. What we have done, continue to do, and may do again must not trigger us to withhold acceptance, love, and forgiveness from ourselves. We must stop judging the things we do not like about ourselves. If we will not open our hand and release ourselves back into God, we will not do it for others.

Faith is difficult for any believer who is still acting as a magistrate thinking that it is their place to judge and condemn.

Jaque's Journal

> *Jaque, where there is no humility there is no fruit, no learning, and no growth. It takes humility to even begin to take an honest look at your life with a willingness to see your own motives, insecurities, and reasons for acting and reacting. There is no wisdom without humility. Humility is an attitude, a disposition of heart and mind that is open to divine counsel for everything. It is looking at something as a child would look, asking questions, and open to learn as if nothing other was already known. Humility is being open to the truth, willing to be placed in another place than what you think is the right place. I have put you in another place, Jaque, I transferred you from Satan to Christ, from rebellion to submissiveness, from anger to forgiveness. You would not have been transformed and transferred unless you were humble enough to receive what I offered. To 'ask what you will' means to 'ask what you are willing to have.' Jaque, humility makes you willing. Humility opens your will and*

allows it to be actively involved in each transfer between us. If you are asking for peace, it is because you are ready and willing to have peace. This is true because, in order to make the transfer, you must also be willing to let go of everything that does not make for peace. Holding a grudge, resentment, or holding on to your right to feel angry, does not make for peace. To 'hold on' is to be unwilling. If you hold on to insult or injury, then you are willing war, not peace. You are willing unrest, not peace. If you want love, you must be willing to receive love, and to receive love you must be willing to give love.

If you are not willing to forgive yourself and to receive grace because of your own judgments against yourself, you are not humble or willing to cooperate with the dynamics through which love enters. If you cannot get past yourself, if you cannot deem yourself worthy of love just as you are, then you will never be able to get on with loving others, not really, truly, or from the heart.

Humility shuts down the 'False Judgment Center' and hangs an 'Out of Business' sign on its door when you let go of that old way of conducting commerce. The enemy will notice that you have gone elsewhere to live and serve; you have gone into 'Humility' and are learning a new way to transact with others and yourself. You have moved to the town of 'Wisdom,' to live nobly and with good works. You will eat the fruit of repentance and humble pie will be sweet. As you abide in the Vine, your fruit will be abundant and you will have plenty to share with others.

Jaque, your new vocation is your new ambition; you will be positively obsessed with dwelling in My presence and being with Me all the days of your life. You will sincerely 'will it' and will be open to the truth that I will show you. You will be a field ripe for the harvest and you will bring forth abundant crops. You will know yourself to be whole-hearted, straightforward, and with no suspicions or doubts about where you are going and what you should be doing. You will make peace with yourself, so you also make it with others. You will be free from conflict and agitating passions, and will be a fruitful tree of righteousness. When you make peace in yourself, Jaque, you make peace in others. There is no confidence without peace. You are free to be fearless, free of what other people might think of you. You are a pool of peace that others begin to resource.

We become a resource that others can draw from; we are God's Profit and Loss Statement and the fruit of the Spirit is His bottom line. He suffered the loss of His only begotten Son to profit our life as His own. When we are bearing fruit, we are bearing Christ in our bodies. We are surrendered vessels who allow His fruit to grow on our branches. This fruit is love, joy, peace, patience, kindness, goodness, faithfulness, gentleness (humility), and self-control. It is His work in the midst of our surrender.

Anything that is profitable for use is fruitful. God's fruit stems from the Vine of Truth; as we receive it, lies and strongholds of the Liar are cut off and burned in the fire. When we are not consciously abiding in Christ or eating of His fruit, we languish in lies. We become dry branches when we do not partake of the glory of Vine Life. Our souls will never enjoy the ecstasy for which God made them until His love for us is in full bloom in our hearts. When this fruit is at full bloom it will be complete and overflowing. We will watch it overflow as it sacrifices for others. There is no greater love than to lay down our lives for others.

We are part of a Kingdom that is here right now; we are in fellowship with our Lord and Master, Who is to be heard, reverenced, and respected each day. He is pleased when, as His Profit and Loss Statement, His wealth can be read by anybody who looks at our lives.

In His Image

We are made in the image of God. The Greek word for image is *eikon*, and involves two meanings; representation and manifestation.

> *But we all, with unveiled face, beholding as in a mirror the glory of the Lord, are being transformed into the same image from glory to glory, just as from the Lord, the Spirit.*
>
> 2 CORINTHIANS 3:18 (NASB)

Being changed into the same image as Christ means much more than 'being like' Him or resembling Him. It is an actual representation and manifestation of all that He is! The mirror only reflects or manifests what it sees Christ (the Image) doing. In the fall, mankind tried to become the Image rather than the reflection. In the true Spirit of Christ, we behold in a glass the glory of the Lord. Where is His glory? His glory is in earthen vessels that were made to carry the Image of God.

Think of it. We are vessels that are made to carry the image of God, not a life *like* His but His very life. What is Jesus doing in us, *as* us? We are vessels bearing an image; we are not the image. The mirror is the word of God, and as we look in the mirror of His Word, we see that we are reflections of His actual image. The image of God is clear when we give, do, respond, and reflect only that which is truly Christ. This occurs when we are truly beholding Him.

If we look to the Old Testament, the Ark of the Covenant carried the actual presence of God. In the New Testament, He chose to make us His final sanctuary. We are the ark, earthen vessels, and He elected to make His home within us and among us.

Jesus is going to reveal who He is, *through* us! Christ experienced the *loss* of His earthly life so we could experience the *profit* of His heavenly life and give it away to others *(what duplication, what profit)*! We are God's fruit, we bear His image as apples on an apple tree - when we see Him, we shall know we are like Him. Christ is Himself in us; He still lays down His life for His friends as His life manifests through us!

Profit for Use

There is great profit to abiding in Christ. He has died, been buried, and has risen in us. He lives in us, and we profit greatly from His life *in* us, *as* us. In fact, our life is becoming all profit; and all that is earthly and devilish is becoming all loss. This profit is His glory; this loss is the gaining of our real life. A profit and loss statement shows us where we are at the end of any given quarter. When we look at our lives for fruit, to see if we are walking the talk, the bottom line tells all. If we presently show a ten percent increase, we shall yet hope for thirty, sixty, and one hundred percent! There is always more gain, and each day offers new goals and godly endeavors.

We bear the fruit of His Spirit, which results in active goodness toward ourselves and others.

☐ DAY 2 - REFLECTION

What is your understanding of what it means to be God's Profit and Loss Statement?

His dying (loss) and laying down His life (to live in us, as us) produces great gain through multiplication of Himself

☐ DAY 2 - JOURNALIZING ASSIGNMENT

I am the true vine, and my Father is the gardener. He cuts off every branch in me that bears no fruit, while every branch that does bear fruit, he prunes so that it will be even more fruitful. You are already clean because of the word I have spoken to you. Remain in me, as I also remain in you. No branch can bear fruit by itself; it must remain in the vine. Neither can you bear fruit unless you remain in me. I am the vine; you are the branches. If you remain in me and I in you, you will bear much fruit; apart from me you can do nothing.

JOHN 15:1-5 (NIV)

[Jesus didn't come to the women at the well to tell her to be born again, he spoke of her thirst, the emptiness. Fill her with Living water and
She will be in the Kingdom of Heaven NOW! (not some day)

LESSON 7, DAY 3 - *When His Word Becomes 'Presence'*

☐ DAY 3 - READING ASSIGNMENT

In scripture, the presence of God equated with the fear of God, is always expressed in behavior. A person living in the fear of God demonstrates a lifestyle of love, joy, peace – and above all, freedom from fear.

MALCOLM SMITH, FREEDOM FROM FEAR

Love, joy, peace, and all the fruits of His Spirit equate to freedom from fear. His fruit, by nature, is fearless, and equips us to live in the midst of a fearful generation, or a perverse society, without alarm. Beholding ourselves in His mirror, we realize that the image we see is Christ in us, our hope of glory. We behold His glory in earthen vessels, His presence fills the ark, and we become partakers of His divine nature. We profit. We partake of His glory; it is not our glory, we did not earn or produce the glory. The glory we experience is God, looking out into the world through our eyes. The privilege of having His presence abiding in us is beyond measure. Not only present, He will also talk with us day or night.

Jaque's Journal

Do not call conspiracy [or hard, or holy] all that this people will call conspiracy [or hard, or holy]; neither be in fear of what they fear, nor [make others afraid and] in dread. The Lord of hosts - regard Him as holy and honor His holy name [by regarding Him as your only hope of safety], and let Him be your fear and let Him be your dread [lest you offend Him by your fear of man and distrust of Him]. And He shall be a sanctuary [a sacred and indestructible asylum to those who reverently fear and trust in Him]; but He shall be a Stone of stumbling and a Rock of offense to both the houses of Israel, a trap and a snare to the inhabitants of Jerusalem.

ISAIAH 8:12-14 (AMPC)

Jaque, do not call hard or holy what others call hard or holy, and do not fear what they fear. Fear and regard Me as holy and honor My name by regarding Me as your only hope of safety. To fear man is to distrust Me; it is offensive.

Jaque, only I am to be your sanctuary, your sacred and indestructible asylum. At one time, you were unaware of My presence within you, you did not know My word or the sound of My voice. You could not cherish what you did not know - but now you are learning to abide in the conscious awareness of Who I am in you and in My word. In spirit and truth, you are learning to cherish the words that have become life to you. The words I speak usher you into My presence again and again, until you are able to come in even when I am silent.

My words have transformed into presence, they are living manna inside of you now. My words are like the ingredients of a cake, when the cake is finished you can no longer see the eggs, flour, oil, sugar, powder, salt, and flavoring separately. That which was known as separate from one another is now known as one - it is cake. It required the mixture of all the proper ingredients for cake to become cake. All of My words are ingredients for the cake of life. When your life is cake, no one can discern you apart from Me. You are a spiritual woman who has many ingredients inside. You taste differently than any other cake because the mixture is composed uniquely. My words have transformed into living presence in you, you are no longer as prone to worry or fear. This is the manifestation of My glory. Happy Birthday, Jaque, we are having a party and you are the cake. However, if someone (or even you) behaves in willful resistance, they will not like this cake; it will taste bitter in their mouths. The flavor of their own willfulness alters their ability to taste and see that I, in Jaque, am good. There are those who hate Me without cause, but they are the cause of their own hatred.

We change when His word becomes *presence* within us. When His word is manna that sustains our life, then we experience life-altering effects, and we exhibit the wonders of His love.

Jaque's Journal

Jaque, grace releases you to repent, it forgives you, then it changes you. If you allow the forgiveness of grace then you can expect change. If you harbor resentment (against others or yourself), you will get earthly and devilish repercussions. Enter the narrow gate that denies you the right to resentments, self-absorbed feelings, and stubborn resistances. Take up the cross, where self-denial is the way out of the hell you have known. Love the truth and let it be the most important love of your life. Speak the truth through the eyes of love. Speak it to yourself, others, and to those in your group. Be willing to have truth as your best friend no matter what it costs you, then peace will rule your heart. Abundant provision will grow from your branches.

A group will build a company and the company comes together dwelling richly in all teaching, singing, serving, and sharing its gratitude. It wills the will of the Lord; it forgives, releases, and returns to the will of God continually. Fields are ripe for harvesting, Jaque. Open your eyes and look at the fields; there are people all around you that want to know what you know - but they do not realize that they can know it. Seeds have been planted in hearts, but there is so much more.

Go and harvest the fields, Jaque, pray them in and pray yourself out to where they are. You may say that you want people to come, hear, and learn the truth. However, are you willing to have them? When you ask for an increase, does that include people that you do NOT know - or are you asking only for those you know. I want to know if you are willing to receive a harvest of people that you do not know. Go beyond your circles of influence and pray yourself across the lines and into the places where you do not feel comfortable. I will be your comfort when you are uncomfortable.

Jaque, go out into the highways and the byways and bring in the lost and the lonely. I will show you who, where, and when, but you must be willing to have them. Be willing to have 'these people,' the ones that you do not know. Be willing to have them into your home in order for them to find Me. Be willing to invite, care for, and to share with strangers, and you will reap souls. A group will build a company, a company will build a battalion, a battalion will build a regiment, and a regiment will build an army…all to the praise of My glory.

Lord, I will it. I am a safe place; help me in my lack of safety. I believe, help my unbelief. I will it, help my unwillingness. I ask for it, be my ability to receive it.

When we have hope for our friends and family, we cannot help but hope that they will find the intimacy with the Lord that we may have found. God will take care of our loved ones as we continually surrender them into His hands. In the meantime, we must be willing to receive people who are not a part of our familiar cliques and circles. We spend so much time, energy, and focus hoping for our own freedom that we have forgotten that there is a hurting world in need of hope.

When we come to the fullness of hope, we realize we are not fully hoping until we are pregnant with the hopes and needs of other people. We do not need to know their names yet - we just need to know that there is a harvest of people and we will love them as soon as we go to them or in the instance that they find their way to us. We need to stop limiting God and begin to look out to the harvest, and say, "Lord, we pray for peace, confidence, and boldness in ourselves and in each other so that we can go out with the courage to speak to people that we do not know." If we carry the presence of God, then we carry hope to the hopeless, light to the darkness, and peace to the chaos. As those who bear His Image, we will become more able to speak to people without being afraid of them. If we remain in fear of their unknown faces, then they remain in fear of ours. Their hearts still ache, nobody is welcoming the other, and the enemy is laughing.

We need to go out beyond ourselves. Whatever we are willing to do today paves the way for tomorrow. Whatever was in our life yesterday, paved the way for today. If we do not like where we are, then we have to do something different today. Anything we dream to do or become always involves loving others. This is why we desire to *be* our true selves, because we know that who we *really* are, loves more.

☐ DAY 3 - REFLECTION

Are you willing to have 'these people' (the ones that you may not know) in your study group? Why or why not?

Absolutely! I love learning more about who God is through meeting, loving, hosting, hearing and serving new hearts & minds it is thrilling.

☐ DAY 3 - JOURNALIZING ASSIGNMENT

Now faith brings our hopes into reality and becomes the foundation needed to acquire the things we long for. It is all the evidence required to prove what is still unseen. This testimony of faith is what previous generations were commended for. Faith empowers us to see that the universe was created and beautifully coordinated by the power of God's words! He spoke and the invisible realm gave birth to all that is seen.

HEBREWS 11:1-3 (TPT)

Suppose one of you had a hundred sheep and lost one. Wouldn't you leave the ninety-nine in the wilderness and go after the lost one until you found it? When found, you can be sure you would put it across your shoulders, rejoicing, and when you got home call in your friends and neighbors, saying, 'Celebrate with me! I've found my lost sheep!' Count on it—there's more joy in heaven over one sinner's rescued life than over ninety-nine good people in no need of rescue.

LUKE 15:4-7 (MSG)

LESSON 7, DAY 4 - *Christ, the Fruit*

☐ DAY 4 - READING ASSIGNMENT

The new creation is 'Christ in us' and He is God's fruit. Christ is the fruit of the Spirit, when He appears He manifests in our lives as fruit. When He appears in, through, and as us, we appear as love, joy, peace, patience, kindness, goodness, faithfulness, gentleness, and self-control. The scripture that says that when we *see* Him we will be *like* Him (1 John 3:2) is not reserved just for future days in heaven. We can bear His image on this earth. We see Him in His word (as in a mirror), and we see the manifestation of His presence when we bear the fruits of His Spirit. We will see Him in us before we see Him anywhere else. He reveals Himself as fruit because He *is* our fruitfulness.

If we are still trying to mimic Him (be like Him, or try to figure out 'what-would-Jesus-do?') then our likeness is short-lived. No one can act like Christ for very long. When we surrender to Him, Christlikeness is long lasting because He knows how to be Himself in and through us. He is in us, as us. He will do what we cannot do; He will live. He will do what we cannot do; He will love. He will do what we cannot do; He will be self-controlled. He will do what we cannot; He will manifest Himself.

Unless a seed goes into the ground and dies it abides alone. All fruit springs forth from death. Our only instruction is to believe on the Son. Through our death in Christ we live in Christ and through our death in Christ we bear fruit in Christ.

The seed of Christ is inside of us; we are like a shell or hard casing around the seed. As the shell stays buried in Christ, its hard casing cracks open and the seed of Christ takes root, grows, and appears in His new form. He appears as me, and He appears as you. He is coming up and out of our ground, even now, to reveal His glory and to bring forth fruit; we bear His image as He bears His own image in and through us.

We have hoped for much, and have seen desires occur. We have learned that we must define our desires and the importance of staying pregnant with vision. We have learned what it means to be able to name our desires (like naming our own children). The desires of Christ will manifest differently through each personality. True hope, desire, and prayer, is always the request for Christ in some shape. We are always hoping for Christ, whether we are hoping for His character to come through us, or for His creative expression to manifest through our art, literature, music, dance, business, family, ministry, or any other possible form. We ask for Him in a thousand ways. Our need and desire for Christ may look diverse and distinct in each of us, but we are all asking for the same Christ. We are asking to see Him as He is in us, and as He is in one another. When we know Him in ourselves, we know Him in others. We find Christ everywhere, even in places we do not expect to find Him.

The greatest gift we give another person is to believe in the One Who is in them. To recognize and acknowledge Christ in one another is life-affirming. We are most encouraged by those who concede the unique expression of Christ in us. More than what people do, say, or give to us, it is when they believe in how Christ is *in us* that we are most heartened. When people see Him (even if we cannot) then their confidence makes His presence more obvious to us. He is drawn out of us, pulled up from our core. We grow when people treat us like Christ in our unique form.

We honor Christ when we honor His presence in one another. When we expect Christ from one another, we are more likely to get Christ. If we expect flesh and ego, we will get flesh and ego. We get what we expect. Grace helps us to see past mistakes, flesh, and broken humanity. Yes, it is all there in each of us. So, what? Christ, the Seed, chose to plant Himself amid our broken humanity. The Seed will go into our ground, crack open, and He will come out again. Let's look for Him in each other. Let's look for Him in the harvest. There are multitudes that are waiting for someone to believe in Who is in them and to call Him up and out of them. People need us to see Christ in them, even before they see Him, because they do not even know that He is there. They do not believe there is anything noble in them. We draw the seed of Christ up and out of them, and they see Him. He is there and He wants to find them, and they want to be found. There are many ways they have to be told, and many ways for them to respond. He needs to be seen, discovered, uncovered, and lifted up. Recognizing God's glory and the latent Christ, even in 'unbelievers' is one way to lead them to Christ. When God's dignity is what we choose to commend, people will see Christ lifted up; they will be drawn to Him. When they are, they will receive the full message of His death, burial, resurrection, and ascension. They will see the message in His life in heaven and on earth, and they will recognize the reoccurrence in His life-giving Spirit in themselves.

Real Fruit Bearers

> *Bring forth fruit that is consistent with repentance [let your lives prove your change of heart].*
>
> MATTHEW 3:8 (AMPC)

Our lives prove that our hearts have been changed. To go from a heart of stone to a heart of flesh changes how His words and directives are received. A heart of flesh wants to obey His Lordship. Obedience is not optional because it is love's privilege and incentive. If we think like a slave we will look at obedience as a law, a legalistic 'I have to' do what He *demands* of us. If we think like a son or daughter we will look at obedience as a privilege, a gracious 'I get to' do what He *desires* for us. One stems from fear and obligation, the other stems from love and earnest. Disobedience is dismaying; obedience becomes the indisputable best course of action. We belong to love now; obedience is no longer a difficult task to perform. Instead, obedience is an act of loving response to the love He loves us with. We obey because He first loved us.

We have the grace to obey because we have a heart of flesh that wants to repent and adhere. God is not impressed with self-effort and self-righteousness whether those traits are in believers or non-believers. God is impressed by Christ. When He sees Christ living His Lordship through humbled and surrendered hearts, God is pleased. Christ bears fruit through us that is consistent with repentance because of Who He is.

☐ Day 4 - Reflection

Is obedience optional? Why or why not?

☐ Day 4 - Journalizing Assignment

But what happens when we live God's way? He brings gifts into our lives, much the same way that fruit appears in an orchard - things like affection for others, exuberance about life, serenity. We develop a willingness to stick with things, a sense of compassion in the heart, and a conviction that a basic holiness permeates things and people. We find ourselves involved in loyal commitments, not needing to force our way in life, able to marshal and direct our energies wisely. Legalism is helpless in bringing this about; it only gets in the way. Among those who belong to Christ, everything connected with getting our own way and mindlessly responding to what everyone else calls necessities is killed off for good - crucified. Since this is the kind of life we have chosen, the life of the Spirit, let us make sure that we do not just hold it as an idea in our heads or a sentiment in our hearts, but work out its implications in every detail of our lives. That means we will not compare ourselves with each other as if one of us were better and another worse. We have far more interesting things to do with our lives. Each of us is an original.

Galatians 5:22-26 (MSG)

He took our sin-dead lives and made us alive in Christ. He did all this on his own, with no help from us! Then he picked us up and set us down in highest heaven in company with Jesus, our Messiah. Now God has us where he wants us, with all the time in this world and the next to shower grace and kindness upon us in Christ Jesus. Saving is all his idea, and all his work. All we do is trust him enough to let him do it. It's God's gift from start to finish! We don't play the major role. If we did, we'd probably go around bragging that we'd done the whole thing! No, we neither make nor save ourselves. God does both the making and saving. He creates each of us by Christ Jesus to join him in the work he does, the good work he has gotten ready for us to do, work we had better be doing.

Ephesians 2:5-10 (MSG)

LESSON 7, DAY 5 - *A Good Pace*

☐ DAY 5 - READING ASSIGNMENT

We have come this far for bearing God's fruit. In Christ, we are His trees of righteousness, and we bear the fruit of His Spirit. We are His, and we have been planted for His purposes alone. God made and created us for Himself; He is entitled to enjoy fruit from the trees He has planted. He has given us a hope, which is none other than Christ in us, our only hope of glory. We have this hope as a sure and steadfast anchor of the soul. It cannot slip, and it cannot break down under whomever steps upon it. This hope reaches further and enters the very certainty of His presence within the veil (Hebrews 6:19). Hope goes into the very presence of God, and faith brings the revelation home. Fruit is conceived in and brought forth from the presence of God.

We have been on a journey of receiving, learning how to dig for treasure, learning how to incubate desires, and learning how to enter His presence where true desires are sifted, sorted, defined, and refined.

We must let ourselves be clearly seen by Him, and of course, that means that we must let Him show us everything about ourselves that we have tried *not* to see. There may be things that were too good to be true, and so we refused to face them. There may also be things that were too awful to admit, and so we refused to face them. Either way, Jesus will reveal who He is and who we are; but He will never leave us nor forsake us. When it is time to face light or darkness, we are not alone. We are safely nestled in the righteousness of Christ.

We are God's Profit and Loss Statement, and our surrender to God is the fruit that is at full bloom in our hearts. As we practice surrender each day, we develop a lifestyle of repentance, obedience, patience, love, joy, peace, and anything else that God calls fruit.

Fruit born from a surrendered heart is sweet and humble. We are able to admit that we do not know what we think we know, and we are able to let go of any false idea, feeling, opinion, hope, or judgment. A humble heart can live at the cross of Christ for the sake of forgiveness of self and others.

Each time we catch ourselves in that false nature, thinking and feeling along with the false and the flesh, then we ask Christ to remind us of who we are, and to Whom we belong. He tells us again that someone new is growing up in us. We yearn for this new creation.

We practice being open vessels. God is eager for us to be open, and to expand the receiving place within us. He is eager for His Kingdom to grow here. He is eager for His blessings to come onto the earth for His children. He is eager to show Himself strong in us, in whosoever's heart is pointed towards Him. He is eager for His dignity and love to belong to us. God is our beloved and we are His; He is all generosity, all goodness. Because He is good and generous, it is important to Him that He can be revealed in the earth through our hopes and desires and through their fulfillment. This is why it is important to Him that we receive the desires of our heart and that they are fertilized and properly incubated and hatched.

It is important that we name our desires and that we ask for those things that we desire; we must define them, so that we can recognize them as our own when it comes time to receive them.

The image we bear is His Image of Himself. We are His mirrors, reflecting His Image. Now, if a mirror were made to reflect our own image, the reflection would look like you and me. Spiritually speaking, however, every one of us was made to reflect God, not ourselves. We are made in His Image. He desires to reflect His holiness from the inside out. He is Spirit, and if we want to see Him, we need to look at each other, for He intends to manifest His Spirit through us. We are meant to reflect His Image through our thoughts, words, deeds, and surrendered hearts. He has chosen, in fact He delights in, the revealing of Himself through all the different image-bearers He has created.

When we are full of His Spirit, we are the actual representation and manifestation of all that He is. He is going to reveal Himself to us, through us. It is within our own room, or from our own secret place, that we emerge as our true selves in Christ. For this is where He is, as a new creation growing up on the inside of us.

Resurrecting out of what was once only death, now life is coming forth from the grave. Christ receives all the glory and honor for it was all by His power. This is a God story. It is about Him. It is not about us. There is great profit to our abiding in Christ; God profits, our lives profit, and others profit. No matter what is going on, friends, we are able to have peace and joy. We can experience goodwill, patience and an even temper. We have learned to wait and to hope on Him.

Patience is a secret weapon at our disposal; it is the mystery behind self-control and every other fruit of His Spirit. Patience will allow His fruit in our lives to manifest as active goodness toward others and ourselves.

There are many fruits that He wants bear through Christians. God bears fruit in the hearts of those born from above, whether we are in the church, or outside of the church. Buildings do not matter - we are the Church, we are Christian. Christ lives here. Christ bears fruit that is consistent with repentance. We have hearts that are constantly changing and turning towards Him, wanting more of Him, all the time. Obedience is our complete and heartfelt surrender in each new moment.

What are we confronting from day to day? Is it congested traffic that hinders our commute, a slow train, a busy check-out line with too few checkers, unresolved conflict, feeling out of control? We can learn to love 'what is,' just the way it is. The Lord will take 'what is,' flip it over, turn it around, shift our outlook, and turn 'what is' into a vision of love. He opens our eyes to see love transforming 'what is' into what He says it is. Suddenly, a slow train is an opportunity to wait on Him, to pray for others, or to speak life. Feeling out of control is an opportunity to rehearse the truth that control is an illusion and that we can trust God with 'what is.' We are in Abba's arms and can safely trust His big love.

☐ Day 5 - Reflection

What are you afraid that God might want you to see, admit, or acknowledge about yourself?

☐ Day 5 - Journalizing Assignment

So if you're serious about living this new resurrection life with Christ, act like it. Pursue the things over which Christ presides. Don't shuffle along, eyes to the ground, absorbed with the things right in front of you. Look up, and be alert to what is going on around Christ - that's where the action is. See things from his perspective. Your old life is dead. Your new life, which is your real life - even though invisible to spectators - is with Christ in God. He is your life. When Christ (your real life, remember) shows up again on this earth, you'll show up, too - the real you, the glorious you. Meanwhile, be content with obscurity, like Christ.

Colossians 3:1-4 (MSG)

LESSON 7, DAY 6 - *Walking in Love*

☐ DAY 6 - READING ASSIGNMENT

On day four, we talked about obedience, but we need to remember that if we obey His rule of *love*, then love will take care of every other rule. To walk according to the will of the Lord, is to pursue His royal command of loving others. Loving others means that we seek the highest and the best for others and ourselves. We 'do no harm,' we are gentle and exercise tenderness of conscience. When we honor others in this way, we wear the same authority as Jesus, because His love, the highest law, is reigning supreme through us.

The obedience to walk in love is more often quiet than loud, not needing words because each loving act of obedience speaks louder than words. Christ treasures our obedience to His golden rule because it is the surest evidence that His life is coming through our surrendered life. The spoken word is less important than God's word in action. The times when we remain silent may be the Lord closing our lips. He is more 'God' in us than we have realized. He is bigger than the life we have lived thus far.

Jaque's Journal

Jaque, you bear faith and love, the fruit of which is the joy of abiding in your truest, deepest, 'want to.' Grace has heightened your godly want to's; it has enabled you to take your desire to the finish line. The offspring of faith is love, exuding, expressing, and exercising kind action toward others and yourself with quiet, confident authority. You are a beauty to behold, Jaque; I love you so completely just as you are, and I am completely pleased that you are at your peaceful best in Me.

Jaque, you have been with Me from the first, for I have always known you in My love, and now you know what has been known from the beginning. Your only effort, Jaque, is to stay awake and aware of My love. Grace is the gift that makes you know that love is here. All I ask is that you keep yourself in My love, doing your best to live loved everyday. Do all you can think of to nurture your mind in love.

Jaque, you have often read about the narrow gate that leads to my Kingdom, but for the sake of simplicity, let Me say that the narrow gate leads to your heart. The gate is compressed, like a pinhole, and connot be penetrated by the flesh, or the false ego-driven self. Few find it because few return to innocent perception. Few empty themselves of judgment in order to enter in and listen to the heart that speaks only the language of love and loving others. Those who find it, have done so by embracing simplicity, and they are the happiest, and most peaceful people on earth.

Lord, the meek inherit the earth! I will enter and I will learn to choose in favor of my heart. When you talk to me like this, I realize that every journal holds a vision of what I should be hoping for. How to manifest each hope-filled vision is a matter of planning. Right now, I see that my plan is the plan to hear Your voice for You impart the vision and the plan of action.

Jaque, your plan is a good one for communion with Me is communion that is good for your mind. Communion happens through a point of contact that you choose - such as a journal. Communion occurs as you receive truth, in your journals or any other truthful input. Communion is for awareness and awareness is an expanded experience of My presence. As your spirit remains open, and your pose non-judgmental, you will thrive.

Jaque, there are times when you read scripture and either feel like the words are all you want, or that they are not enough. That is because you are only at home in Me.

> *Studying scripture cannot be enough. You journalize because My love is an infinite supply of words within you. Scripture prompts you, and then journalizing is a training method for discovering the words that are written on your heart. The fruit of repentance is the humility to receive them.*

> Lord, sometimes I feel I would rather study the Bible or prepare a lesson than to wait for Your presence. Thomas Merton prayed, *"Untie my hands and deliver my heart from sloth. Set me free from the laziness that goes about disguised as activity when activity is not required of me, and from the cowardice that does what is not demanded, in order to escape sacrifice. Give me the strength that waits upon You in silence and peace. Give me humility in which alone is rest, and deliver me from pride which is the heaviest of burdens. Possess my whole heart and soul with the simplicity of love."* My brother's words have made this another day for returning my heart to You, oh Lord.

We often think of the ego as being big and loud, and it is, but it is also subtle and crafty. The ego invented our false identity (any identity apart from who we are in Christ) from the beginning, using circumstances to create problems that stole our joy. The ego is the separated entity, the entity that fell from grace. We are not that ego or the identity it constructed. We are love. The permanence of the love of Christ in us, defines us. The ego, that prefers to take definition from temporary feelings and emotions, does not define us.

We are made in God's image, and love is who God is. The ego craves work; work that the ego believes will make it feel more important, or more dedicated to the cause, more deserving of praise and applause. The ego fuels feelings of independence and separation from the God of Love. Love, however, rests in simply being what it is in and through us. Love never needs to work to be what it is; it just is. Love is happy with itself, but ego never is. Ego is a striving entity requiring busy-ness in order to remain distracted from love. Ego hates love. Remember this;

the ego hates God, else how could it prefer separation? The greatest work to be free from despair, and to be full of hope, is to abide in Christ until we cannot believe in the hopelessness of any situation ever again!

Love defines us; we hope for the manifestation of His love through us in any given moment. The greatest work we can do embodies wisdom as its foundation. We seek God, we expect love to come to us and to come from us, and in wisdom, we keep it that simple.

☐ DAY 6 - REFLECTION

How would you explain the idea that 'loving others' is our greatest act of obedience?

God is in All things, when we Choose to love others (w/o judgement) we are choosing (obedience) to Love God, as others.

☐ DAY 6 - JOURNALIZING ASSIGNMENT

Let no debt remain outstanding, except the continuing debt to love one another, for whoever loves others has fulfilled the law.

ROMANS 13:8 (NIV)

With tender humility and quiet patience, always demonstrate gentleness and generous love toward one another, especially toward those who may try your patience. Be faithful to guard the sweet harmony of the Holy Spirit among you in the bonds of peace, being one body and one spirit, as you were all called into the same glorious hope of divine destiny. For the Lord God is one, and so are we, for we share in one faith, one baptism, and one Father. And He is the perfect Father who leads us all, works through us all, and lives in us all!

EPHESIANS 4:2-5 (TPT)

Real wisdom, God's wisdom, begins with a holy life and is characterized by getting along with others. It is gentle and reasonable, overflowing with mercy and blessings, not hot one day and cold the next, not two-faced. You can develop a healthy, robust community that lives right with God and enjoy its results only if you do the hard work of getting along with each other, treating each other with dignity and honor.

JAMES 3:17,18 (MSG)

LESSON 7, DAY 7 - *Writing and Waiting*

☐ DAY 7 - READING ASSIGNMENT

When it comes to hope, it is born in the furnace of God. God's furnace burns away that which is false to preserve that which is true. We wait on God and we write; we write and we wait on God. He wants His words to be in us so that we can keep ourselves in His love for us and for each other. He wants to remain clear and present to us. God Himself is the eternal word spoken from before the earth was ever formed. His words are inspired words, God-breathed words, and they are written and re-written in many works and in many ways. Hearing God speak to us is important because His words help form our hopes, our identity, our convictions, and our faith. Words bring shape and form.

Do we want our relationships to take shape? Yes, and so we capture His vision for our relationships. When we want to shape a painting, we use ideas, brushes and paint. When we want to shape a relationship, we use ideas, actions, and words. Scripture is our greatest resource for words. With the ego out of the way, we can hear His voice and follow His lead.

Jaque's Journal

Jaque, journalizing could easily downgrade to manipulation. You do not want that to happen, but it will happen if you mix My words with wit and well-crafted phrases. My words carry their own meaning. Forcing words to sound in your mind, the way they were formed in the spirit is dangerous. When I speak, you speak. When I am silent, you remain silent. The essence of our relationship is 'you' hearing 'My' voice so that I can shape and form you. It is not for you to shape and form My words to fit your ideologies.

Jaque, the point is that practicing faith is one thing, but pretending a 'word' or using a journal to 'project an image' to people and calling that 'faith' is dangerous. The ego would invent ministry in My name in order to 'show' or

> *'appear' important to others. May it never be so. I create words; you repeat them. When you write, you record words coming from your spirit, not from your mind. Writer's block, Jaque, is when the mind gets stuck and can't think of what else to create. But here, in* <u>*My*</u> *arena, the mind is not the creator, it is the responder. Your spirit 'creates' by My Spirit and your mind takes dictation because it is only a servant. Train your mind to faithfully serve My Spirit, Jaque, and refuse the ego every time it rears its head. Live from Christ, for He has nothing to prove and no false image to project.*

> Lord, I have felt the burden of pride many times. I know it as the false ego. When I see it, it shall be slain. When I do not see it, expose it by any means necessary. Create in me a clean heart, oh God, for I continue to trust You in the process. You are bigger than the ego; I will not let the possibility of an occasional untruth hinder the probability of the truth on a regular basis.

Where there is no pride, there is no source of unrest. The load was left at Calvary and now all sin or doubt can be revealed and, in time, repented. We leave all fear, doubt, and unrest 'out there' as it is, never afraid of being 'wrong' again, for, in Christ, we can no longer be wrong at the core. We can only have a wrong reaction, and so what? There is mercy, grace and love to help in time of trouble. Therefore, we delight ourselves in the Lord and watch how He delights Himself in us.

We are new. We trust the One who lives through us, giving all honor and praise to Him. To know Christ as our life is a completely new attitude that will keep our thoughts accountable to the truth. If we are but a vessel (and we are) then there will never be another thing for us to boast in. We are an expression of Christ; He gets the glory and we don't have to be trapped by the ego ever again.

We really do get to be 'no one' while Christ is all. We really do get to live a love life that is all for others. We get to be free to use our hands to create and our thoughts to think of others and our actions to meet the needs of those around us. We really do get to sell everything we have to buy this field! Oh glorious revelation of Christ in us as us!

Truth comes in waves as we learn to trust the One who lives in us. No more looking at our actions as if they are separate from Christ. By faith, we realize that what we do is what Christ does. The leap of faith is the shift from seeing us as the one doing everything to recognizing Christ in us doing it through us. We learn to relax in the work that He gives us to do - which is that which is right in front of us to do. This is love in action - finding safety and acceptance within ourselves, which gives us freedom of movement.

Hope is the bearing of the fruit of righteousness, peace, and joy. Repenting or turning away from that which is not fruit becomes lessons in humility and surrender. God is clearing our disposition of pride and replacing it with humility. What lessons are yet to be learned!

Soul Peace, God's Plan for Mankind

The fruit of the seed sown is righteousness, always sown in peace by those who make peace in themselves and others. Fear and reverence for God is the beginning of this wisdom, and this reverence is full of abandoned trust. The fruit of this trust is peace and harmony, living every day without disturbance in our inner man, peace that is free from fear, from agitating passions and moral conflicts. Peace that enters into the presence of God in the Holy of Holies, peace that no past, present or future event can disturb. God is a God of peace. This is what the world is searching for in every other way. They are blindly choosing to love the things in the world, for they have yet to find depth of life, peace, the fruit of love, joy, or ecstasy of mind and heart. They toil and spin just to make ends meet or to fill their barns for the day of retirement - which to them is the only rest they believe they are entitled to have in this life.

As for any other future, well, they just do not know if they believe in that or not. Without hope, they are not really living at all, they are the walking dead, but the Lord would say to those who do believe and to those who do not yet believe:

I am the God who breathes life into dead things and call those things that be not as if they already are. I am the resurrection and the life, and My seed is in you and for you. I want to manifest Myself through your prayers, for I want you to be My voice in this dry and barren land. Give Me your heart, and lend Me your tongue. Open your heart and find the grace to obey Me; then watch what I, the Lord your God, will do in this land! Know Me in this day, and in the days to come you will know Me like never before. Watch the glory of the Lord cover the earth as I send forth My fruit bearers! You shall multiply as I pour out My Spirit on all flesh, and you shall be full of joy and exceedingly glad. Know that you are graced to endure whatever comes your way with patience and tireless long-suffering, that you are graced to forgive...readily. Let My peace and soul harmony act as umpire continually in your heart. My peace will decide and settle with finality, all the questions that arise in your minds, for you were called to live in peace. My Word, living at home in you, will dwell in you richly, and you will admonish, you will teach, and you will train others in all insight and wisdom. Do everything in dependence and trust in Me, for I am Christ the Lord, and the Life of someone new...in you.

☐ DAY 7 - REFLECTION

In what ways have God's words to you been shaping and forming your true hopes and desires?

It has been showing me how to love, forgive, trust, and be in Awe of Him who moves in me.

☐ DAY 7 - JOURNALIZING ASSIGNMENT

Since we are now joined to Christ, we have been given the treasures of redemption by his blood - the total cancellation of our sins - all because of the cascading riches of his grace. This superabundant grace is already powerfully working in us, releasing within us all forms of wisdom and practical understanding. And through the revelation of the Anointed One, he unveiled his secret desires to us - the hidden mystery of his long-range plan, which he was delighted to implement from the very beginning of time. And because of God's unfailing purpose, this detailed plan will reign supreme through every period of time until the fulfillment of all the ages finally reaches its climax - when God makes all things new in all of heaven and earth through Jesus Christ. Through our union with Christ we too have been claimed by God as his own inheritance. Before we were even born, he gave us our destiny; that we would fulfill the plan of God who always accomplishes every purpose and plan in his heart.

EPHESIANS 1:7-11 (TPT)

Lesson 7 - Heart-Work

The Heart-work is a valuable part of your inner work. Taking the time to give heartfelt responses to the following questions is beneficial for you and beneficial for sharing with others who are in your study group.

Putting it All Together

1. What is the fruit that must be at full bloom in your heart and why?
2. Why is it so important to God that you receive the desires of your heart?
3. Write a brief overview of this teaching on 'hope' using a few of your favorite parts.
4. Please share your journalizing experience this week with regard to heart and frequency. How was your desire for discipline grounded in grace this week?

Note: If you are in a VI class, please include one journal from this week with the Heart-work you submit for coaching.
If not, please bring your Heart-work and a journal to share with others in your study group.

Evaluation Questions

Having completed the study, consider the following questions to help evaluate if the study was beneficial to you.

1. How has your intimacy with God deepened by journalizing the assigned scriptures in this study?
2. In what ways did you experience the light of Christ through others who may have participated in your study group?
3. How did the discipline and accountability you experienced during this study enrich relationship and deepen community?
4. What was the most life-changing revelation that you received during this study?
5. Would you recommend this study to a friend? Why or why not?

JOURNALIZING

Thus says the Lord, the God of Israel, "Write all the words which I have spoken to you in a book."

JEREMIAH 30:2 (NASB)

We are going to journalize God's word every day during this study. To journalize means to write what your inner ear hears when you meditate on God's word. It is done by faith, as though Christ is speaking and interpreting the truth into your life. With repetition, you will come to *know* the truth and the truth *you know* will set you free. What you only hear with your ears you will forget; what you simply see with your eyes you *might* remember; but what you hear, write, *and* see on paper will give your heart a triple braid of understanding. Statistics reveal there is seventy-five percent to ninety percent memory retention for people who write things down. If our life in Christ is worth living, it is worth recording and understanding.

> *All this the Lord made me understand by the writing by His hand upon me, all the work to be done according to the plan.*
>
> 1 CHRONICLES 28:19 (AMPC)

Journalizing is not the end, but a means to the end. It is as a car or any other means of transportation that gets you to your destination, which is intimacy with God. Keep your heart open and willing; it's a prerequisite to *learning* from Jesus. That is why Scripture says:

> *"God opposes the proud but shows favor to the humble." Submit yourselves, then, to God. Resist the devil, and he will flee from you. Come near to God and he will come near to you. Wash your hands, you sinners, and purify your hearts, you double-minded. Grieve, mourn and wail. Change your laughter to mourning and your joy to gloom. Humble yourselves before the Lord, and he will lift you up.*
>
> JAMES 4:6-10 (NIV)

What Journalizing Does

The Holy Spirit will use journalizing to change your life. Our reactions to Christ's Lordship (and life in general) are filled with a wide range of fears, absurdities, and emotional outbursts. God's presence will stabilize your emotions as you allow His word to be written as personal dialogue to you. At its core, journalizing will:

- ❖ Lead you to trust God's action in you.
- ❖ Show you over and over again the nature of His heart.
- ❖ Show you your heart and its desire to please God.
- ❖ Reveal the grace that causes you to obey.
- ❖ Guide you toward maturity through a daily disciplined plan of action.

How to Journalize

When you are ready to start, come with a sense of expectation, trusting that God wants to reveal Himself even *more* than you want Him to do so. Remember, too, that your ability to see God rests with Him. This isn't about how well *you* can hear, it's about *His* ability to speak and to make Himself known to you. In other words, when you feel as if you just can't hear, shift your focus *off* yourself and *onto* Him by reminding yourself that He is God and your part is simply to surrender and give Him your willingness to hear.

Journalizing is similar to eavesdropping on a conversation already in progress and recording what you hear. As you write, some things may sound strange, but you must write them anyway in the moment you hear them. Keep writing without stopping the flow. Do not judge what you are writing; allow yourself to be spontaneous. The Holy Spirit will sift it and will teach you what it means later. Accumulate thoughts, not judgments. Later you will check one verse against another to see if what you are hearing is accurate. For now, get it on the page. If you are willing to keep writing, eventually you will be unblocked from fear and condemnation; you will not know exactly when or how it happened, but you will know that Jesus is narrating salvation into your heart.

When you begin journalizing, focus and meditate on the Scriptures assigned for the day. After thinking about the verse or verses, pick up your pen and write whatever you feel in your heart, and do not judge as to whether or not you *should* feel it. Then ask Him to direct your thoughts with His word, and, in faith, write what you believe He is saying to you. When you are finished with that, write your reply. Keep going back and forth until you are finished.

Remember that God will speak in accordance with what you read in Scripture and that the essence of the Scripture is written on your heart by the Spirit of God. It is Christ *in* you coming up from your own heart. Be sure to let Him call you by name as another step of faith. If your mind bombards you with doubt or fear, speak out loudly to your tempters. Say something such as, "Get behind me, Satan, I belong to the Lord and have a heart to hear His will alone. I desire to see God and to do His will, and, therefore, I will know it." (See John 7:17.)

If you are stuck from the beginning, start by paraphrasing the Scripture, as though God were speaking that verse directly to you. For example, John 3:16 might read this way: "*(Your Name),* I love you so much that I sent My Son for you. If you will believe on Christ and put your trust in Him, you will not die but will know what it means to have eternal life. I love you, *(Your Name),* and always will. Love, your Father." Do not worry about whether or not these words are really from God. *Only believe.* Just keep writing what comes, and trust God to be big enough to reveal Himself and to prove Himself to you. He will correct any error in your thinking. Remember, He wants to be known by you. He will interpret Scripture into the very fabric of your being, little by little, every day. Do not let your intimate enemy get away with robbing you of this intimate experience.

Enjoy the journey. Journalize in awe of God. Your goal is to hear the heart of God; journalizing will help you listen clearly.

> *As for you, the anointing you received from Him remains in you, and you do not need anyone to teach you. But as His anointing teaches you about all things and as that anointing is real, not counterfeit—just as it has taught you, remain in Him.*
>
> I JOHN 2:27 (NIV)

> *But the Counselor, the Holy Spirit, Whom the Father will send in My name, will teach you all things and will remind you of everything I have said to you."*
>
> JOHN 14:26 (NIV)

Disclaimer

Journaling is a term widely used in the world today as a tool of self-discovery and self-transformation and to develop a relationship with 'self.' In life or death, Jaque Banas Shank and family, do not support or take any responsibility for any spiritual experience or action that does not have God as its source, His word as its support, and the wholesomeness of His faith as its result.

Scripture tells us that when we believe in Jesus and accept His sacrifice for our sin, we receive God's Holy Spirit, who comes to dwell within us. Being born from above in this way is a prerequisite to listening prayer and true inner healing. For this reason the tool of journalizing will be used correctly, only in the hands of those who are born from above (See John 3:3-6). We have the capacity to tune in to hear Him because, as new creations in Christ, we are a dwelling place for God. He has given us the mind of Christ and His Spirit within interprets His Word into our lives (See 1 Corinthians 2:11-16).

'Journalizing' - the way that was taught by Jaque Banas Shank - is *not* about subjectively delving into self-awareness based only on knowledge, experience and thought processes. It is grounded in a meditative reading of Scripture as the Holy Spirit of God 'works the earth of the heart.' Journalizing is not an intellectual procedure; it is about listening to, and entering intimate relationship with the Spirit of the Living God within us. He is speaking, and the direction, insights, correction, and revelation we receive as we read His Word and listen to Him will be Truth. If it is not, then it has not come from the purity of His Spirit. We develop relationship with our Creator King, not with our 'self' and we experience His love in the spirit of humility.

Jaque knew that what we hear, write, and act on in faith must tie in with the whole of Scripture as found in the Bible. The Holy Spirit opens our spiritual ears to hear, as we faithfully *combine* journalizing with reading and living from sound biblical principle and practice.

It is not safe to isolate from the body of Christ and then claim a word or vision from God, for He keeps His lambs safe within "the fold." To experience the full measure of discipline, accountability, relationship and community that are cultivated through Jaque's studies, we recommend a group study to help ensure humble compliance with God's word through one another.

Journalizing, Heart-work, and Using the Study Manual

- ❖ Commit yourself to a time of focused attention. Be still and listen for the Lord's voice during a specified time each day. Dedicate the time and the place that works best for you.
- ❖ Humble your heart before Him and invite Him to make His presence known. Take as much time as you need to prepare your heart for Him.
- ❖ With a teachable spirit, read the lesson for the day.
- ❖ Read the assigned Scriptures but do not try to journalize each verse separately. This is a combined reading assignment. Ask Him to speak to your heart; hear what He wants to say personally to you, and write it.
- ❖ There are "Heart-work" questions at the end of each chapter. Find the rhythm and pace that helps you complete the questions with heartfelt consideration. If you leave them until the end of the week and they are rushed or you feel pressed for time, then perhaps the discipline of answering one per day may be better for you. These questions are intended to stimulate your thought process. The Lord will use them to summarize what you are learning and help you enjoy this study that much more.

Other Study Manuals

The following studies are transformational; they integrate the daily practice of personal dialogue with the One who lives in the heart of born again believers.

Miracle in the Mirror

A Christian's plague is the sin of unbelief. Most of that unbelief centers on our perception of who we think we are. This study helps us let go of that sin and to place greater reliance upon the life of Christ within each believer. It is time to stop swatting at cobwebs and to go after the spider - our self-view. We are new creations in Christ - we will walk it out as we are renewed in the spirit of our mind. As we learn to listen to who He says we are, His voice becomes undeniable and wholly recognizable.

Hope and the Purple Onion

This study is about vision and purpose, and creating the habit of permanent expectancy. Hope is filled with the visions God has for us; when one is born, His next desire awaits us. We are living from His hope for our future. This study will teach us to brood over hope, like a hen sitting on her eggs. Even a purple onion has purpose! The working out of hope's specifics becomes a personal story for each of us. Christ pursues His unique plan in and through the individual lives of His children.

Reflections in Righteousness

Christianity has become a religion of do's and don'ts for many who suffer under the crushing weight of what they believe they *ought* to do for God. This study reveals the foundational heart of the Gospel and the result is life-changing faith in Jesus Christ. Throughout the study, we will magnify the cross of Christ until we recognize what happened on our behalf before we were ever born into this world. When we finally see Him, we will be like Him - in fact, He Himself will be our life.

God's Money Highways

Prepare for a radical position on stewardship, living debt-free, giving the first fruits of our income, and trusting God as the ultimate defender of our fiscal wellbeing. Where there is no conviction, there can be no change. This study will stimulate a pricking of the conscience. We may find ourselves saying, "God, reveal *Your* values. Show me how to manage *Your* money. " Its intention is dialogue with God that will create a contrast between His way and the world's way.

The Character of God

Who is God? What is the essence of His Being or the attributes of His divine nature? We start by thinking we know more than we do about God, but the answer to these questions changes everything. The Lord reveals Himself through His character. Infinite beyond our imagination, we cannot know any more about God than He chooses to reveal. He is that big; you and I are that small. This study is meant to broaden our view of God so that He might broaden our view of everything else.

Prayer, the Power to Possess What You Already Own

Is there such a thing as unanswered prayer, or are prayers just aborted? Why do we lose heart and give up on requests when met with delay? When delayed, do we seek the Lord's counsel? Are we asking for stones and scorpions instead of asking for the Holy Spirit? In this study, we learn that prayer undergoes a purification process; it turns out that knowing who we are facilitates knowing how to pray. God already provided everything in Christ; prayer is learning to possess what we already own by knowing who we already are.

Love, the Only Diet There Is

Thoughts choose emotions, emotions regulate chemistry, and chemistry determines physical health. Addiction can form when we take emotional comfort in substance or behavior in an effort to avoid pain. It is the repetition of certain intakes, conditions, and times. God's first commandment is His invitation is that we would choose our addiction rather than letting it choose us, for we are going to be addicted to something. Let's get addicted to His love and let it eliminate the ache of an empty life.

The Way of the Visionwriter

With a heart for God to purify our view, this study will reveal that the keys to God's kingdom are often cloaked in mystery; they are not hidden *from* us, but *for* us. In dialogue with the Holy Spirit, we will explore what we do not yet understand, and receive keys for opening the door wide enough to see that Christ *in* us, is actually living *as* us. We will learn to detect, admit, release, and communicate that which He reveals as either a building block to hold onto, or a hindrance of which to let go.